the symbol stones
of scotland

the symbol stones of scotland

*A social anthropological resolution
of the problem of the Picts*

Anthony Jackson

with drawings by
Helen Jackson
and diagrams by
Anne Leith Brundle

THE ORKNEY PRESS
1984

Paperback edition 1987
ISBN 0 907618 16 2 (paperback)

Published by The Orkney Press Ltd, Victoria Street,
Stromness, Orkney

Printed by the Kirkwall Press, *The Orcadian* Office,
Victoria Street, Kirkwall, Orkney

Bound by James Gowans Ltd, Glasgow

The publishers wish to acknowledge
the assistance of the Publication Fund
of Aberdeen University's Extra-Mural
Department.

In token of the 80th anniversary of
Romilly Allen's most famous publication:
The Early Christian Monuments of Scotland

Salve atque vale

CONTENTS

Maps

Figures

The cover design by Keith Laird is based on a stone from the Knowe of Burrian in Harray which is now in Tankerness House Museum, Kirkwall (Table 2A:3).

Tables

Photographs

The frontispiece and Plates 11 and 13 appear by courtesy of the Scottish Development Department, Plate 4 by kind permission of the Sutherland Trust, and Plate 14 by kind permission of Moray District Council. The help of the staff of Inverness Museum and of Ross and Cromarty Tourist Board is also gratefully acknowledged.

Foreword

The symbol stones of Scotland constitute, I have long thought, one of the most neglected glories of our British heritage. Belonging to a period which in Scotland is effectively prehistoric (or at least proto-historic, in the sense that there are just a few fleeting references to the Picts in contemporary texts), they constitute a rich and enigmatic series of monuments, which no-one has yet succeeded in explaining satisfactorily. They are at once the best-known source of information about those mysterious and shadowy people, the Picts, and the least understood.

For many years I have felt that one of the most desirable scholarly contributions in British archaeology would be the compilation of a new and full corpus to succeed Anderson and Romilly Allen's great, but now outdated, work of 1903. This we do not yet have, but Anthony Jackson has provided us with a provocative and ingenious analysis of the monuments and of the symbols themselves, which boldly challenges the assumptions made by Charles Thomas (and before him by F. C. Diack) in the only previous attempt at a systematic treatment of the material.

Anthony Jackson questions the widely accepted view that the symbol stones were funerary monuments, each making a statement "Here lies X, remembered by Y". Instead he proposes that they are collective announcements to the living, proclaiming permanent political alliances through marriage between members of different Pictish lineages.

His approach utilises a systematic quantitative analysis of the co-occurrences of the symbols. He states, very persuasively, that only those designs which occur in combination with others should be regarded as symbols in the sense of conveying encoded messages. His ensuing analysis of the frequency of occurrences (and co-occurrences) of the signs shows a number of patterns which have never hitherto been noticed, and to my mind break exciting new ground. The proposal that the pairing of the symbols on the stones represents a pairing (through marriage) of Pictish lineages is an ingenious hypothesis. It predicts various regularities in the actual distribution of the symbol stones across the Pictish territories, and again his analysis does indicate spatial patterning of what seems to be a significant kind.

Perhaps when he comes to assign a specific meaning to the individual symbols depicted, the arbitrariness of the procedure leads to some less compelling proposals — but he is at pains to stress that these proposed meanings constitute only a model for the interpretation of the individual symbols, not a definitive solution.

Anthony Jackson has produced a book bursting with ideas, many of them drawn from the field of social anthropology, on a subject neglected for too long by all but a few meticulous scholars. He is altogether undogmatic about his conclusions, speaking appositely of "provocative forays" into the field of Pictish scholarship. But while some of his findings are speculative (and will certainly provoke controversy), in a number of ways his work is progressive and in harmony with modern archaeological thought. In the first place, he is willing to take on the challenge of working in the cognitive field, with symbols and patterns of meaning. Secondly, he starts from a quantitative analysis of the symbol-occurrences, which is instructive and revealing. And finally, he sees the symbol stones as playing an active role in society, not simply as funerary monuments. Here it is relevant to refer to one of the few comparable bodies of sculptured stones from pagan northern Europe, the runestones of Scandinavia. As Klavs Randsborg has shown on his *The Viking Age in Denmark,* such monuments have an active socio-political role, even when (as in the case of most runestones) they did indeed serve as funerary monuments. The possibility that the symbol stones of Scotland were not associated with burial at all is an altogether refreshing one. With several other of the author's suggestions, it is a proposal which is certain to generate lively and rewarding debate.

COLIN RENFREW
Disney Professor of Archaeology
University of Cambridge
1.12.84

Preface

Southwest China is the unlikely origin of this book on the Picts! I had just completed my researches on the Na-khi, a remote highland tribe near the Tibetan frontier, when my attention was drawn to the fact they shared many of the social features and even the fate of the Picts. Both tribes were matrilineal, each had invented a unique symbolic script, they were consumed by fierce internal quarrels about succession to the throne, they had extensive royal genealogies, both had been converted to an alien religion, while each tribe were finally subjugated by a powerful neighbour and made to renounce their traditional marriage system, inheritance patterns and their native beliefs. These parallels were so astonishing in their specificity that I naturally became greatly intrigued by the Picts despite their distance in space and time from my researches.

Social anthropologists rarely stray into the distant past for an object of study, but they have made valuable contributions to our understanding of archaic cultures thanks to their expertise in pre-literate societies. In the present case there is no direct connection between the Na-khi and the Picts other than the shared societal features which interested me. I decided to explore what we knew about the Picts and it did not take long to discover our abysmal ignorance.

I decided to concentrate on the Pictish symbol stones since they are the *only* body of data of known Pictish origin. In 1971 I wrote a paper on these stones suggesting a possible explanation, and this received favourable mentions. Although the basic idea was correct I was unable to prove it and so I spent several years of fruitless endeavour looking for a solution. It was only after attending a conference on the Picts which was held in Glasgow in 1982 that I suddenly realized why so little progress had been made: this discussion by archaeologists was *still* being conducted on the same lines and with the same assumptions that were current a century ago.

If there is anyone to be held responsible for this state of affairs it is Anderson and Romilly Allen whose large tome: *The Early Christian Monuments of Scotland* (1903) both set the seal of approval on Pictish studies and simultaneously ended all further advance in our understanding of the symbol stones. This impasse is due to Romilly Allen's painstaking description of the stones and his adherence to the quite misleading system of classification devised by Anderson. Romilly Allen's major error was to assume that all the Pictish designs he picked out were symbols without ever asking himself what a symbol really was. The net result is that we have 50 or 60 'symbols' which, understandably, has left everyone confused.

I have broken away from this tradition by starting with a definition of a Pictish symbol, *viz* any design that combines more than once with another design to form a pair is a symbol. In this way one can reduce the number of real symbols to just 28 and it then becomes possible to make sense of the entire Pictish symbol system. The proof of this claim is the substance of this book.

As regards the so-called 'problem of the Picts', this is partly of the experts' own making. *Their* problem in understanding the Picts has three causes: 1) their vagueness about the symbols, 2) their acceptance of Western individualism and hence the belief that symbols refer to the dead, 3) their difficulties in dealing with 'timeless' societies, i.e. those without history. Only in some such way can the complete lack of progress in explaining the symbols be accounted for.

My approach to the Picts is radically different to conventional studies but it is based on publicly available data. In the course of my exposition I have made use of many tables which, though not always the most exciting reading, provide a direct link with reality: the actual Pictish stones themselves. (Attention is called to the note on p.23 which refers to the single enumeration system employed in this book to distinguish between sets of related items.)

My thanks go to the Scottish Society for Northern Studies for first allowing me to voice my heretical thoughts at a memorable conference on the Picts at the University of Dundee, several years ago. I also wish to thank various critical members of the Society—Anna and Graham Ritchie and Ian Keillar, amongst others—for their encouragement to pursue these thoughts *but with care and moderation!* I hope that I have now done this. I am also grateful to my editor, Howie Firth, for his careful examination of the whole argument and his suggestions for the better clarification of the text. However, the responsibility for any other errors is my own.

I would also like to thank my daughter, Helen, for her skill in drawing all the symbols and Sueno's Stone, freehand. I am also indebted to my wife, Maja, for putting up with this minor obsession of mine over the last few years. Those of you that have been gripped by Pictomania will appreciate the problems that this causes! It is simultaneously absorbing, but it is *utterly* time-consuming. So my thanks go to all my encouraging friends with their respective warnings.

As I have already indicated, this book is the result of quite a chance coincidence of circumstances, since I had never really contemplated writing on the Picts. I have, all the same, enjoyed pursuing this problem, and hope that others may derive benefit from my observations. I have attempted to arrange the chapters in a logical order that represents the successive discoveries I have made. In this way, I hope to persuade my readers to work their own way through the evidence and convince themselves that the conclusions are valid. This makes heavy demands upon the reader to be alert and to follow through complex arguments—not an easy task! I make no apologies for this method of presentation, since I believe, in this particular case, that we need to proceed as carefully as possible, since we know so little about the Picts.

This is not a book to read once only; it must be double checked. Is it consistent and self-supporting? Not only must it be self-sufficient but it must not be *that* out of line with recent discussions on the Picts—the bibliography is a handy check-list for this. What I am asking my readers is: do not believe what I say—check it first *but* if you can find no contrary and counter-arguments then I may well be right! *You* have to decide whether or not I have proved my case, for you do not have to rely on experts since the evidence is there for all to see.

I would like to conclude on a slightly different note. To-day is the first day of the Pictish New Year and it is also the 13th centenary of the edict that caused the setting up of the symbol stones. In 683 A.D. king Bridei (son of Bili) proclaimed that all lineages should erect stones recording their alliances/marriages. This event, alas, was not recorded and hence is not historically verifiable, but the proof remains in the existence of several hundred symbol stones. The reasons for this remarkable edict lie before you!

Edinburgh 1.11.1983

Note on spelling

There is no standard rendering for the names of the Pictish king-lists, and disagreements continue over the possible original form of many—Brude or Bridei, Unuist or Oengus, and so on (cf M.O. Anderson). The same situation also exists in the case of the tribal names given by Ptolemy, which are transcribed by different writers (e.g. Henderson and Duncan) in different ways.

Part One

... ONLY CONNECT !

Everything goes in twos; or the sharks will bite

Lau (Fijian) saying

Class I : Drimmies   (Table 2A:106)

CHAPTER 1

The background to the historical Picts

Scotland has been continuously populated for eight millennia, during which time numerous waves of settlers have made it their home—the most significant of whom, in this context, were the Celts. Linguistically, the Celts are divided into two branches: Q-Celtic and P-Celtic; the labels derive from the fact that the former tongue preserves the Indo-European *qu* whereas P-Celtic transformed the *qu* into *p*. Examples of Q-Celtic are the Goedelic languages: Irish, Scottish Gaelic and Manx. P-Celtic includes Gaulish and Brittonic: British, Welsh, Cornish and Breton. It is difficult to establish exactly when these differently speaking Celts arrived in the British Isles. Some evidence suggests that Q-Celts had reached Ireland by the 6th century B.C. while P-Celts were in Britain by the 4th century B.C. or even much earlier—in the Bronze Age. As for the previous inhabitants we have no idea what language they spoke.

The first tribal map of Scotland (cf Map 1) is given in Ptolemy's geography, a 2nd century A.D. compilation of 1st century data, which shows that there were some 14 different tribes here. However by the 4th century A.D. we learn that the Picts were divided into two peoples, the *Dicalydones* and the *Verturiones,* who presumably lived north and south of the barrier of the Mounth. This political division of the Picts continued for the next five centuries until the end of the Pictish kingdom. [1]

[1] See end notes for these references

Class I : Strathpeffer (Table 2A:40)

Map 1: The tribes of North Britain
in the Roman period

ORCADES

CORNOVII

CAERENI

LUGI

CARNONACAE

SMERTAE

DECANTAE

CREONES

CALEDONII

VACOMAGI

TAEZALI

VENICONES

EBUDAE

EPIDII

ANTONINE WALL

DAMNONII

VOTADINI

SELGOVAE

NOVANTAE

HADRIANS WALL

BRIGANTES

There is no way of knowing if any or all of these early 1st century A.D. tribes were Celts or some other pre-existing peoples but at all events it is clear that all these tribes had amalgamated over the three centuries into just two groups. On the basis of Ptolemy's map it would appear that the *Caledonii* tribe had absorbed all ten of the minor northern tribes into the *Dicalydones* people while the three southern tribes, *Vacomagi, Taezali* and *Venicones* became the *Verturiones* people. Why or how these confederations were formed is open to question but it seems to be related to the attempts of the Romans to pacify Scotland between the 1st and 4th centuries.

B.C.
c.300   The Greek voyager Pytheas mentions Orkney

A.D.
43   Orcadian chiefs submit to Claudius
80-84   Agricola leads the first Roman invasion of Scotland
139-154 The Antonine wall
c.150   Ptolemy's tribal map of Scotland
208-221 Severus campaigns in Scotland
297   The Picts first named by Eumenius
306   Constantius invades Scotland
360   Ammianus Marcellinus says the Picts are divided into two
         peoples
c.400   The Romans leave Britain
c.500   The Scots settle in Dalriada
554-584 King Bridei (son of Maelchon) receives Columba near
         Inverness
658   The Northumbrians occupy southern Pictland
683*   King Bridei (son of Bili) issues edict on symbol stones?
685*   Northumbrians defeated by the Picts under Bridei (son of
         Bili)
741*   Dalriada crushed by the Picts under Oengus (son of
         Fergus)
842*   Sueno's stone erected to denote the end of Pictish
         sovereignty?
843   Unification of Picts and Scots under Kenneth MacAlpin

* period of Pictish monumental sculpture

Table 1: A brief chronology of some major events in Pictland and
Scotland

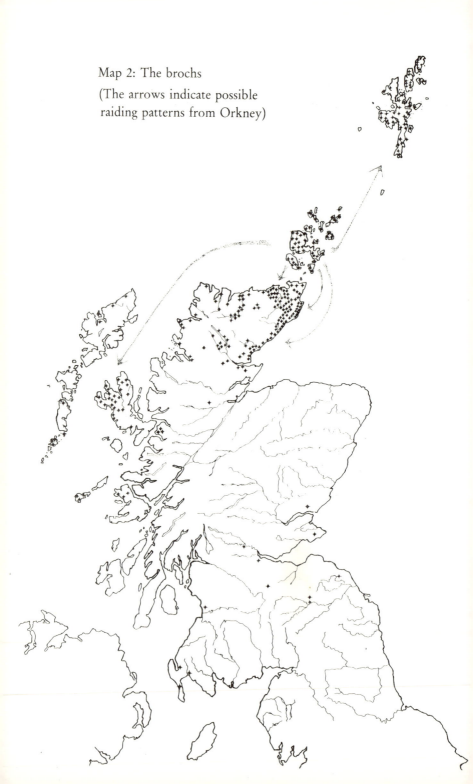

Map 2: The brochs
(The arrows indicate possible
raiding patterns from Orkney)

To anticipate my argument, it is just possible that these 14 tribes in ancient Scotland could have been the basis for the 28 Pictish symbols and the 7 main Pictish lineages of historical times. My reason for making this connection now is that I hold that the erection of the symbol stones was to signify alliances between different lineages. Thus the task of the *Caledonii* in binding ten different northern tribes to themselves into one confederation would have been greatly simplified if there was some system of controlled intermarriage and hence political alliances. It is not suggested that the symbols themselves were formalised as early as the 4th century although the different tribes may well have had distinctive emblems—a common feature of totemic, tribal societies. Nevertheless, we need to bear in mind what possible mechanisms there were available in tribal society for maintaining confederations of different tribes—it did not just happen!

Returning to Ptolemy's map, it shows, interestingly enough, the two groups of islands—the Hebrides *(Ebudae)* and the Orkneys *(Orcades)*—where between 100 B.C. and 100 A.D. a remarkable series of large structures—brochs—were erected. There are some 100 brochs or broch-sites in each of the Orkney and Shetland isles, 40 in the Western Isles and 230 in Caithness and Sutherland—most heavily concentrated opposite Orkney. These brochs are massive defensive towers that functioned to defend the local settlements against some sea-borne raiders. Yet, where in the first century B.C. would that enemy have sailed from? The most plausible suggestion is that they came from Orkney itself since most brochs are within easy sailing distance from Orkney (cf Map 2).

There can be no doubt that Orkney has played a key role in Scottish history from the 4th century B.C. to the 11th century A.D. yet it had an important role long before that. Orkney has one of the longest records of continuous occupation of anywhere in the British Isles as its rich archaeological sites testify.[2] So perhaps it is not surprising that it gets a mention as early as c.300 B.C. by the Greek voyager Pytheas who obviously thought it was important. He added that the British Isles were called the Pretanic Islands and that the cape opposite Orkney was Cape Orcas. Kenneth Jackson derives the name *Pretanic* from a people the *Pritani*, who are identifiable as the Picts while the name *Orcas* comes from **orci*, a Celtic word meaning 'the young pigs'.

The history of Orkney shows it to have been a thorn in the side of many would-be rulers of Scotland. The submission of Orcadian chiefs to Claudius in 43 A.D. is a significant fact in itself since why should it be mentioned unless Orkney was a force to be reckoned with in the conquest of Britain? (However, doubts have been expressed about the authenticity of this statement concerning the Orcadian chiefs.) In 84 A.D. Agricola sent his fleet up north to specially subdue the Orkneys and it is highly significant that this raid marks the beginning of the end of the brochs as purely defensive structures. King Bridei of the Picts, near Inverness, held hostages from the 'king' of Orkney in 564. Sixteen years later king Aed of Dalriada is waging war on the Orkneys. After a century we find the Pictish king Bridei laying waste Orkney in 682. By 800, Orkney had become the staging post for Norse attacks upon Ireland and maybe they were correct in calling the Pentland Firth—*Pettaland fjord:* Pictland Firth. Of course at that time the Picts were in Orkney and it is noteworthy that the very first Pictish settlement to be discovered was at Buckquoy, excavated just a few years ago by Anna Ritchie.

The evidence, then, all points to Orkney as being possibly the cradle of the Picts, as no other part of Scotland can make such a claim. This was of course the traditional view of the origin of the Picts, as given by Bede, that they came from Orkney and first conquered Caithness before subduing the rest of the country. Bede's view that the Picts themselves originated in Scythia is somewhat far-fetched but that they were P-Celtic invaders is not impossible. The Picts were never a single tribe but a confederation of tribes which had been welded together by the most powerful of their numbers. The Orcadians may well have been that tribe, as evidenced by the brochs, besides which as islanders they must have been good sailors from early times and were probably engaged in trade at the time of Pytheas since they must have had something to offer to get a mention by a Greek. The presence of brochs in Caithness, Sutherland and the Western Isles could be the result of an expansion of the Orcadians from their original strong island base. More likely, they were a common defensive structure erected against raids *from* Orkney, with the capture of slaves for sale to Rome being a possible prime motive for such incursions.

A far more sinister possibility exists—the Orcadians may have been head-hunters. To the Celts, the head was the seat of the soul and we know that they practised the cult of the severed head. Like many other head-hunting tribes the object of obtaining heads was two-fold: a) to give status to warriors and b) to promote the fertility of the village.

Agricola's punitive expedition to Orkney could well have been triggered by the newly-felt revulsion that the Romans had developed against Celtic human sacrifice but it is more likely that it was because of Orcadian piracy and slave-raiding. The reasons are unclear but one does not go to such great lengths as making an expedition without strong cause so the only conclusion must be that the Orkneys posed a considerable threat to the Roman conquest of Scotland. That threat had to be a naval one since one cannot imagine an Orcadian army marching down through Caithness and Sutherland, let alone further south.

The decline of the brochs after Agricola's raid could be due either to a drying-up of the slave trade or a change in inter-tribal raiding patterns. It should be pointed out that head-hunting and slave-raiding were more frequently carried out against one's neighbours than distant folk, so it is not surprising that brochs were built everywhere in this area—Orkney itself included; it is a cultural trait that has a circumscribed area. A significant feature about many trading societies is that they are often matrilineal, so it could well be that this particular element of Pictish society derived from Orkney and is not an aberrant or non-Indo-European custom. The abandonment of the brochs suggests that the northern tribes were slowly being united, possibly under the leadership of Orkney, thanks to their command of the sea and coastline—a unification process spurred on by the Romans.

The first Roman invasion of Scotland began in 80 A.D. under that brilliant Roman governor, Agricola, who established a series of forts between the Forth and Clyde after having crushed the *Votadini* and the *Selgovae* to the south. In 84 A.D. he pushed northwards, defeated the *Caledonii* at Mons Graupius and went on to the Moray Firth while his fleet subdued the Orkneys. However an uprising in 105 forced the Romans to retreat back to the Tyne in order to protect their colony. A dozen years later Hadrian decided to build a wall to separate the *Brigantes* in the south from the *Selgovae* and *Novantae*. The next emperor, Antonius Pius, reversed this policy and so in 139 the Romans advanced once again to the Forth/Clyde line and built a new *limes*—the Antonine wall. After only a few years this new frontier had to be abandoned after a new revolt by the *Brigantes* in 154. Fifty years later even Hadrian's great wall had been breached, and this provoked Severus to campaign again in Scotland between 208-211; this had the effect of making peace on the northern frontier for the rest of that century. New trouble eventually broke out and Constantius was forced to re-invade Scotland in 306 to quell its unruly people. Yet in 360 the Picts (as they were then called) were again on the rampage, and in alliance with the Scots from Ireland they plundered the districts near Hadrian's wall which they pierced in 367. The wall itself was abandoned in 400 and after that the Roman province had to shrift for itself. Thus this period of 300 years (80-380) of Roman involvement in Scotland was probably the most important element in the creation of the Picts as a unified set of tribes.

The Picts are first mentioned by name by Eumenius in 297

A.D. when he talks of 'the Caledones and other Picts'—indicating that the northern Picts were dominant under the leadership of the Caledonii. It is Ammianus Marcellinus in 360 who says that the Picts are divided into two peoples—*Dicalydones* and *Verturiones.* The meaning of the name *Pict* is obscure: it could refer to 'painted people' *(picti)* or it could be the Latinized version of a native name.

As this brief account shows, the Picts were a troublesome lot to the Romans beyond Hadrian's wall in the 4th century, even though they lived well beyond the Forth/Clyde line, with the semi-pacified Britons in between. Roman policy was to treat only with the most important tribes and either by bribery or fear try to make them keep the lesser tribes in order. While the discipline of the Roman army would have been impressive, it is not likely to have been followed by the Picts, yet they had a need to co-ordinate their attacks upon the Romans in order to defeat them and so the idea of a confederation under a single war leader may have evolved out of this experience. Hitherto the Picts and other tribes had only been fighting themselves in small engagements so the pickings from a combined attack on the Romanized settlements may have proved to be an irresistible lure, although 'protection money' might have been equally rewarding!

Up until the 6th century when the truly historical period of the Picts begins and which also introduces a new people—the Scots—into Scotland, there were only two indigenous peoples: the Picts and the British who, according to Eumenius, were enemies. Kenneth Jackson suggests that both the Picts and British were P-Celts; their main difference being that the British were pacified by the Romans in 297 and the Picts were not. Pacification also meant acquiring a taste for civilized living and with the recognition of Christianity in 313 it meant that the Romanised Britons south of the Forth/Clyde line were also offered a new religion. Apparently both these acquisitions were reinforced after the Roman withdrawal which further deepened the differences between the Picts and the British. The claims that the southern Picts were also converted to Christianity are nowhere substantiated despite Bede's statement that "the southern Picts who live on this side of the mountain" (i.e. the Mounth) were converted by Nynia (a Briton) in the 5th century.

When Bridei, son of Maelchon, (554-584), was reigning as king of the Picts near Inverness, he received a visit from Columba who, it is said, converted the king to Christianity. Columba had travelled from Dalriada where the Scots were now firmly entrenched and they were already Christian. So on the face of it there were three Christian tribes: the Picts, the British and the Scots, all at daggers drawn. However, there is no concrete evidence that the Picts were ever fully converted until the 8th century and even then it was only the southern Picts. It is quite likely that some Pictish households became Christian during this time but little more.

The situation in Scotland was quite altered in the 7th century when the Angles of Northumbria gradually advanced up south-east Scotland and colonised the area up to the Forth. They also overran southern Pictland. So for the next few centuries the battle lines were drawn between all four peoples in Scotland: the Picts, British, Scots and Angles. There was a constantly shifting pattern of alliances as they tried to defeat each other. Perhaps the three most significant events in this long period were: the defeat of the Northumbrians in 685 by the Pictish king Bridei, son of Bili; the crushing of Dalriada in 741 by the Pictish king Oengus, son of Fergus; the unification of the Picts and the Scots in 843 under Kenneth MacAlpin. (See Table 1 for summary).

It was at some period between the reign of Bridei, son of Maelchon, and that of Kenneth MacAlpin that the Pictish sculptured stones were erected—the subject of this book.

The purpose of this chapter has only been to sketch in the background to the Picts, and much detail (available in the standard histories) has been omitted as it is not germane to the symbol stones. As for the archaeological evidence, which is pretty scanty, it does not throw much light upon the Picts and practically none on the sculptured stones. Historical sources are equally disapointing as the stones are not even mentioned once.

We are unlikely to discover exactly how the tribes of 1st century Scotland were transformed into the Picts by the beginning of the 4th century, although there is some consensus of opinion, ancient and modern, that the impetus towards unification came from Northern Pictland. I endeavour to show in Chapter 6 that there are some grounds for this notion. It seems quite possible that sea-power lay at the root of this drive; this is hinted at in the following chapter. It is partly for this reason that I have laid stress on the importance of Orkney here and ventured an explanation of the role of the Orcadians in this matter. There can be little doubt that the broch-builders and the Picts are strongly connected in some way that goes beyond identity of place. Whatever the reason, the fact is that the centre of Pictish power had moved near to the Moray Firth by the 6th century, and further south to the Mearns by the 8th century. This gradual drift southwards implies a steady decline in the power of the Northern Picts—a point that will be discussed in Part II. [3]

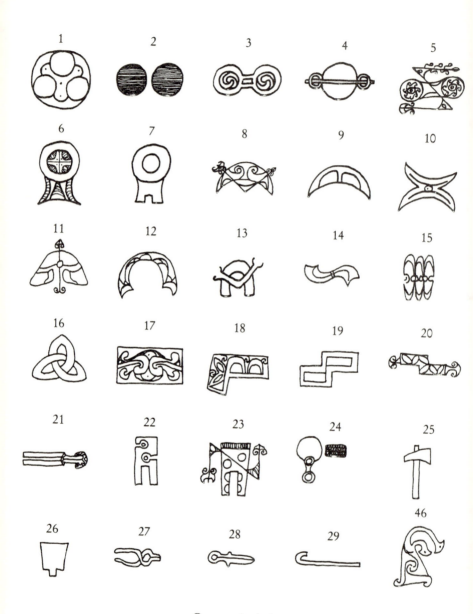

Geometric designs
(the *Caledonii* of Northern Pictland?)

Figure 1: The Pictish

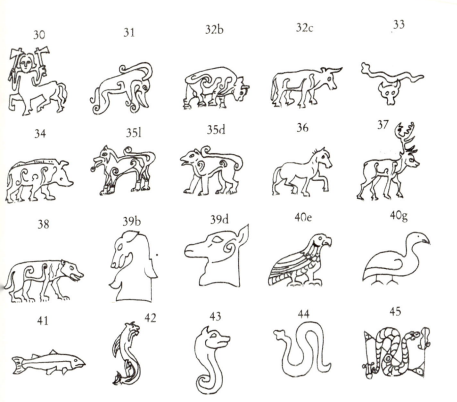

30   31   32b   32c   33
34   35l   35d   36   37
38   39b   39d   40e   40g
41   42   43   44   45

Animal designs
(the *Maeatae* of Southern Pictland?)

designs (after *ECMS*)

CHAPTER 2

The sculptured stones

Just over a thousand years ago Pictish society disappeared as a distinctive entity but they left behind, as silent witness to their existence, a remarkable series of sculptured stones that is without parallel in Europe. The prime purpose of these standing stones was to display symbolic messages about their society but these, once public, statements are now most secret. Perhaps the messages were so obvious, trivial and commonplace that it did not seem at all noteworthy to contemporary Christian commentators. However to us they are a puzzle that more than a century of devoted scholarship has failed to explain.

The Pictish sculptured stones exhibit a high standard of craftsmanship, technical skill and aesthetic merit that was outstanding for its time. The two main techniques used were incised patterns and relief carvings while the subjects depicted were abstract geometrical designs, animals, men and the Christian cross, all in various combinations. The sculptures were executed on stone of every kind—some roughly dressed, others carefully shaped into slabs or free-standing crosses. The very high degree of uniformity of the designs throughout Pictland suggests that the masons used a pattern-book: actual or mental. This stereotyping indicates that some of the designs must have carried the same meaning everywhere in the Pictish world, while deliberately setting the stones upright meant that they were to be publicly seen. The only question is why, and what do they mean? (cf Fig 1).

No immediate answer to that question springs to mind when one surveys the range of designs on the several hundred Pictish sculptured stones scattered over the landscape, since the collection seems so various in its composition. Indeed until the 19th century nobody had ever considered the totality of the Pictish stones since nobody was aware of its breadth and scope. All this changed with the publication of Stuart's *Sculptured Stones of Scotland*, 1856 and 1867, (hereafter called *SSS*), for it brought to public attention for the first time an array of some 300 stones (not all of them Pictish) in a magnificently illustrated volume on our heritage of Scottish monumental sculpture. The stones were sketched, sometimes inaccurately, and reproduced in sepia wash together with a commentary. The illustrations are not presented in any particular order and they cover stones from all over Scotland and the English border counties.

SSS was a remarkable achievement, for it contains more than half the stones we know about today and was instrumental in awaking such interest in Pictish stones that four or five new stones were reported every year up to the turn of the century. The intriguing nature of these stones led to attempts to systematise our knowledge, and this eventually resulted in that all-time classic of Pictish studies: Anderson and Allen's *The Early Christian Monuments of Scotland*, 1903—hereafter *ECMS*.

It was Anderson (p.xi) who first suggested that the Pictish stones could be grouped into three classes:

> Class I. Monuments with incised symbols only.
> Class II. Monuments with symbols and Celtic ornaments carved in relief.
> Class III. Monuments with Celtic ornament in relief, but without the symbols of the other two classes.

He further opined (p.cxiii) that Class I were roughly 7th and 8th century, Class II were 9th and 10th century, while Class III had ended by the 12th century.

It was left to Romilly Allen to describe and analyse the monuments according to this scheme, so the major credit for *ECMS* goes to him. Very sensibly, what Romilly Allen did was to take over Stuart's catalogue plus all the recent finds and group them into the three different classes. Furthermore, he abstracted all the incised designs and relief designs of a geometrical or animal nature from the Class I and II stones to make a list of 46 designs which he proceeded to analyse.

At this point we must pause because Romilly Allen's decisions were to have fateful consequences for our current understanding of the Pictish symbol stones. The sheer magnitude of *ECMS*, its detail of analysis and the fact that it actually ordered all those puzzling stones in a reasonable way has lent it an almost sacred quality—it is even jokingly referred to as 'the Bible'. But we have to be on our guard against simply accepting what *ECMS* tells us, because it contains two serious errors despite its excellence otherwise. In a sense we ought to stop the clock at 1900 and pretend that *ECMS* never really happened since it has misled every scholar this century with the resulting impasse in our studies of the Pictish symbols.

The first error concerns the terms of reference of both *SSS* and *ECMS*. As their titles imply, they are both concerned with Scotland which is legitimate in its own way; however, their simple mistake was to assume that present-day Scotland was somehow co-terminous with Pictland at the time of the erection of the three classes of stones. This quite deliberate confusion of Pictland with the whole of Scotland was also at the centre of a heated debate between the Scots and the English right throughout the Middle Ages concerning their respective claims to the territory north of the Cheviots. These nationalistic claims were quite as mythical as the belief that we can learn anything about the Pictish symbol stones by looking *outside* traditional Pictland. There can be no doubt whatever that the main aim of both *SSS* and *ECMS* was to account for the Pictish symbol stones—Classes I and II in Anderson's classification—and *not* simply to make a register of monuments in Scotland.

Had the true desire of these authors been to examine Dark Age and Middle Ages sculptures, then they would have had to include Northern England, Wales, South-west England and Ireland which have many fine examples that closely parallel the Class III stones here. Thus by extending their surveys from Pictland to the whole of Scotland they have inadvertently expanded the Class III category beyond all reasonable limits such that it is just a rag-bag of Christian monuments. Indeed the very title of *ECMS* begs the question as to its true purpose. There was another very popular myth in the Dark and Middle Ages to the effect that the whole of Scotland was Christian by the 6th century and much propaganda went into upholding that view. Did Romilly Allen fall victim to a similar myth about the conversion of the Picts? He added nearly 200 Class III items to Stuart's list that gave him a staggering 300 Class III artefacts! Hence he could well have said that 75 percent of all the sculptured stones were Christian but what he actually claimed was: "On the whole, it is quite obvious that the associations of the monuments are Christian rather than Pagan" (p.19). Yet if we were to subtract from his Class III all those stones which do not have any sculptured figures of men or beasts upon them then we are left with only 90 stones for the *whole* of Scotland! The remaining 210 stones are either plain crosses or mainly fragments of some monument or other that could have come from any period up to the late Middle Ages. If, now, with only 90 Class III sculptured stones we make the comparison of the number of Pagan designs to the number of Christian crosses on the stones we find, strangely enough, that 75 percent of the stones have *Pagan* associations! Is it just conceivable that those several hundred fragments of Christian sculpture were deliberately added to justify an ancient myth and the title of *ECMS?*

It is always possible to justify the inclusion of these superfluous 200 Class III stones on the grounds that the decorative designs on them might show links with the Pictish stones. In point of fact, Romilly Allen's exhaustive analysis of the designs only proves that *every* Christian stone is different in composition. Since 80 percent of *ECMS* Class III stones are extremely unlikely ever to have been Pictish at all, the whole category is highly misleading and simply bemuses the reader. Had Romilly Allen been more modest in scope and not allowed himself to be carried away by Stuart's example he could easily have shown that Classes II and III *in Pictland* are very closely related and quite distinct from the spurious stones with which he clutters up his Class III.

So the first recommendation is that Class III be redefined as:

> *Monuments with figures of men and beasts in relief but without the symbols of the other two classes.*

There are less than a hundred examples of this new Class III and only 60 appear in traditional Pictland. Interestingly enough, about one third of these stones have a representation of a man on horseback and these are given in Table 2E. A full listing of this new Class is not given since it is not relevant to the present task but with these numbers it is at last possible to speak sensibly of Class III which, hitherto, has been an utterly incomprehensible category.

Romilly Allen's second error is even more serious since it quite confuses all attempts to understand Classes I and II. When he compiled his list of designs upon these stones he arrived at a total of 46 designs which, *without any justification whatsoever,* he declared were symbols. On this basis he then proceeded to analyse these 'symbols' in terms of frequency, distribution, etc. However he confused at least six different designs and grouped them as only three *viz.* no. *35* is both a dog and a lion, no. *39* is a beast's head and a deer's head, no. *40* is a goose and an eagle. So really he was dealing with 50 'symbols' and, unfortunately, more designs have been discovered and added to his canon of 'symbols' so that the grand total is nearly 60.

These two false premisses have made *ECMS* a monumental source of confusion that has plagued everyone who has attempted to make sense of the Pictish sculptured stones right down to this very day. *ECMS* has been elevated into the position of being *the* touchstone of all Pictish studies, yet while it is a good reference book it is a bad guide. Hence it is little wonder that scholars have fought shy of re-examining the plethora of Class III stones and are extremely reluctant to do anything more than recapitulate what *ECMS* has to say about Classes I and II. Very few people have dared even to speculate on the meaning of the 'symbols', which is hardly surprising seeing that there are so many of them nowadays!

The chief objection to Romilly Allen's list of 'symbols' is that it was arrived at by the simple process of accumulation, much like the Class III stones; each new example was just added to the list without any prior conditions being laid as to what constitutes a symbol. This *ad hoc* method defies the very *raison d'être* of any symbol system, namely that symbols are specifically chosen to represent something and that *taken together* they form a system. To borrow an example from heraldry which is capable of an infinity of representations, there are some basic rules governing the creation of a blazon. There are standard arrangements of the designs that are widely recognized as having specific meanings *in themselves*, irrespective of the content of those designs. Now the real Pictish symbols are nowhere near as complicated as heraldic marks since there are fewer of them and the number of possible rules of combination are also limited, but both have underlying rules governing their use which makes them into systems.

What we have lacked hitherto is any notion of what kind of system the Picts employed. The one simple and obvious way of finding out does not seem to have crossed anyone's mind and that is to analyse the distribution and the various combinations of the 'symbols' themselves. For if the symbol stones were announcing important and unambiguous messages to an illiterate society, then surely the sum total of these messages must give us a clue to their decipherment. Having carried out this analysis (cf Table 3) it is plain that the majority of the designs occur in pairs and so the second recommendation is that:

> *a design that combines more than once with another design, in a pair, is a symbol.*

Using this one criterion, there appear to be *only* 28 true Pictish symbols out of the 60-odd designs assigned to this category. The theoretical reasons why pairs of symbols were used is given in Chapter 5.

Starting with Class I stones, where one is not distracted by any extraneous designs, it is clear that (with three exceptions) every *undamaged* stone has *two and only two* designs on its sides. An immediate qualification must be made concerning no.24—the mirror and comb symbol—which has a special and different

significance as will be discussed below. There are also a number of
damaged stones that only have a single symbol upon them, but it is
important to note that these symbols always occur elsewhere in
pairs. With only four exceptions, all pairs consist of two different
symbols. Furthermore, both of the two symbols *almost touch each
other* as if to indicate they are linked, one above the other, and so
actually constitute a single entity.

A peculiar feature of symbol *24*, the mirror and comb, is that it
always is placed at the bottom of a pair of symbols and is almost
touching the lower symbol. Thus *24* is a special kind of symbol
which tells us about the relationship between the other two
symbols above it. Sometimes the comb is missing, apparently, but
this does alter the function, which will be discussed in Chapter 4.
In terms of the paired-symbol hypothesis, symbol *24* is 'invisible'
and does not count in the same way as the 28 other symbols.

Very occasionally on Class I and II stones we find an array of
four or eight symbols arranged vertically above each other. In the
case of four symbols: A, B, C and D, the array could either be
reckoned as A/B & C/D or, more likely, A/B, B/C, C/D for
reasons explained in Chapter 5. What we are dealing with are still
pairs of symbols and not sets of four or eight symbols.

It should be noted that A/B and B/A are saying different things
about A and B although the *position* of one symbol above another
is making the same general statement about the top symbol with
regard to the bottom symbol. In the rare cases where A/X appears
but the design X is never found again it is unlikely that X is a true
symbol. Similarly, where we find design Z only occurring by itself
then it has no claim to being a symbol for it cannot be stressed
enough that Pictish symbols are always found in pairs and cannot
act alone like, say, the Christian cross can and *always* does:
Christianity is monolithic but Pictish symbols are dualistic.

This 'two or nothing' criterion for Pictish symbols discards half
of the 'symbols' in *ECMS* but to no great loss, since half of these
only appear once while another half are only found on Class II
stones. Two of these 'symbols' occur in a pair—once. It is difficult
to imagine anyone springing to the defence of these rejected designs
apart from the near 'mass-produced' Burghead bulls which have
won the hearts of the art-historians. Reluctantly, until it is found
yoked up to another symbol, and despite its high artistic quality,
there is no good reason why it should be accepted as a symbol.
What is important is the message, not the style. In any case there
are some poorly executed cows or bulls as well, so obviously the
Burghead breed were a pedigree herd and they will now be
certified, but not as symbols.

We can, in fact, certify that a total of 30 (!) of these *small* bulls were discovered in Burghead harbour, near the Pictish fort—oddly similar to other bull designs that have also been found near forts. This is a unique hoard of bull stones found, as they were, in a most unlikely water-meadow. *In any other context* there would be no question but that these were simply votive tablets that had been cast into the sea or down a well for ritual purposes, since this has been such a common practice in European cultures down the ages. The fact that these designs *happen to be Pictish,* curiously alters people's perceptions about the true functions of these particular stones. They are raised to the status of Art (for they are extremely well done) and then labelled symbols on no better grounds than that Romilly Allen declared them to be so! Thus the Burghead bulls are set alongside the equally well-executed true (on my definition) animal symbols as having the same purpose. Nobody seems to have wondered why such a huge quantity of *single* designs should be found in a single watery grave? There is no precedent for any other designs having been made in such large numbers in one place by this cattle-keeping, artistic, ritualistic and warlike people. Surely, the very circumstances of their discovery—*in* the sea, *near* a fort—and the fact that all the cattle designs, everywhere, are *also* single designs, might have raised the suspicion that they could be quite different in purpose from the much larger stones, with two designs, *that are firmly embedded upright in the soil of Pictland?* This is a point of some substance since it affects the interpretation of all the Pictish designs while not affecting their artistic merit (cf pp. 75-76). If the Burghead bulls were *not* votive tablets at some annual, animal sacrifice (a practice that continued long after the Picts), then what possible alternative explanation is there? This was not Art for Art's sake, neither was it an underwater factory.

With the two recommendations just made about Class III and the symbols as our guide, it is time to reassess the contributions of *SSS* and *ECMS* to our understanding or lack of it! Separating out those stones which do not have a genuine symbol on them and discounting all Class III stones without any sculptured figures, we arrive at the following table. The question marks indicate a wrong classification by Romilly Allen and his followers.

	I	I?	II	II?	III	III?
SSS 1856	53	4	33	10	50	45
SSS 1867	15	9	9	5	15	22
ECMS 1903	38	2	12	0	27	140
post 1903	40	14	3	3	?	?
Total	146	29	57	18	92	207

Stuart, of course, did not classify his stones, and it is Romilly Allen who placed them in these categories, but 16 percent of Class I are wrongly placed while most of the misplaced Class II stones should have been somewhere in Class III. As can be seen, Romilly Allen did quite a good job apart from his gross over-exaggeration of Class III and his lumping of all cave-art and *art mobilier* into Class I (not reckoned in the above table). However, the cumulative effect of these misclassifications is dramatic for *nearly one half* of all the generally accepted sculptured stones are of dubious value when it comes to considering genuine Pictish sculptures. Genuine is here defined as referring to stones that bear true symbols and/or figures. It may well be that the Picts also carved other designs like the bulls and even made decorated crosses without accompanying figures but it should be clear that retaining all these stones in the *ECMS* classification system is distinctly more confusing than enlightening. A reclassification on the lines suggested by the above table is necessary if we are to make any progress in explaining Pictish symbolism, because we have been overburdened far too long with a superfluity of 'symbols' and stones masquerading as Pictish.

Another thing the above table shows is that three Class I, one Class II and one Class III stones were discovered every couple of years from 1856 until 1903. Since then only one Class I stone has been found every two years while hardly more than a handful of Class II and Class III stones have turned up, curiously enough. As it happens, half of the Class I stones we now have are damaged but only one third of those recorded by Stuart were, so it looks as if we are discovering many more damaged stones. The significance of this is that half of these despoiled stones bear only one symbol—it is as if the other symbol was smashed off! An examination of these damaged stones shows that the 'surviving' symbol is generally in its 'home' territory, as will be shown later.

Employing the new classification proposed above, Tables 2 list all the currently known stones in Classes I and II by county, grid reference, bibliographical reference, the symbols found, location of discovery and present whereabouts if different, besides indicating if they are damaged.[4] Each stone is numbered and ordered geographically from north to south, as far as possible.[5] The stones that fall into the dubious categories are separated into adjoining tables. A full listing of the 90 sculptured Class III stones has not been given as they are mainly peripheral to the study of symbols. However, those stones that bear a horseman upon them have been given, as these riders function as a kind of symbol on both Class II and III stones.

The stones are given on the distribution maps 3-5 in accordance with their sequence number in the tables.[6] The maps show that the Mounth forms a natural division: in Class I, most stones are to the north of the Mounth while the reverse is the case for Class II and III. There is an apparent tendency for stones to cluster together as if they had found some centre of excellence—this tends to be a museum or a churchyard. Little can be deduced from the fact that a third of Class I and II stones are near churches, since churches are normally placed in the middle of a settlement on common ground where public notices would also have been placed before the arrival of Christianity.

At present more than half the Pictish stones are in private ownership or in museums; the remainder are in churchyards or in the open. The former were simply collected and removed to private residences or institutions while we may also suspect that the Church did the same. For obvious reasons most of Class III are at religious sites and more Class II than Class I stones are near churches, although the actual numbers are the same—25.

Attempts have been made to associate symbol stones with burials but very few of the 200 stones seems to be directly connected with this practice. Some stones are near interments which is hardly surprising since the stones were not put up in the wilderness but in, or close to, settlements where some of the hundreds of thousands of Picts must have been buried or disposed of over the centuries. It is most likely that the stones were erected in sacred areas, possibly places of pagan worship, where the Christians were also very careful to build their own churches. However, the most significant feature about the location of the stones is not their orientation but their frequent presence near water—the sea, rivers, springs and wells. This could simply be a consequence of the settlement pattern but maybe there is more to it than that (cf Chapter 7).

Lastly, one must consider the actual frequencies of the combinations of the symbols. Even with only 28 symbols there are 756 possible ways of forming pairs of symbols but *only 12 percent* of these options are taken up by the Picts. We find there are just 90 *different* pairs of which one third are repeated a half a dozen times on average. Close examination reveals that just three symbols —5, 8 and 31—are a constituent part of 2/3 of all symbol pairs in Class I and II stones and we find that their combination with 18 other symbols accounts for most of the repeated pairs. As for the remaining pairs, they are formed from the other 25 symbols and only represent 8 percent of the possible combinations, which indicates that these unique pairs are very rare.

The combinations are shown in Table 3 where it can be seen that the combination of symbols is heavily skewed so that just 14 symbols are involved in 98 percent of all pairings and that even their own intercombinations account for 70 percent of the total. [7] The main conclusion is that these 14 symbols are highly significant while the remaining 14 symbols only play a minor role, although a necessary one. It is not without interest to note that there is absolutely no place in this scheme for any of the 20-odd rejected 'symbols' of Romilly Allen's for they would be right out on a limb. The *actual* pairings are given in Figure 2. [8]

Whatever the purpose of these paired symbols was, the geographical and statistical distribution of the symbols makes plain one fact: no symbol pair was ever used twice in the same place.

The purpose of this chapter is to pave the way for a possible solution to the problem of the symbol stones by presenting the data in a new way. Simplification has been the aim and, by just using two criteria, the huge accumulation of stones and symbols has been effectively halved. There should be few regrets at losing all this spurious data which has for too long blurred our vision. Some people may object on principle against this paring down, although it would be hard to find a good reason for keeping misleading data. Anyway it is now up to the defenders of the *status quo* to make a case for the retention of the excluded stones and 'symbols'.

As an object lesson in what happens if one keeps the whole panoply of *ECMS,* consider some of the proffered interpretations to be found in the next chapter.

Note on the enumeration system used in this book

a)	I, II, III	the three classes of Pictish monument
b)	*I—VIII*	the eight sets of four symbols grouped into geometric and animal designs (pp. 72-73)
c)	i—ii	the two provincial moieties
d)	*i—viii*	a dualistic arrangement of the eight sets of four symbols (p. 66)
e)	1,2,3, . . .	frequencies, enumerations, dates *(passim)*
f)	*1,2,3, . . .*	symbol reference numbers (Figure 1)
g)	A,B,C,D	the four sets of the basic seven symbols (Tables 3 & 5)
h)	*A,B,C,D*	the four sections of Sueno's Stone (pp. 166-175)
i)	M & N	hypothetical lineages (pp. 126-127)
j)	P,Q,R,S	hypothetical paired lineages (pp. 83-92, 155-156)
k)	W,X,Y,Z	the geographical areas called provinces (Maps 3-6)

95(14)

143

121(12)

89

109
109

9

67

76(34)

108

100(52)

6(1)

107

61(16)

23

33

36(5)

65

40

106

75

47

85

3

81(4)

54

31(4)

103

82

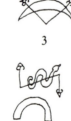
48

77

Figure 2: The symbol pa

135

62

55

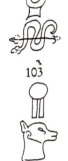

103

72

45

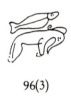

80

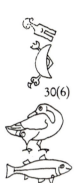

30(6)

138

78

91

96(3)

51

49

24

112

11

53

86

128

86

17

43(2)

8

1

90

130

94

127

75

(Class II in brackets)

26

 114

 68

 46

 124

 (44)

 (17)

 (21)

 (38)

 (15)

 (45)

 (54)

 (42)

 (8)

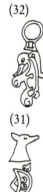 (32)

 (5)

 (3)

 (23)

 (16)

 (31)

 (6)

 (29)

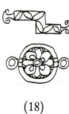 (36)

 (5)

 (43)

 (37)

 (26)

 (18)

(3)

 (39)

TABLE 2: CATALOGUE OF PICTISH SYMBOL STONES

CLASS I, II, and III

Arranged according to geographical location from the North southwards

NOTES

1. The grid references give the reported sites of the stones.

2. The present locations of the stones are at the grid references unless mentioned otherwise in the comments.

3. *Only Class III stones with horsemen are given.*

4. Class I and II stones that do not bear common true symbols are mentioned separately, together with other artefacts that bear symbols.

Caution: Symbol stones have a remarkable mobility. They are frequently removed from where they were discovered, to private houses, churches and museums. This process has not yet ceased and hence this catalogue must be regarded as provisional. Furthermore, free access to some stones is not always possible.

TABLE 2A: CLASS I

Notes:
a) No. in County

b) ECMS   *Early Christian Monuments of Scotland (page numbers).*
     RCAMS   *Royal Commission on Ancient Monuments of Scotland Inventory (for area).*
     PSAS   *Proceedings of the Society of Antiquaries of Scotland.*
     DES   *Discovery and Excavation in Scotland.*

If no reference is given, it means that no entry was made in the RCAMS files, and the source must be from their own inspectorate.

c) Symbol   / pair; // two sides; II between pairs; + mirror; * mirror & comb; — side by side.

d) Comment: Locations   D — Dunrobin Castle; De — Dundee; E — Edinburgh; El — Elgin; F — Falkland Palace; I — Inverness; P — Perth Museum.

★ damaged.

TABLE 2A: CLASS I

CLASS	SEQUENCE NUMBER	COUNTY	NO. IN COUNTY	GRID REF.	ECMS REFS.	SYMBOL	COMMENTS		NAME
I	1	Shetland	1	HU 190570	4/5	17/12+	Lost	?	Sandness
I	2	Orkney	1	HY 2537 2678	RCAMS	40e	Lost	?	Broch of Oxtro
I	3	Orkney	2	HY 308168	PSAS LXXIV	40e/8+	Kirkwall		Knowe of Burrian
I	4	Orkney	3★	HY 379170	20	17/8		E	Firth nr. Kirkwall
I	5	Orkney	4	HY 542031	PSAS LVIII: 297	7/8+		E	St. Andrews, Greens
I	6	Orkney	5★	ND 449931	20/1	17/8//8/7		E	St. Peter's
I	7	Sutherland	1★	NC 75 64	45	44? or 45?		?	Kirtomy
I	8	Caithness	1	NC 9226618	29/30	15/7*	Lost		Sandside House
I	9	Caithness	2	ND 025701	30	8/12	Lost	?	Thurso Castle
I	10	Caithness	3★	ND 339584	27	7?/15		E	Birkle Hill, Keiss
I	11	Caithness	4★	ND 339584	28/9	41/17	Ogham	E	Keiss Bay
I	12	Caithness	5	ND 349550		17		E	Ackergill
I	13	Caithness	6★	ND 198334	PSAS XCII: 40	8		?	Latheron
I	14	Sutherland	2★	ND 0420 1615	PSAS 102: 136, 143	4?		D	Navidale
I	15	Sutherland	3★	?	PSAS XL: 128	12?	Lost	?	Langdale
I	16	Sutherland	4★	NC 930080	43/4	14+		D	Kintradwell 2
I	17	Sutherland	5★	NC 930080	43	14/7		D	Kintradwell 1
I	18	Sutherland	6★	NC 930080	45	21?		D	Kintradwell 4
I	19	Sutherland	7★	NC 930080	44/5	8*		D	Kintradwell 3
I	20	Sutherland	8	NC 914069	39/40	12/8+		D	Clynemilton 1
I	21	Sutherland	9★	NC 914069	40/1	23*		D	Clynemilton 2
I	22	Sutherland	10★	NC 894060	39	17/8+		D	Clynekirkton 2
I	23	Sutherland	11	NC 894060	38/9	8/17		D	Clynekirkton 1
I	24	Sutherland	12	NC 851007	42	14/21*		D	Dunrobin Castle
I	25	Sutherland	13	NC 833008	PSAS LXXVII: 26-30	8/31*		D	Golspie 2

TABLE 2A: CLASS I

CLASS	SEQUENCE NUMBER	COUNTY	NO. IN COUNTY	GRID REF.	ECMS REFS.	SYMBOL	COMMENTS	NAME
I	26	Sutherland	14	NC 847003		10/45*		? Golspie 3
I	27	Sutherland	15★	NH 814965	47/8	8?		D Little Ferry Links 4
I	28	Sutherland	16★	NH 814965	45/6	17?		D Little Ferry Links 1
I	29	Sutherland	17★	NH 814965	46/7	12/8?		D Little Ferry Links 2
I	30	Sutherland	18	NH 787983	41	21/8/46	Pillar	D Craigton
I	31	Ross	1★	NG 800771	PSAS LXXXVI: 110-11	40e/41		Gairloch
I	32	Hebrides	1	NG 421491	RCAMS: 640	8/5*		Snizort
I	33	Hebrides	2	NG 241465	RCAMS: 640	8/1		Dunvegan
I	34	Hebrides	3	NG 330340	PSAS LXI: 241-3	5/8		E Fiscavaig
I	35	Hebrides	4	NF 800560	110/1	1/17		E Benbecula
I	36	Hebrides	5	NL 607875	111/3	8/46		Pabbay
I	37	Ross	2★	NH 709851	57/9	41/5	Pillar	Edderton
I	38	Ross	3	NH 663712	PSAS LXV: II	3/3?		Nonakiln
I	39	Ross	4	NH 681690	60/1	19?/8?/21?	Pillar	Roskeen
I	40	Ross	5★	NH 485585	59/60	12/40e		Strathpeffer
I	41	Ross	6★	NH 549589	56/7	5/8/8//1?/8		Dingwall
I	42	Ross	7★	NH 559949	106	5/5		Torgorm
I	43	Inverness	1	NH 511453	PSAS 101: 288-9	15/8		I Wester Balbair
I	44	Inverness	2★	NH 511319		8/?		Garbeg, Drumna-drochit
I	45	Inverness	3	NH 655412	103/5	6/34	Pillar	Knocknagael
I	46	Inverness	4★	NH 647395	DES 1968: 23	34?/3?		Essich House
I	47	Inverness	5★	NH 638402	PSAS XCII: 39-40	23/12*		Cullaird, Dores
I	48	Inverness	6★	NH 510300	98/9	45/3		E Drumbuie 1
I	49	Inverness	7	NH 510300	99/100	41/6*		E Drumbuie 2

TABLE 2A: CLASS I

CLASS	SEQUENCE NUMBER	COUNTY	NO. IN COUNTY	GRID REF.	ECMS REFS.	SYMBOL	COMMENTS		NAME
I	50	Inverness	8	NH 798315	PSAS LXVIII: 56	8/5		E	Invereen
I	51	Moray	1	NJ 149691	124/6	12?/8*//40g/41		E	Easterton of Roseisle
I	52	Moray	2★	NJ 223696	124	8		E1	Drainie
I	53	Moray	3	NJ 185576	128/9	39b/41*			Upper Manbean
I	54	Moray	4	NJ 206586	118/9	40e/23			Birnie
I	55	Banff	1	NJ 284469	151/2	6—23			Arndilly
I	56	Banff	2	NJ 323392	PSAS LX: 274-8	31/?			Mortlach
I	57	Moray	5	NJ 202423	127/8	1?/8/8			Knockando 1
I	58	Moray	6	NJ 202423	127/8	44/?+	Pillar		Knockando 2
I	59	Banff	3	NJ 183376	DES 1964: 23	8/31			Inveravon 4
I	60	Banff	4★	NJ 183376	154	31			Inveravon 3
I	61	Banff	5	NJ 183376	153/4	8/4*			Inveravon 2
I	62	Banff	6	NJ 183376	152/3	6/40e*	Pillar		Inveravon 1
I	63	Inverness	9★	NJ 142353	PSAS XL	8/6			Advie
I	64	Banff	7	NJ 149259	152	1			Balneilean
I	65	Inverness	10	NJ 058262	96/7	12/31	RH)		Congash 1
I	66	Inverness	11	NJ 058262	96/7	5/11	LH) jamb		Congash 2
I	67	Moray	7★	NJ 026260	101/2	8/23			Inverallan
I	68	Moray	8	NJ 049288	126/7	37/17?		E	Grantown
I	69	Moray	9	NH 994254	101	23/8		E	Findlarig
I	70	Inverness	12★	NH 951206	105	8			Lyncburn
I	71	Aberdeen	1	NJ 930631	187/8	40e/23			Tyrie
I	72	Aberdeen	2	NJ 987508	164	?/6/4	Illegible		Fetterangus
I	73	Aberdeen	3	NJ 969481	162	17/8	Lost		Old Deer
I	74	Aberdeen	4★	NJ 720490	187	5		?	Turriff

TABLE 2A: CLASS I

CLASS	SEQUENCE NUMBER	COUNTY	NO. IN COUNTY	GRID REF.	ECMS REFS.	SYMBOL	COMMENTS	NAME
I	75	Aberdeen	5	NJ 745378	184/5	12/1		(Rothie Brisbane
I	76	Aberdeen	6★	NJ 768377	164/5	8/31+		(Fyvie 1
I	77	Aberdeen	7★	NJ 768377	165/6	3/40e	Fyvie Church	(Fyvie 2
I	78	Aberdeen	8	NJ 529464	185/6	40g/6+		Tillytarmont 1
I	79	Aberdeen	9	NJ 521469		8/5	Whitehills	Tillytarmont 2
I	80	Aberdeen	10	NJ 521469		9/1	Whitehills	Tillytarmont 3
I	81	Aberdeen	11	NJ 521469		40e/31	Whitehills	Tillytarmont 4
I	82	Aberdeen	12	NJ 521469	DES 1974: 5	45/12*	Whitehills	Tillytarmont 5
I	83	Aberdeen	13★	NJ 529399	166	12	Pillar – illegible	Huntly 1
I	84	Aberdeen	14★	NJ 558376	167	5		Huntly 2
I	85	Aberdeen	15	NJ 557282	505/6	31/21+		Ardlair
I	86	Aberdeen	16★	NJ 539260	157/8	4/5+	Knockespock House	Clatt 1
I	87	Aberdeen	17★	NJ 539260	158	5		Clatt 2
I	88	Aberdeen	18★	NJ 539260	PSAS XLIV: 208	12/31		Clatt 3
I	89	Aberdeen	19	NJ 610302	167/8	5/45+		Insch
I	90	Aberdeen	20★	NJ 604258	177/8	17/38*	Pillar	Newbigging Leslie
I	91	Aberdeen	21★	NJ 535264	181/2	41/12		Percylieu
I	92	Aberdeen	22★	NJ 490263	182	5/?	?	Rhynie 2
I	93	Aberdeen	23★	NJ 490263	183	31/8+	Illegible	Rhynie 4
I	94	Aberdeen	24★	NJ 499266	183/4	39b/5*	Lost	Rhynie 5
I	95	Aberdeen	25★	NJ 499266	184	5/8+		Rhynie 6
I	96	Aberdeen	26	NJ 490263	182	41/31		Rhynie 1
I	97	Aberdeen	27	NJ 497262		31/?	Pillar	Barflat
I	98	Aberdeen	28	NJ 664295	178/9	3/45		Newton House
I	99	Aberdeen	29	NJ 694280	PSAS L: 279-85	6/?/10	Pillar	Newton of Lewesk

TABLE 2A: CLASS I

CLASS	SEQUENCE NUMBER	COUNTY	NO. IN COUNTY	GRID REF.	ECMS REFS.	SYMBOL	COMMENTS	NAME
I	100	Aberdeen	30	NJ 703258	175/6	8/3		Logie Elphinstone 1
I	101	Aberdeen	31	NJ 703258	176/7	8/5	Ogham — Pillar	Logie Elphinstone 2
I	102	Aberdeen	32	NJ 703258	176/7	31/8		Logie Elphinstone 3
I	103	Aberdeen	33★	NJ 780206	168/9	8/6/45/5	Pillar	Inverurie 1
I	104	Aberdeen	34★	NJ 780206	169/70	?/5		Inverurie 3
I	105	Aberdeen	35	NJ 742238	PSAS 49: 334	5		East Balhaggardy
I	106	Aberdeen	36★	NJ 742235	162/3	12/14*		Drimmies
I	107	Aberdeen	37	NJ 759288	161/2	8/9*	Mounie castle	Daviot
I	108	Aberdeen	38	NJ 761225	506/7	8/45	Ogham	Brandsbutt
I	109	Aberdeen	39	NJ 779201	170	5/41*		Keith Hall
I	110	Aberdeen	40	NJ 779197	160/1	31/8	Pillar	Crichie
I	111	Aberdeen	41★	NJ 804249	157	8/5*		Bourtie
I	112	Aberdeen	42	NJ 793163	171/2	41/4//8/31	Pillar	Kintore 1
I	113	Aberdeen	43★	NJ 793163	172/4	31/5//31+	Back upside down	Kintore 2
I	114	Aberdeen	44	NJ 793163	174	10/21		Kintore 3 *E*
I	115	Aberdeen	45★	NJ 748096	PSAS XLIX: 33-43	6*		Nether Corskie
I	116	Aberdeen	46	NJ 821144	170/1	1/8		Kinellar
I	117	Aberdeen	47	NJ 875154	163/4	31/5		Dyce
I	118	Aberdeen	48★	NO 790980	180/1	23/8*		Park House
I	119	Aberdeen	49★	NJ 640024	159/60	?/44/41	Pillar	Craigmyle House
I	120	Aberdeen	50★	NJ 430048	179/80	23/8		Mar Coldstone
I	121	Aberdeen	51★	NO 390975	186/7	5/31+		Tullich
I	122	Angus	1★	NO 470537	206	45	Kimblethmount House	Baggerton
I	123	Angus	2★	NO 638473	DES 1965: 4	8/31+	*De*	Inverkeillor
I	124	Angus	3	NO 508488	206/7	46/5*	Pillar	Dunnichen

TABLE 2A: CLASS I

CLASS	SEQUENCE NUMBER	COUNTY	NO. IN COUNTY	GRID REF.	ECMS REFS.	SYMBOL	COMMENTS		NAME
I	125	Angus	4	NO 522555		12/31	Pillar	De	Aberlemno 4
I	126	Angus	5	NO 524556	205	44/5*			Aberlemno 1
I	127	Angus	6	NO 395466	221	37?/44+	Re-used in II		Glamis 1
I	128	Angus	7	NO 385468	221/3	44/41+	Re-used in II		Glamis 2
I	129	Perth	1	NO 290504	282/3	12/31	Pillar		Bruceton
I	130	Angus	8★	NO 273398	207/8	38/5+	Pillar		Keillor
I	131	Angus	9★	NO 465337	208	31	Lost?		Linlathen
I	132	Angus	10	NO 374362	208/9	8/31		De	Strathmartine
I	133	Perth	2	NO 212328	PSAS XCV: 221-2	?/31*			Collace
I	134	Perth	3	NO 306299	DES 1966: 38	2?			Longforgan
I	135	Perth	4	NO 191213	PSAS XCII: pl.III	3/41//21*//41/44	On three sides, Ogham P		St Madoes
I	136	Perth	5★	NO 188166	282	21/8			Abernethy
I	137	Fife	1	NO 260163	343/4	4/8+			Lindores
I	138	Fife	2★	NO 209101	DES 1969	21/39d			Strathmiglo
I	139	Fife	3★	NO 2384 0732	DES 1971: 21	21/2?		F	Westfield Farm 1
I	140	Fife	4★	NO 2384 0732	DES 1971: 21	6/6		F	Westfield Farm 2
I	141	Fife	5★	NO 360090	334/5	40e/3?			Walton
I	142	Perth	6	NN 924097	PSAS LXXXI: 2-7	40g/?			Blackford
I	143	Perth	7	NN 818654	285/6	5/12?			Struan
I	144	Midlothian	1★	NT 252736	421	8/5		E	Edinburgh

TABLE 2B: DUBIOUS MONUMENTS (NO COMMON SYMBOLS) & OTHERS

Notes:a) No. in County

b) ECMS *Early Christian Monuments of Scotland (page numbers).*
RCAMS *Royal Commission on Ancient Monuments of Scotland Inventory (for area).*
PSAS *Proceedings of the Society of Antiquaries of Scotland.*
DES *Discovery and Excavation in Scotland.*
If no reference is given, it means that no entry was made in the RCAMS files, and the source must be from their own inspectorate.

c) Symbol ✸ damaged. / pair; // two sides; II between pairs; ° possible mirror and/or comb; — side by side.

d) Comment: Locations D — Dunrobin Castle; E — Edinburgh; SV — St Vigeans; M — Meigle; I — Inverness; El — Elgin; F — Falkland Palace; De — Dundee; P — Perth Museum.

TABLE 2B: DUBIOUS MONUMENTS (NO COMMON SYMBOLS) & OTHERS

CLASS	SEQUENCE NUMBER	COUNTY	NO. IN COUNTY	GRID REF.	ECMS REFS.	SYMBOL	COMMENTS		NAME
I	1	Shetland	1	HU 608985	4/5			E	Uyea
I	2	Shetland	2	HU 475415	3/4			E	Lerwick
I	3	Shetland	3	HU 398096				?	Dunrossness
I	4	Shetland	4	HU 369209		5	Stone Disc	E	Dunrossness
I	5	Orkney	1	HY 763514	25/6	8//7	Bone		Broch of Burrian
I	6	Orkney	2	HY 763514	25		Pentacle	E	Broch of Burrian
I	7	Orkney	3	HY 383268	PSAS I.VIII: 295-7		Scratched figures	?	Broch of Aikerness
I	8	Orkney	4★	HY 37232640	PSAS 101: 130-3	o		?	Sands of Evie
I	9	Sutherland	1★	NH 814965	47	o?		D	Little Ferry Links 3
I	10	Ross	1★	NH 644743	55/6	38		I	Ardross 1 Roskeen
I	11	Ross	2★	NH 644743	55/6	39d	Deer — 37	I	Ardross 2 Roskeen
I	12	Inverness	1★	NH 6643	102/3	32		I	Inverness
I	13	Inverness	2★	NH 6643	103	32		I	Inverness
I	14	Inverness	3★	NH 600350	97/8	34?		E	Dores — Clune Farm
I	15	Moray	4	NJ 494444	95/6				Balblair
I	16	Moray	1	NJ 109690	119/20	32		E	Burghead 1
I	17	Moray	2★	NJ 109690	119/20	32			Burghead 2
I	18	Moray	3	NJ 109690	121	32		El	Burghead 3
I	19	Moray	4★	NJ 109690	122	32			Burghead 4
I	20	Moray	5	NJ 109690	122	32	British Museum		Burghead 5
I	21	Moray	6★	NJ 109690	123	32		El	Burghead 6
I	22	Moray	7	NJ 190710	129/31	41/8//46/15//8/6// 19/6 5/15//pentacle//	Cave		Covesea
I	23	Banff	1★	NJ 560464	154/5	?			North Redhill
I	24	Inverness	5★	NH 821048	100	39d	Deer — 37		Dunachton
I	25	Aberdeen	1	NJ 898140	199	14	Chain	E	Parkhill
I	26	Aberdeen	2	NJ 790162	DES 1975:5				Kintore 4
I	27	Aberdeen	3	NJ 780206	169	o?			Inverurie 2
I	28	Aberdeen	4	NJ 780206	170	36			Inverurie 4

Class I : Aberlemno 1   (Table 2A:126)

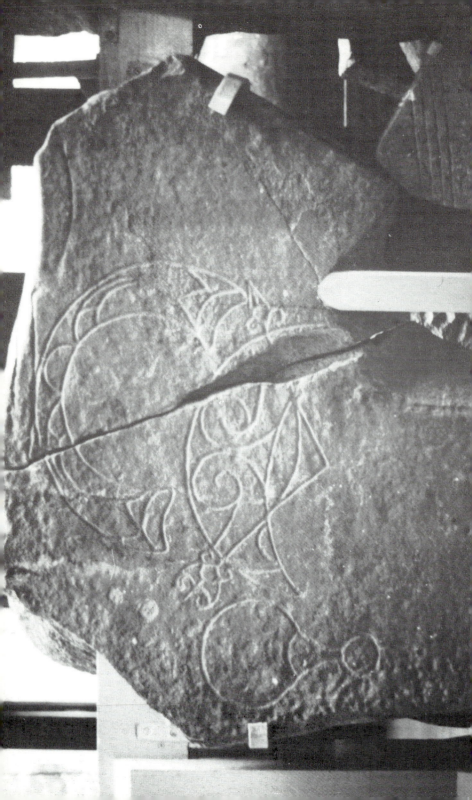

TABLE 2B: DUBIOUS MONUMENTS (NO COMMON SYMBOLS) & OTHERS

CLASS	SEQUENCE NUMBER	COUNTY	NO. IN COUNTY	GRID REF.	ECMS REFS.	SYMBOL	COMMENTS	NAME
I	29	Aberdeen	5	NJ 495270	182	?/?		Rhynie 3
I	30	Aberdeen	6★	NJ 464047	159	5		Corrachree House
I	31	Kincardine	1	NO 882846	200	41	Banchory House garden	Stonehaven 1
I	32	Kincardine	2	NO 882846	200/1	?	Banchory House garden	Stonehaven 2
I	33	Kincardine	3	NO 882846	201		Banchory House garden	Stonehaven 3
I	34	Kincardine	4	NO 882846	201	2?	Banchory House garden	Stonehaven 4
I	35	Kincardine	5	NO 882846	201	5//46°	Banchory House garden	Stonehaven 5
I	36	Kincardine	6★	NO 882846	201			Stonehaven 6
I	37	Kincardine	7	NO 823908			Ogham	Auquhollie Farm
I	38	Perth	1	NN 995425				Dunkeld
I	39	Perth	2	NN 818497	DES 1971: 34			Camserney
I	40	Angus	1	NN 692463				W. Mains of Ethie
I	41	Angus	2	NO 601406	205/6			Arbilot
I	42	Angus	3	NO 537577			?	Aberlemno 5
I	43	Perth	3	NO 160345			?	Cargill
I	44	Angus	4	NO 492349	283/4	8//5/39b	Bronze Plate — lost	Caiplie
I	45	Fife	1★	NO 599058	280/1	12?/?	Cave	Norrie's Law
I	46	Fife	2★	NO 409073	PSAS XCIV: 324	5/39b	Plaque, Beast E	East Wemyss
I	47	Fife	3★	NT 334958	368/9	?.?	Caves	East Wemyss
I				NT 242969	370/3	?.?	Caves	East Wemyss
I				NT 343920	370/3	?.?	Caves	East Wemyss
I				NT 344971	370/3	?.?	Caves	East Wemyss
I				NT 345972	370/3		Caves	East Wemyss
I	48	Fife	4	NO 244062	PSAS 60: 32	32	Pillar E	East Lomond Hill
I	49	Roxburgh	1	NT 437140	431/2	41		Roberton
I	50	Selkirk	1	NT 3924	472/3	5/22	Chain E	Over Kirkhope
I	51	Lanark	1	NS 824196	477/8	5/43	Rock	Whiteclough
I	52	Kirkcud- bright	1	NX 598560				Anwoth
I	53	Argyll	1	NR 837935	PSAS LXIV: 112	34	Rock	Dunadd
I	54	Argyll	2	NM 864099	PSAS XCV: 37	37		Glen Domhain

Class I : Clynemilton 1   (Table 2A:20)

D

TABLE 2C: CLASS II

CLASS	SEQUENCE NUMBER	COUNTY	NO. IN COUNTY	GRID REF.	ECMS REFS.	SYMBOL	COMMENTS	NAME
II	1	Orkney	1★	HY 238285	RCAMS	6/8/31/40e	→ 3 Warriors E	Brough of Birsay
II	2	Caithness	1	ND 132621	30/3	43 — 43 II 15/8	→ Horse Thurso	Halkirk
II	3	Caithness	2	ND 336419	33/5	(31/41 II 8/35d) (19/43 II 3/10)	← Horse	Ulbster
II	4	Caithness	3	ND 200336	PSAS XXXVIII: 534-8	40e/41	← 2 Horsemen	Latheron 2
II	5	Sutherland	1	NH 787983	48/50	17/31 II 35d/41 II 46/8 II 3/44	Ogham, Man, Ogham D	Golspie
II	6	Ross	1★	NH 915840	73/5	8/21/45/31?	→ Horseman	Tarbat
II	7	Ross	2	NH 870760	61/3	5/8/2/*	← Female rider and 3 Horsemen	Hilton of Cadboll
II	8	Ross	3	NH 865747	68/73	3/31	→ 3 Horsemen	Shandwick
II	9	Ross	4	NH 804722	75/83	40e/31	→ Horseman	Nigg
II	10	Ross	5★	NH 737576	63/8	8/8 II 5/8 ++		Rosemarkie
II	11	Hebrides	1	NG 540360	PSAS XLI: 435	21/8	Cross also on rock below	Portree
II	12	Nairn	1	NH 930420	115/6	31/8/5/31	Archer hunting	Glenferness
II	13	Moray	1	NH 989584	132/5	43 — 43 II 31/5	Oghams	Brodie
II	14	Moray	2	NJ 221630	135/6	5/8	← 4 Horsemen	Elgin
II	15	Banff	1	NJ 324394	155/6	43 — 43 II 40e/44	← Horseman	Mortlach
II	16	Aberdeen	1	NJ 875154	189/90	8/4 — 6/5		Dyce
II	17	Aberdeen	2	NJ 703247	190/1	23/31*	Pillar	Maiden Stone
II	18	Aberdeen	3	NJ 7015	192/4	19/4		Monymusk
II	19	Aberdeen	4	NJ 436068	191/2	5 — 13	← Horseman	Migvie
II	20	Kincardine	1★	NO 726783	201/3	/5	← 3 Horsemen	Fordoun
II	21	Angus	1	NO 522555	209/14	23/4	→ 3 and ← 2 Horsemen in battle	Aberlemno 2

Direction of horsemen is shown by arrows.

TABLE 2C: CLASS II

CLASS	SEQUENCE NUMBER	COUNTY	NO. IN COUNTY	GRID REF.	ECMS REFS.	SYMBOL	COMMENTS		NAME
II	22	Angus	2	NO 522559	214/5	8/5	← 4 Horsemen		Aberlemno 3
II	23	Angus	3★	NO 517566	242/5	3/18	← 2 Horsemen	E	Woodwray
II	24	Angus	4	NO 389544	226/7	* 18?	Seated Man		Kirriemuir 1
II	25	Angus	5	NO 389544	227/8	5	→ 2 Horsemen		Kirriemuir 2
II	26	Angus	6	NO 334550	226	* 19/9	Seated Man	E	Kingoldrum
II	27	Angus	7★	NO 400500	216/8	8/5	→ 2 pairs of Horsemen		Cossins
II	28	Perth	1★	NO 244487	286	5			Alyth
II	29	Perth	2	NO 286446	296/7	41/45*(39b+31)	Beast, ← 5 Horsemen	M	Meigle 1
II	30	Perth	3★	NO 286446	299/300	31/8	← 2 Horsemen	M	Meigle 4
II	31	Perth	4★	NO 286446	300/1	6/31	← Horseman	M	Meigle 5
II	32	Perth	5★	NO 286446	301/2	3/9	← Horseman	M	Meigle 6
II	33	Perth	6★	NO 286446	302/3	5*		M	Meigle 7
II	34	Perth	7	NO 292308	306/8	8/31	← 5 Horsemen		Rossie
II	35	Angus	8	NO 352474	218/9	31/5	→ 3 men with rods		Eassie
II	36	Angus	9	NO 395466	221	4/46	Also used in Class I		Glamis 1
II	37	Angus	10	NO 385468	221/3	39d/4	Also used in Class I		Glamis 2
II	38	Angus	11★	NO 374375	215/6	31/45	← 2 Horsemen		Balluderon
II	39	Angus	12	NO 378352	231/2	18/31			Strathmartine 3
II	40	Angus	13★	NO 378352	233	5			Strathmartine 5
II	41	Angus	14★	NO 378352	233/4	31			Strathmartine 6
II	42	Angus	15	NO 499325	228/9	3/5*		E	Monifieth 1
II	43	Angus	16	NO 499325	229/30	39d/8		E	Monifieth 2
II	44	Angus	17	NO 638429	234/9	5/9*	→ Archer hunting	SV	St. Vigeans 1 & 1a
II	45	Angus	18	NO 638429	239/40	3?/? II 45/40e		SV	St. Vigeans 2
II	46	Angus	19★	NO 638429	240	5		SV	St. Vigeans 3
II	47	Angus	20★	NO 638429	240/1	3?		SV	St. Vigeans 4

Direction of horsemen is shown by arrows.

TABLE 2C: CLASS II

CLASS	SEQUENCE NUMBER	COUNTY	NO. IN COUNTY	GRID REF.	ECMS REFS.	SYMBOL	COMMENTS	NAME
II	48	Angus	21	NO 638429	241	?/5	SV	St. Vigeans 5
II	49	Angus	22	NO 638429	241/2	5	SV	St. Vigeans 6
II	50	Perth	8 ★	NO 196212	292/6	8 – 5/31	← 3 Horsemen	St. Madoes
II	51	Perth	9 ★	NN 967520	291/2	45	← Horseman	Logierait
II	52	Perth	10	NN 950560	286/9	31/? II 3/8 II 8/31	2 Seated men and → Horseman	Dunfallandy
II	53	Perth	11 ★	NN 928240	289/90	5/8	← 3 Horsemen	Fowlis Wester
II	54	Perth	12 ★	NN 973183	290/1	45/46	← 2 Horsemen Moncrieff House	Gask House
II	55	Perth	13 ★	NO 096392	PSAS LXXXV: 175	8/31	P ← 3 Horsemen	Murthly
II	56	Fife	1 ★	NO 419033	344/7	5/31	Polton	Largo
II	57	Fife	2	NO 384018	347	31/?	E → 3 Horsemen Ogham	Scoonie

Direction of horsemen is shown by arrows.

TABLE 2D: DUBIOUS MONUMENTS (NO COMMON SYMBOLS) — CLASS II?

CLASS	SEQUENCE NUMBER	COUNTY	NO. IN COUNTY	GRID REF.	ECMS REFS.	SYMBOL	COMMENTS	NAME
II	1	Caithness	1	ND 960654				Sandside House
II	2	Ross	1	NH 711846				Edderton
II	3	Aberdeen	1	NJ 59566	A.J. ii: 100		Stave	? Portsoy
II	4	Aberdeen	2★	NO 570980	188/9	+	Ogham	Mo Aboyne Castle
II	5	Angus	1	NO 628854	219/21		2 Snakes	Farnell
II	6	Angus	2	NO 609903	225		2 Snakes	Kinell
II	7	Angus	3	NO 379353	230/1		2 Snakes	Strathmartine 2
II	8	Angus	4★	NO 378352	232/3	?		E Strathmartine 4
II	9	Angus	5	NO 374375	234		Monster	De Tealing
II	10	Angus	6	NO 273398	224/5			Kettins
II	11	Perth	1	NO 286446	303		2 Monsters	M Meigle 8
II	12	Perth	2	NO 286446	303/5		2 Monsters	M Meigle 26
II	13	Perth	3	NO 094392	305/6		2 Seahorses	E Little Dunkeld

Notes: a) **No. in County** ★ damaged.

b) **A.J.** *Antiquities Journal.*

c) **Symbol** / pair; // two sides; II between pairs; + mirror; * mirror & comb; — side by side.

d) **Comment** El — Elgin; F — Falkland Palace; Mo — Montrose; D — Dunrobin Castle; E — Edinburgh; SV — St Vigeans; M — Meigle; I — Inverness Museum; De — Dundee.

TABLE 2E: CLASS III WITH HORSEMEN

CLASS	SEQUENCE NUMBER	COUNTY	NO. IN COUNTY	GRID REF.	ECMS REFS.	COMMENTS		NAME
III	1	Shetland	1¶	HO 522424	5/10	→ Horseman between 2 clerics with crosiers	E	Bressay
III	2	Ross	1	NH 719843	83/4	→ Horseman over 2 armed riders		Edderton
III	3	Moray	1★	NJ 108692	138	→ Armed horseman	?	Burghead 8
III	4	Moray	2★¶	NJ 223694	143	→ Horseman	El	Drainie 3
III	5	Moray	3★¶	NJ 223694	148	→ 2 Horsemen over 5 men	El	Drainie 13
III	6	Moray	4	NJ 046595	149/51	Many horsemen and warriors: "Sueno's stone"		Forres
III	7	Angus	1	NO 534644	263/4	→ Armed horseman above another		Menmuir 1
III	8	Angus	2★	NO 534644	264/5	→ Horseman		Menmuir 2
III	9	Angus	3¶	NO 574580	245/7	→ Armed horseman below 2 seated clerics		Aldbar
III	10	Angus	4¶	NO 709968	223/4	→ Armed horseman	Mo	Inchbrayock 1
III	11	Angus	5¶	NO 709968	254	→ Armed horseman	M	Inchbrayock 2
III	12	Angus	6	NO 709968	255	→ One horseman above → another, hunting Craig Manse		Inchbrayock 3
III	13	Angus	7★	NO 639429	275	→ Horseman	SV	St Vigeans 17
III	14	Angus	8★¶	NO 639429	277/8	→ Armed horseman	SV	St Vigeans 22
III	15	Angus	9	NO 499325	229/30	→ Horseman	E	Monifieth 3
III	16	Angus	10¶	NO 384545	258/60	→ Armed horseman above another		Kirriemuir 3
III	17	Angus	11¶	NO 333328	247/9	→ Armed horseman above another		Benvie
III	18	Angus	12	NO 348304	255/7	→ Armed horseman	E	Invergowrie 2
III	19	Perth	1	NO 284449	297/8	→ Horseman over 3 riders followed by one more rider		Meigle 2
III	20	Perth	2	NO 284449	298/9	→ Armed horseman		Meigle 3
III	21	Perth	3	NO 284449	331/3	→ 3 Horsemen in a row		Meigle 11
III	22	Perth	4¶¶	NO 284449	334/5	→ Armed horseman		Meigle 16
III	23	Perth	5¶	NO 025426	317/2	→ One horseman followed by another above 4 men, under whom are 3 prostrate men — one is beheaded		Dunkeld 2

TABLE 2E: CLASS III WITH HORSEMEN

CLASS	SEQUENCE NUMBER	COUNTY	NO. IN COUNTY	GRID REF.	ECMS REFS.	COMMENTS	NAME
III	24	Perth	6 ¶	NO 053188	319/23	← Armed horseman above 4 warriors. Free standing cross	Dupplin
III	25	Perth	7 ★¶	NO 052175	326	← Armed horseman	Forteviot 4
III	26	Perth	8 ★¶	NN 806493	315	← One armed horseman followed by another — preceded by 6 warriors E	Dull
III	27	Fife	1	NO 225180	367	← Horseman above another, above 2 more riders, hunting. Free standing cross.	Mugdrum
III	28	Fife	2 ¶	NO 236968	364/5	← Armed horseman	Dogtown
III	29	Fife	3 ¶	NO 616083	368	← 1 Horseman above another	Sauchope
III	30	Fife	4 ¶	NT 130830	367	← 1 Horseman above 2 others Lost	Inverkeithing
III	31	Kinross	1 ¶	NO 055008	375	↑ Horseman hunting E	Tullibole
III	32	Perth	9 ¶	NN 782014	315/6	↑ Armed horseman	Dunblane 1
III	33	Lanark	1 ¶	NS 550656	459	↓ Horseman ?	Jordanhill
III	34	Lanark	2 ¶	NS 550656	462	↓ Armed horseman hunting. Sarcophagus.	Govan 1
III	35	Lanark	3 ¶	NS 550656	464	↓ Horseman	Govan 5
III	36	Dumbarton	1 ¶	NS 400730	451	↑ Horseman G	Mountblow
III	37	Renfrew	1 ¶	NS 406690	455/7	← Armed horseman. Free standing cross.	Barochan
III	38	Bute	1 ¶	NS 089645	416	← Armed horseman	Rothesay 2
III	39	Bute	2 ¶	NS 095534	407	← Armed horseman	St. Blanes 2
III	40	Bute	3 ¶	NS 095534	410	→ Horseman	St. Blanes 6

Notes: a) **No. in County** ★ damaged; ¶ crude carving.

Direction of horsemen is shown by arrows.

b) **Comments** E — Edinburgh; El — Elgin; M — Meigle; SV — St Vigeans; G — Glasgow Museum; Mo — Montrose.

Table 3: Symbol combinations

* Class I
° Class II

A

	5	8	12	23	31	40e	45
5*	1	4					1
5°		4					
8*	4	2	3	3	3	1	
8°	4	1			2		
12*	1	1		1			1
12°							
23*		1			1		
23°							
31*	1	6	4	1		1	1
31°	3	4	1			1	1
40e*					1		1
40e°					1		
45*	1	1			1	1	
45°							

B

	5	8	12	23	31	40e	45	3	6/7	9	21	40g	41	44
3*		1			1	2	2	1						
3°		1					1							
6/7*	4	1		1	1	1	1		1			1	2	
6/7°	1													
9*	1	1						1						
9°														
21*		3		1	1		1							
21°		2												
40g*			1											
40g°														
41*	1		1		1	1	1		1			1		2
41°					1	1								
44*	1				1	1		1				1	1	
44°														

Top matrix (label C):

										4	14	15	17	38	39b	39d
4*		1						1								
4°	1	1														
14*			1													
14°							1									
15*		1														
15°		1				1										
17*		5	1	1											1	
17°																
38*	1															
38°								1								
39b*	1						1									
39b°																
39d*									1							1
39d°																

Bottom matrix (labels C, B, A / D):

	4																	17
1*	4	1						1						1				1
1°																		
10*				1		1								1				
10°																		
19*				1	1					1								1
19°																		
37*																		
37°																		
34*			1	1														
34°																		
43*																		
43°																		
46*	1				1													
46°	2 1																	

A × A
45*
(71)
26°

A × B	B × B
22*	11*
(36)	(13)
14°	2°

A × C	B × C	C × C
13*	7*	1*
(18)	(7)	(2)
5°	0°	1°

A × D	B × D	C × D
9*	5*	2*
(11)	(8)	(4)
3°	3°	2°

Table 3a: Summary of symbol combinations by sets

*   Class I

°   Class II

Table 3b: Frequency of inter-set combination

Set A = 89* + 47° = 136   80%

Set B = 45* + 19° = 64   38%

Set C = 23* + 8° = 31   18%

Set D = 16* + 8° = 24   14%

N.B. Sets A & B account for 98% of all symbol pairs while even their self-combination amounts to 70% of the symbol pairs.

Table 3c: Frequency of mirror & comb

Set A has 67%

Set B has 25%

Set C has 8%

Table 3d: The number of paired and single symbols

Class	Pairs	Singles	Total
I	120	35	155
II	54	14	68
Total	174	49	223

CHAPTER 3

Previous interpretations

Currently, on the basis of *ECMS* and taking into account later finds, it is widely assumed that there are 250 sculptured Pictish symbol stones that bear nearly 60 different symbols upon them in differing combinations. What have scholars made of all this and what do they suggest the symbols mean? Cruden, in his *The Early Christian and Pictish Monuments of Scotland,* 1964, sums up some of the possibilities: the symbols may be pagan idolatry or they may be secular—identification marks, badges of rank, indicators of social status; perhaps they describe the dead. These are all plausible but they cannot all be true so which, if any, is the correct interpretation?

One might have expected to learn the answer in one of the major works on the Picts *viz:* Anderson and Allen's *The Early Christian Monuments of Scotland* (1903), Wainwright's *The Problem of the Picts* (1955) and Henderson's *The Picts* (1967). Surprisingly enough, everyone carefully sidesteps the issue and no interpretation is forthcoming; it surely is very curious that scholarly prudence restrains everyone from even hinting at a possible meaning for this remarkable collection of symbol stones. Are there then other reasons which inhibit even an inspired guess? To understand why so few interpretations are forthcoming, it is best to review what has been written on the matter.

The first scholarly attempt to come to grips with the problem was Joseph Anderson's pioneering work, *Scotland in Early*

Christian Times, written a century ago. This, together with his subsequent Rhind lectures for 1892, laid the foundations for *ECMS,* written in collaboration with Romilly Allen. Although their great achievement was to bring together everything that was then known about the Picts, neither author ventured an interpretation of the symbols.

Anderson notes that the remarkable constancy in form of the symbols prevents any attempt to trace back the symbols to their origin—not that this prevented later scholars from attempting precisely this! It thus follows that the intention behind these representations must be the same and *so* if the geometrical figures are conventional symbols then all the other designs—mirror, comb, the animals, etc.—must also be symbols and not simply pictorial representations. This means, argues Anderson, that *we have to provide a meaning for every representation,* not that he attempts it, mark you! The logic behind this argument is hard to follow: why should constancy of form imply *meaning* in designs? It may be true in many cases but not *necessarily* in all. However, this *obiter dictum* of Anderson's has had the most enervating effect possible upon Pictish studies: it meant one had to explain *every single one* of Romilly Allen's 46-odd symbols. No wonder that nobody was very enthusiastic over the prospect and interest waned to such an extent that very few people even bothered to try.

Anderson's other comments were, although trenchant, hardly likely to encourage anyone to attempt an interpretation because it made the whole subject quite intractable. Looking at the combinations of symbols, Anderson remarks on some of the peculiarities of the floriated rods as an example. He notes that they are only combined with certain symbols but there must be a rule operating that makes it appropriate for the V-rod to combine with the crescent symbol but not with the double-disc symbol; similarly the Z-rod combines with the double-disc but not with the crescent symbol. It follows that the rods have no intrinsic significance and are only important when in combination with symbols that can, indeed, stand alone. Next, he observes that the mirror and comb symbols are always placed last or lowermost in combination with other symbols and that they *may* have a female reference. The three commonest symbols—crescent, double-disc and the 'elephant' —rarely occur singly, while when they are in pairs they normally occur with the mirror and comb. Hence these pairs must apply to males and females alike but are definitely female when the mirror and comb are added. Here, Anderson is deliberately misleading because these three symbols do occur alone quite frequently—in fact, they comprise 2/3 of all single symbols or roughly 12 percent of all stones! As for the combinations with the mirror and comb, this is hardly 'normal' if it only happens in 20 percent of the combinations! As for his illogical conclusion that pairs could refer to either sex but *must* be female when the mirror and comb is present—this is presuming that the symbols refer to *individuals* and that the mirror and comb really *are* feminine.

Anderson goes on to say that the combinations of symbols are rarely repeated in the same order and that when this does occur it is in different places and that it is not something personal and localised but a widespread general statement. While his conclusion may be true, the premises are highly contentious because he is implicitly assuming that *the symbol stones are really about individuals.* The obvious conclusion, that others have drawn, is that the stones therefore must be about something general, like status. Having tried out various ideas, Anderson reaches the inevitable conclusion that no consistent theory can be constructed from the circumstances of the occurrence of the geometric symbols on the monuments concerning their origin and significance. That, then, would appear to be that as far as Anderson is concerned but he does qualify this by saying "A system of symbolism so extensive and so elaborately constructed can scarcely be supposed to have been invented and practiced over a wide area for the expression of trivial or commonplace ideas. Its characteristics are those of a carefully designed system of monumental symbolism, which must have embodied some corpus of ideas universally applicable and universally intelligible over the whole area and throughout the whole period in which it was prevalent." Wise words.

Anderson has a few further observations. No symbols on Class I monuments are associated with any Christian symbols (of course not, his category forbids it) while this is the case with Class II! From this it follows, says Anderson, that the symbols were capable of supplementing *(sic)* Christian symbolism, probably having the same meaning in both cases, and hence could *not* be distinctively pagan. At this point Anderson is encouraging some impersonal interpretation of the symbols by his rather restricted view about what constitutes paganism. Even if he conceived of paganism in terms of gods, he is mistaken in asserting that one cannot have two faiths at once. Furthermore Anderson asserts there is in Class II an increase in animal *symbolism* that he mistakenly derives from the preoccupation of early Christian sculptors with subjects from the Bestiary with all its fabulous beasts. As for Class III, the earlier symbols have disappeared and have been replaced (!) by pictorial representations of Biblical subjects.

It should be remembered that Anderson was a pioneer, a forefather of Pictish studies, and that neither he nor

Romilly Allen was omniscient. Their immense work, *ECMS*, is impressive but it is not sacrosanct even if it is still regarded as such by many. Empirically it is excellent, but it offers no guidance to what constitutes a symbol nor what the symbols might mean.

One might have expected that by the mid-century, with the publication of the proceedings of the conference on the Picts, edited by Wainwright, we would find some discussion of the symbols, but no. Only Stevenson discussed the symbols in his chapter on Pictish art, and he confines himself to the origin and sequence of artistic styles.

Henderson tends to treat the symbols as art forms and welcomes Stevenson's discovery of the 'declining symbol' *viz* that there is a correct form for each symbol and this will be the earliest example, and any decline from this standard will be later. Stevenson's study of the decorative infilling of the crescent and V-rod comes to the surprising conclusion that the most elaborate example is the *earliest*. Curiously, the majority of the examples are all Class I stones and hence the 'decline' seems to be confined to this period. Less than half the total examples of this symbol are examined by Stevenson and so the problem is: what does one do with those cases where is *no* decoration—like the majority of the other symbols? This is a vital point: the ordinary symbols were undecorated. Why were certain symbols, especially the crescent and V-rod, singled out for special decoration?

Stevenson has usefully pointed out that there are three distinct styles of decoration on the crescent and V-rod symbol, so if we add in the 'plain' or undecorated style, there is a total of four styles. As I will argue later on, this particular symbol plays a key role in symbol combinations and it is likely that these four styles represent four different branches of the same lineage. Stevenson argues that the elaborate form was earliest because it subsumed all the other designs and hence was predominant in setting the style. I would accept that this elaborated form was primary but for political reasons; in my terms elaborate = power. Hence the more elaborate the internal decoration then the higher stood this lineage (symbol) politically and since most lineages were subservient they had no internal decoration whatever. Thus I would re-interpret Stevenson's 'declination' more in terms of political power and not as indicating chronological lateness. Such a revision of art styles might make better sense of the interrelationships between symbols e.g. the key patterns in symbol *8* (Hilton of Cadboll) and in symbol *31* (Nigg). Such comparisons might reveal some unsuspected connections between symbols and places.

After this inconsequential survey, is there not anyone bold

enough to give an interpretation? Well, there are two scholars who have stuck their necks out: Diack in his *The Inscriptions of Pictland,* 1944, and Thomas' 'The Interpretation of the Pictish Symbols,' 1963. There is a remarkable similarity of approach between these two essays despite the 40 years that separate them, for Diack originally wrote his piece in 1922, although it was not published until two decades later. For this reason they will be taken together. Both Diack and Thomas hold that the Picts were Gaels (though it is not clear whether they were P- or Q-Celts) and that the symbol stones were sepulchral monuments. Diack and Thomas, arguing from Classical writers that the Picts tattooed themselves, suggest that the symbols are simply these tattoo designs belonging to each individual, varying with his rank, repeated on his stone for his burial. In addition Thomas believes that the symbols are identifiable with the material cultural objects of the Pict's Iron Age ancestors. Both writers reject cave art and *art mobilier* as being in a different category from the other symbols because they are not *true* funerary monuments.

The main reason why Diack and Thomas identify the Picts with the Gaels is that it enables them to smuggle in the assumption that the Picts are similar to the old Irish society recorded in the myths and stories about old Ireland. No justification is offered for this bland statement which, taken at its face value, raises some problems about the later relations between the Scots and the Picts. Linguists would probably take exception to this assumption. In fact what both Diack and Thomas want to do is to lift the Irish social structure and transplant it to Scotland so that they can equate the symbols with the 26 titles of honour found in old Irish society. All that then remained was to find out which symbol corresponded to which rank; here the shade of Anderson is walking!

Diack enunciates one sensible rule about Class I stones: they normally have only two figures but where there are three then the third is the mirror and comb which comes last and probably denotes a female—a conclusion that Thomas agrees to. Diack also raises the vital question: why should there be just two symbols? He thinks it could be that more than one person was commemorated *(sic)* but as this seems unlikely, perhaps one figure denotes the class while the other gives the grade of honour of the person or, even possibly, the classes were not exclusive so that a man could hold two classes, e.g. a man could be both a noble and a bard—a suggestion that Thomas elaborates on at length. As for the frequent presence of the mirror and comb, Diack considers this is connected with the Pictish system of mother-right whereby succession passes from a man to his sister's son—a point that Thomas, most surprisingly, neglects to take up.

Class I : Glamis 2 (Table 2A:128)

As an illustrative example, Diack takes the Class II stone from Dunfallandy where one seated figure is associated with the 'bear' (or elephant) symbol, the other figure with the double-disc and Z-rod, the horseman with the crescent and V-rod and 'bear', while at the bottom of the panel, the anvil and tongs represent the artist who executed the work—apart from the last idea, this simple association is acceptable. For his interpretation Diack suggests that the crescent and V-rod, double-disc and Z-rod, and 'bear' *must be* grades of chiefs *since* (!) they are among the *commonest* symbols and are found in practically every district while the less-common serpent and Z-rod *must* be a *mormaer* (or earl). All one can say is that it is of course possible but no real reason has been offered. It also happens that the double-disc and Z-rod, the 'bear' *and* the serpent and Z-rod appear in equal numbers in the very *few* districts in which they do occur.

Although Diack has some interesting observations, his interpretation does not really carry us very much forward.

Thomas seems to have based his analysis upon Diack's since it follows it very closely, so it may justly be considered to be a simple extension of it.

In his essay entitled 'The interpretation of the Pictish symbols' Thomas puts forward some tentative explanations of the symbols that he, nevertheless, claims are "highly likely to be correct in principle, if not in detail" besides which "it is not easy to see how any radically different explanation could have advanced". As Thomas accepts most of Diack's assumptions, then both hypotheses stand or fall by the trustworthiness of their joint assumptions.

Curiously enough, Thomas, yet again, takes his essay to be primarily an analysis of Pictish *art* although he qualifies this by saying that the designs are not merely artistic motifs but, rather, primitive pictograms or simple messages *commemorating the dead*. Why this should be so, he does not actually explain. However, he claims that a symbol or a group of symbols constitute a 'statement' that is normally placed vertically on the monument; such 'statements' can be classified according to their relative position with regard to each other and by how many symbols are included. It is extremely important to note that Thomas confines himself to Class I monuments *only*.

There are, he states, four classes of 'statements':

S1:- single 'statements' which are normally an animal symbol.

S2:- pairs, where there is an emphasis on objects rather than animals.

Class II : Glamis 2   (Table 2C:37)   E

S3:- triples, which is an extension of a pair with the mirror symbol.

S4:- quadruples, which are pairs with the mirror and comb symbols.

Thomas interprets these 'statements' as follows: single S1 'statements', being generally animals, are group labels that mark territorially-bound areas; S2 'statements' with two animals denote boundary marks between tribal territories; S2 and S3 'statements' with object symbols are memorials to the dead, where the beginning of the 'statement' refers to the deceased and those at the end to the erector of the memorial. The addition of a mirror (in S3) and mirror and comb (in S4) means a female relative.

Thomas asserts there are some 50 symbols: 14 animal symbols and 35 object symbols. He notes the existence of two alternating series: those with or without the V-rod, Z-rod and 'curling tongs' (or 'tuning fork') symbol. He identifies the Z-rod and the V-rod with a broken spear and a broken arrow respectively while the 'curling tongs' is a broken sword. The reason he gives for this alternative series is that they respectively represent the living and the dead. Hence the crescent conveyed the rank of a living Pict while, together with a V-rod, it denotes his status after his death; the implication of this is not very clear if the symbols are *all* memorials to the dead.

Thomas next proceeds to identify the *original* objects upon which the symbols were modelled, leaving aside the animals, for, with the exception of the 'elephant', these *must* be real animals that are represented. Apart from the three symbols already identified above, the others are: the notched rectangle—a chariot and two ponies; the triple disc and bar—a cauldron; the hammer, anvil, pincers, mirror and comb are what they look like, the rectangular figure is a container, the 'flower' is a bronze harness brooch, the triple oval is a bronze armlet, the arch is a hinged bronze collar, while all the other symbols are derived from an even *earlier* unknown art style. As regards the actual interpretation of these symbols, he rightly points out how comparatively rare the symbol stones are, for *if they were* individual funeral monuments then some half a million stones should have been erected between 400 and 700 A.D. Hence, he concludes, the 150 (Class I) stones must be those of Top People which, thus, points the way to their interpretation.

Turning to the four postulated 'statements', Thomas examines each in turn. S1 'statements' could be the territorial marks of a tribe or could even refer to the tribes themselves. Thus the 14 animal symbols might refer to the bipartite division of the seven legendary Pictish tribes but he is unable to detect much connection between these stones and any territorial divisions. The same problem attaches itself to S2 'statements' of the animal/animal type, so he ends up by simply concluding that they may just be cult symbols. Now as there are an *equal* number of single object-symbols as there are single animals, does this mean that *they* denote the territory of the dead or are they cult symbols too?

Having derived his symbols from some pre-existing Bronze or Iron Age people's artefacts, Thomas turns to Irish society to find an explanation of the symbols—on the assumption that all these peoples, the Picts included, are Q-Celtic. Taking the titles of honour from the old Irish accounts, he tries to match them, thus: the double-disc is a king, the crescent is a sub-king, the notched rectangle is a war-leader, the snake and Z-rod is a head magus, the triple oval, the arch, the circular disc, the disc and rectangle are all nobles, the sword is a champion, the triple disc is a magus, the rectangle is a historian, the hammer, anvil, tongs, pincers and 'flower' are all metalworkers, the mirror and comb is a woman, the remaining symbols have 'religious' meanings only, while the V-rod, Z-rod and the 'curling tongs' represent the dead.

Armed with this battery of 'interpretations', Thomas goes on to unlock the secrets of the symbol stones. Thus S2 'statements' would read: "To a Dead (King, etc) of (Animal group label) Group" or "To a Dead (King, etc) of such and such occupation (e.g. historian)". As for S3/4 'statements' containing the mirror and comb symbol, these would read "X, commemorated by Y, commemorated by a woman". As for the few S4 'statements' without a mirror and comb, Thomas creates a special explanation. With regard to the Birsay stone, this "clearly reads 'Grave of a local sub-king of appropriate noble status, also a man of the 'elephant' group and a man of the Eagle group' ". Because this stone breaks Thomas' self-imposed rule of 'one man, one statement', the Picts therefore had to draw three men on the stone to explain away this exception! As for the Inverury S4 'statement' this is translated as reading "Memorial of a man who was first a sub-king, of appropriate noble status, he became famous as a chief magus, and was king of the province when he died."

As this is the most serious attempt yet to interpret the symbols it has been expounded at length here so that we can examine the analysis. The ideas put forward are both bold and highly speculative but the analysis suffers from many defects. For, having carefully classified the relative positions of all the symbols, he has to admit that position does not seem to be significant. In fact, the positions are critically important to an understanding of the symbols. Likewise, he is forced to abandon the S1 and S2 'statements' concerning animals because they do not fit either.

Indeed, how would Thomas explain S4 'statements' that contain two animals and the mirror and comb—"Animal Group X, commemorated by Animal Group Y, commemorated *by a woman*"? Neither is it clear why *only* animals can act as group labels. The upshot is that the animal symbols remain a mystery.

Deriving the symbols from Bronze and Iron Age artefacts is ingenious and full of recondite archaeological knowledge, but it is stretching incredulity to the limit to propose that the geometrical shapes were passed on through countless generations *via* tattooing! Maybe the Picts were tattooed but, if they were Celts and had the same social structure as the Irish, why were the Irish not also tattooed as well? In any case the associations seem highly arbitrary for why, apart from their frequency, should the double-disc and crescent be kings? As for the ascription of death to the V-rod and Z-rod, this is very curious, because it then becomes difficult to explain why we have so many symbols *without rods* on these allegedly commemorative *funeral* monuments. Why are only four statuses honoured in death this way? What are we to make of all those famous silver chains and lappets that have a Z-rod on them—were they just meant as grave-goods?

When one reflects on what Thomas' interpretation really amounts to, it is quite astonishing, for it means that what the Picts are actually commemorating on their symbol stones is not the dead at all but their stratification system! It is as if we buried *our* top people and only recorded that here lies "A King & Poet", "A Prime Minister & War Leader", "An Archbishop & Historian", etc.,—nothing else. Would so ingenious, artistic and warlike people as the Picts be so obsessed by ranks that they would simply scatter the landscape with stones recording all the permutations of status that some *unnamed* persons happened to have had, at some time or other, all through the centuries?

It is also very curious that despite the fact that these Class I stones are supposed to be funeral monuments to kings and top people there are very few burials near these stones. Yet, on the other hand, Class II stones are frequently near churchyards and hence near burials, so why are they not discussed? It is just possible that the early Christians may have looked askance at the presence of chief magi, lesser magi and all those other 'religious' and cult symbols in their midst. Yet it is most likely it was the formidable task of explaining away the eight symbols that occur on some Class II stones that caused the hypothesis to collapse: it implies that some individual had monopolised almost a third of all the Pictish statuses going! Such an interpretation might read "To a Dead King, who early in life was a chief magus; he became a great warrior, and then settled down as historian and poet before turning to metal-working, he later became a sub-king and war leader when he died." This is some biography! Can one conceive of a society that would to record all that for some unnamed *Christian*—just because they had the appropriate status symbols to their credit?

There are still two further problems with this hypothesis. Why is it that there are no undamaged monuments with only *one* symbol on them? Surely over the centuries there must have been hundreds of kings, magi, war-leaders, poets, etc., who only achieved one status as a top person but, alas, they are all condemned to oblivion.

It would seem that only people who achieve two *and two only* statuses would be remembered—a somewhat crippling limitation to Pictish ambitions! Oddly enough, few paired symbols (the common form) are ever repeated so, yet again, there is another limitation: only certain combinations of statuses are allowed.

The last points of criticism can be summarised by Thomas' failure to account for two fundamental and interconnected questions that he completely neglects:

1) Why are there no *undamaged* single-symbol stones?
2) Why do most symbol stones only have just two symbols? (if we forget the mirror and comb)?

The reason why these basic questions go unanswered is that Thomas only gives qualitative and arbitrary explanations of the symbols, for he *never* considers one fundamental fact: the actual distribution of the symbols on the ground.

Although this article was published twenty years ago, Thomas has not altered his position in any way, as can be seen from his recent (1984) article: 'The Pictish Class I symbol stones', where he now wisely sticks to Class I stones only. He proposes that the problem of the symbol stones be split up into six problems, and the answering of these occupies most of the article. I do not propose to detail Thomas' answers, since they are contained in the above analysis of his previous article. However, I will give *my* answer to his questions even if this anticipates my subsequent arguments.

1) "*The nature and character* of the stones"—they were politico-ritual statements that were universally understood.
2) "*The origin of the custom* of picking out, incising, and setting up these stones for display"—the Picts were well aware of other incised monuments and employed skilled masons to execute these stones.
3) "The *purpose,* or *function* (if any) of this display"—to indicate permanent political alliances through marriage.

4) *"The origins of the various individual symbols*—arbitrary, distinctive and apparently (as we see them) stereotyped"—they began as mystical claims to power over abstract and real entities.

5) "The *meaning*—the *semantic values*—conveyed by the symbols, particularly when in pairs and groups"—the position of the symbols indicate the social relationships between two different lineages.

6) *"The length of time,* approximately in absolute dates, between the erection of the oldest class I stones and their assumed supersession by the relief-worked, cross-enriched, Class II"— 693-728 A.D.

Thomas criticises just two 'constructive' *alternatives* to his hypothesis that symbol stones are funerary monuments, *viz* Henderson's (1971b) idea that they are territorial markers, and my (1971) view that they were alliance markers. Thomas dismisses the territorial argument on the grounds that *he* can find no correlation—however, Table 13 supports Henderson's contention. My article is criticised for "taking some liberties with those stones . . . [that] do not conform to [my] model", not explaining why the stones appeared, avoiding any question of dating, not explaining the origin of Pictish art, and for being only an argument by analogy. All that is rectified here. While I agree that this early article had a number of faults, I am as pleased as Thomas is about his article, that it is often mentioned in journals and books!

Support for the funerary monument thesis is also given by Close-Brooks (1984), who attempts to link the symbol stones to graves. For reasons that are not quite clear, she holds that Class I stones are Christian—presumably because it is these stones that are found near graves and which *therefore* could not be pagan! In her article, Close-Brooks does not establish a single firm connection between *any* symbol stone and a contemporary burial. Stones have been found near graves, but this could have been simply because celebrations of *rites de passage*—birth, marriage and death—were held in 'sacred' areas. As Thomas, himself, says (1984, p.175): "Hardly one [symbol stone] has been recorded as having been found in its original and primary association with a burial. They have however been found—I repeat myself—far more often than coincidence should permit, in, under, or around known burial grounds." But what does Thomas mean here? Where—if the stones were *not* funerary markers—were the symbol stones supposed to have been erected? The stones were meant to be seen, for it would not be that unreasonable to place them near some 'holy' place where people came together for some regular, collective ritual occasion.

This new volume on the Picts (edited by Friell and Watson) is basically about how *archaeologists* see the Picts (half the volume is occupied by Alcock, Close-Brooks, Watkins and Solly), while there is no room for historians, linguists or social anthropologists although they *are* mentioned, in passing. Thus this conference was *not* inter-disciplinary like the 'Problem of the Picts' conference, even though representatives of the other disciplines attended: their views were not recorded, although expressed quite forcibly against many of the assumptions taken by the archaeologists giving the talks.

To sum up, we do not yet have any viable interpretations of the symbol stones. Either the task is impossible, which seems unlikely, or we have been misled as to what our objective is. If it is, as Anderson suggests, simply an interpretation of *all* Romilly Allen's 'symbols' *in terms of individuals and if these are commemorative of the dead,* as many people suppose, then we are indeed locked into an impossible set of conditions that will not admit of any answer. Yet we do not have to accept these preconditions at all, as we are free to begin where we will as long as we can explain all the *stones,* not all the 'symbols' that have been wished upon us. We need to look at the Pictish stones with fresh eyes and see what *they* tell us—not what some scholar tells us to do! It is for this reason that this chapter has been so negative: old ideas do not turn out to be necessarily the best.

CHAPTER 4

A new look at the symbols

We have seen in the last chapter that nobody has been able to give a convincing explanation of the symbol stones. This strongly suggests that we must have all been looking in the wrong direction *viz* towards *individual memorials to the dead* when the answer could well have been in completely the opposite direction *viz* towards *collective announcements to the living*. Our particular difficulty in perceiving this possible alternative stems from our Christian civilization's curious obsession with death, which was far from the minds of our pagan ancestors (like the Picts) to whom *life* was the be-all and end-all of existence since it was so short! It is our Christian concept of the soul that is the cause of our concern with death because it involves the judgement of our behaviour here and what will happen, eventually, to the soul. This is not the way that many 'primitive' people see their world since death has no cosmological implications - it is just the end of life.

Obviously, symbols need to have physical manifestations if we are to become aware of them, but that is the least important thing about them. Symbols are simply devices to represent something *other* than that which their actual appearances suggest and so their physical shape is quite irrelevant. Hence all attempts to link the Pictish symbols with comparable artefacts from the past are a monumental waste of labour since it contradicts the very *raison d'être* for the symbols: their power of reference to something over and above their actual design. It is this misunderstanding of what *symbolism* is that is the root cause of failure of previous interpretations. [10]

Symbols are specifically devised to evoke meanings. It may happen that they even closely resemble what they represent, but with a difference. Thus, for example, a drawing or a model of a snake may indeed stand for a snake but the reference could be to a specific clan whose totem is a snake or it might be to a spirit, to the soul, to death or many other things. It is most unlikely that the reference is to a *real* snake. However, only a knowledge of the myths and rituals of the peoples concerned would allow us to know what the snake symbol stands for. We can, though, be fairly certain that a literal interpretation will be false.

If symbols, then, can have multiple and different references, depending on the belief system of the people, it would seem to be a well-nigh impossible task to assign any meanings to the Pictish symbols. Certainly the common custom of giving these symbols arbitrary meanings derived from *outside* the society on the grounds of parallels with *other* societies allows an infinite range of possibilities that the Victorians were not slow to exploit since they were convinced that the symbols were of Oriental origin! Yet, there is a way around the difficulty: we can begin by analysing the total array of symbols as a self-contained system.

We have 28 different symbols and so it follows that there are 28 different connotations involved since it is highly unlikely that the symbols are duplicating each other in meaning. As these symbols are always combined in pairs, then these internal arrangements indicate the limits of the symbol system. So the pairing of symbols *in itself* is significant as is the well-known fact that the Picts had a predilection for the number 7. This suggests that we are dealing with four groups of seven symbols that make up the total set of 28. The dualism implicit in the pairing also suggests that the total set could also be divided in two: giving two groups of 14 symbols, each comprising two groups of 7 symbols. This hypothesis will be shown later to have a statistical basis in the actual numbers of symbols found.

If the Picts had a dualistic mode of thinking, as seems most probable from the evidence: the pairs of symbols, the dual tribal structure, the two historical kingdoms and the naming of the provinces by paired names, then one must consider the nature of dualistic thinking. Although this will be stated in more detail in Chapter 7, it should be pointed out that the most universal form of such dualism is to divide *everything* into two opposed yet complementary pairs. The most basic method is the division of the whole universe into things of the left hand *(sinister)* and those of the right hand *(dextrous)*. There is no written proof that the Picts so thought but, equally, there are no strong grounds for assuming that they are the sole exception to this underlying rule of dualism. What can be disputed is what things go into each category and, in particular, how is the opposition of male/female to be resolved. It will be put forward in Chapter 7 that the Picts are like most dualistically-minded peoples in placing males in the right-hand category.

So far, we have made three assumptions:

1) there are 28 true symbols
2) the symbols are always paired
3) the symbols are divided between left- and right-hand categories.

On this basis, all the symbol designs will be subjected to various alternative arrangements to elicit the rationale of the symbol system as a whole. It will be shown that these three assumptions enable us to place all the symbols in a meaningful pattern. There is a fourth critical assumption:

4) the number 7 is very important, symbolically.

If the Picts had practised a thoroughgoing dualism, then the total number of symbols should have been 32, equally divided between geometric and animal symbols, reflecting the two original tribes that made up the Pictish confederation; but with only 28 symbols, 16 geometric and 12 animal, it would appear that we are 4 animal symbols short of complete equality. Why? It is inconceivable that two similar yet independent tribes would have had an unequal number of available designs to turn into symbols and so it seems that the dictates of unification of the two tribes, under the requirement of observing the mystical importance of the number 7, reduced the actual number of symbols to 28. The mystery of the 'missing' four animal symbols will be discussed after an exploration of the possibilities that 28 symbols offer us: two sets of 14 symbols, four sets of 7 symbols and seven sets of 4 symbols. Each of these three arrangements has statistical significance in terms of the total number of symbols found in Pictland, besides the historical implications these sets have for our understanding of Pictish society. So while it is possible that the two original tribes that eventually made up the Picts could have had 16 designs each, divided between left and right, it is most improbable that they could then have formed a viable symbolic system. Indeed, to add any further symbols to 28—as has been standard practice—actually reduces a coherent symbolic system to a meaningless collection of designs, ¾ of which only appear once! Comprehensiveness inhibits comprehension.

At this stage there will be no discussion of the origin, meaning or purpose of the symbols, since the sole aim here is to examine the internal coherence of the designs and their frequency of occurrence which is taken to be an indicator of the relative importance of the symbols. The present objective is to discover the patterns which will give us some clues as to the meaning of the symbols for, it must be stressed, the meanings cannot be presupposed but have to be deduced from the empirical information that the stones themselves provide.

The historical evidence tells that the Picts were originally two separate but related tribes: the *Caledonii* and *Maeatae* of Cassius Dio (3rd century A.D.), the *Dicalydones* and *Verturiones* of Ammianus Marcellinus (4th century), and the Northern and Southern Picts of Bede (8th century). It was also held that these two tribes held seven provinces which were likewise divided in two and which have come down to us as the seven double-named provinces of Marr and Buchan, Muref and Ros, etc. Myth has it that the first king of the Picts was one *Cruithne* who was succeeded by his seven sons who gave their names to the seven Pictish kingdoms of *Fib, Fidach, Foltaig, Fortrenn, Cait, Ce* and *Circinn.* From old Irish legends and even contemporary Celtic folklore we know that seventh sons of seventh sons were especially gifted in magical arts. It cannot be otherwise than that dualism and the mystic value of 7 were deeply embedded in Pictish thought, to judge by the above evidence. Thus the existence of just 28 symbols on the Pictish stones can be no mere coincidence of the rule enunciated in Chapter 2 that only designs that occur more than once in a pair are symbols. When, additionally, we find that the statistical frequencies also support the importance of 7, then it really becomes almost impossible to doubt that the four assumptions, given above, must have a great element of truth in them to produce such startlingly clear patterns. It should be added that the following tables *emerged from* the statistics and were not consciously planned as the result of pure deductive reasoning from first principles.

In accordance with a world-wide rule of dualism, the right hand is held to be superior to the left hand, and so the tables are arranged that way. The reasons for this will be discussed in Chapter 7 which provides solid support for this arrangement. The disadvantage with this procedure is that it causes some difficulties in grasping the tables because, in our convention of reading from left to right, we tend to give priority to what we first read *viz* the left-hand table. Once one can overcome this peculiarity of English writing then the tabulation should be self-evident.

The symbols and designs are designated by the number, given

in italics, that Romilly Allen used (*ECMS* pp.57-58) but with certain modifications. A distinction is drawn between *32b* (bull) and *32c* (cow), *35d* (dog) and *35l* (lion), *39b* (beast) and *39d* (deer), *40e* (eagle) and *40g* (goose). On the other hand, *6* is taken to be identical with *7*—hence both are called *6/7*, while *42* is thought to be the same as *43*, hence *42/43*.

We now wish to demonstrate that the 28 symbols are related in some unexpected ways, and this will be done by rearranging the symbols in different patterns. These transformations are governed by the four basic assumptions given on p.62, the importance of the dominant symbols (i.e. those with the most wide-ranging combinations—sets A and B, Table 3), differentiation of geometric and animal symbols, while seeking resemblances between particular pairs of designs and correspondences between the symbols. A step-by-step guide to the construction of the first arrangement (Table 4) may help to explain its eventual form.

The 28 symbols as given by sets A,B,C and D (Table 3) are taken as the building blocks, since they rank the symbols in terms of dominance and in groups of seven. The sets are divided in two:

LEFT	RIGHT
Set B	Set A
Set D	Set C

The 14 symbols in these two columns are again dualistically divided into right and left categories such that there are 7 rows, alternately containing geometric and animal symbols and four columns that are alternately labelled left and right.

We begin to fill these rows by starting with the right-hand position of the right-hand column (Table 4b). This prime place is given to the most important symbol of set A *viz: 8*, while its companion on the left goes to *5*. The left-hand column (Table 4a) and its top row is filled from set B such that the left-hand position corresponds to the left-hand position of the right-hand column (Table 4b)—thus *3* is the design that resembles *5* but without the Z-rod. In a similar manner *9* completes the first row, since it resembles *8* without the V-rod.

The next row (*ii*) contains animals. The extreme right-hand position is given to *40e*, not because it is the commonest animal symbol but because it is juxtaposed to the serpent, *45*, in a well-known opposition. The corresponding symbols to the left are *44* and *40g*.

The third row is geometric, and we begin with the left-hand position in the right-hand double column and assign *23* there on the grounds that it places the three Z-rods together. The corresponding design is *6/7*, for this is an equally solid design with two 'feet'. This leaves the more dominant *12* in the extreme right and with *21* as its corresponding design. It should be added that *12* is the only other design, other than *8*, to have a V-rod on it, but this example is not a true symbol. All these designs, in fact, have two downward projections.

The fourth row is animal and the two remaining designs from sets A and B are placed in right-hand positions, with the more powerful *31* on the extreme right, and *41* on the left. This leaves two vacancies to be filled from the two other sets. Since the designs already chosen are aquatic, it is assumed that the other two will be aquatic as well, and so *39b* is the obvious companion for *31* while *42/3* matches *41*.

Next, there is a geometric row, and *17* is assigned to the extreme right on statistical grounds but, for other reasons, it might be better to place *4* there instead of making it the companion of *17*. The corresponding designs to these, in the left-hand pair of columns, are *1* and *19*, on the basis of the circular motifs of *1* and *4* and the rectangular shapes of *19* and *17*.

The sixth row is animal and, again, we begin with the left-hand position on the right side and place *39d* as it links up with the head of *39b* above. The corresponding design is *37* since they are both deer. The other wild animals are *34* and *37* and are placed to the left and right.

The seventh row is geometrical and it is questionable if the ordering is entirely satisfactory, but it has been arranged on the empirical basis that few of the symbols in any of the four columns combine with another symbol within their own respective column. This is why it might be better to transpose *1* and *19* besides *4* and *17* to accord with this new principle, since it would reduce the total incidence of combinations *within* each of the columns to just 8%. In other words, there seems to be a rule operating which prohibits *intra*-columnal combinations while encouraging *inter*-columnal pairings. Despite this consideration, row *v* will be left because there is the equally important parallel that symbol designs *1* and *3* and *4* and *5* all contain circles in their respective columns.

An eighth row of non-symbolic animal designs has been added to the table and this row includes the famous Burghead Bulls, *32b*. These however, should be disregarded at this stage, since they are only placed there for dualistic symmetry as part of a later argument which explains why they never became true symbols.

This concludes the rationale for this transformation of the four sets A,B,C and D into four dualistic columns of 7 symbols. Now, we may just glance at the statistical frequencies of these symbols. It will be seen that, generally speaking, the right-hand symbols on the right-hand side (Table 4b) tend to be more frequent in occurrence than their left-hand counterparts. Correspondingly, the same thing can be said of the extreme left-hand symbols (Table 4a), that they are more numerous than their right-hand counterparts. However, a word of caution is necessary, since these numbers only refer to the *discovered* symbols and not, necessarily, to the actual number produced. It so happens that the estimated theoretical maximum numbers of symbols given in Table 13 broadly support the general distribution given, but the actual numbers found can vary from ⅓ to ½ of the predicted numbers. Hence one must be careful not to draw fine comparisons between pairs of frequencies when the actual numbers appear to be small. Nevertheless, the figures seem to indicate a polarisation such that the extremes (the very left and very right columns) are the dominant symbols in their own respective sets. At the same time it clearly shows that sets A and C are predominant over their counterparts in sets B and D.

The whole purpose of this transformation has been to show that the somewhat arbitrary sets established in Table 3 on grounds of their combinatory powers are in fact linked together. Sets B and C are just pale reflections (in design) of sets A and C, as well as being junior to set A in the array of 14 symbols that constitute sets A and B. Similarly, set D is junior to set C.

We shall regard sets A and B as being the primary group of 14 symbols, since their combinations with themselves and other symbols account for 98% of all paired symbols. Remember, this group of symbols was deduced from their frequency of pairing, and hence they may have no substantive unity or reality—it could be all due to chance!

Row	Left	Right		Left	Right
i	3 (16)	9 (5)		5 (45)	8 (84)
ii	44 (9)	40g (3)		45 (16)	40e (14)
iii	6/7 (21)	21 (10)		23 (10)	12 (18)
iv	42/43 (1)	41 (17)		39b (2)	31 (46)
v	1 (8)	19 (3)		4 (11)	17 (13)
vi	37 (2)	34 (2)		39d (3)	38 (2)
vii	10 (3)	46 (6)		15 (3)	14 (3)
viii	(32c)	(36)		(32b)	(35d)

Table 4a : left   Table 4b : right

Table 4: The basic 28 symbols arranged dualistically

The next step in the argument is to hypothesize that these two groups of primary and secondary symbols reflect some kind of reality in the Pictish world. Despite a certain obscureness about the relationships at the secondary level which rarely combine anyway, we have also noted that symbols are equally reticent to form pairs within the columns. In terms of our junior/senior analogy, it would seem that the symbols within columns are also divided in a similar way, but with the rider that they seem to be one of a 'kind' since they so infrequently combine. In other words, secondary symbols seem different in kind from each other, yet similar to the primary symbols in their columns in kind but different in degree. The question, to be addressed later, is why this should be so?

It might be asked why has the alternation of geometric and animal symbols been built into these assumptions? An answer will be given later but, here, symmetry again is the excuse. However, Table 4 does not look quite so symmetrical, as it is divided at row *iv* in order to accommodate the two sets of 7 symbols! This needs to be rectified.

Having separated out the sets in Table 4 in a series of correspondences, it is now time to rearrange them in a more significant manner. This new transformation involves splitting the simple dualistic table into three—left, right and centre—in order to retain the unity of the four sets of 7 symbols we started with. This split takes place at row *iv* when all four symbols are moved to a central position. The right-hand symbols move leftwards, naturally, while the left-hand symbols move to the right—as shown in Table 5. All four aquatic animals enter centre stage as mediators between the symbols to their left and right. So we have a 'watery' barrier of animals separating the sets internally as well as externally. In relation to the other animals that separate the geometric symbols in their respective sets, these aquatic animals are quite different. In row *ii* we have animals that crawl or fly while in row *vi* there are four-footed *wild* animals (note that row *viii* has four-footed *tame* animals!)

These dividing symbols: *31, 41, 42/3, 39b*, have a symbolic role to play, as will be explained later, with regard to water. Of all the animal symbols it is *31* and *39b* that have attracted the most attention, since they stand in such great contrast to the animal designs as they are not identifiable. Symbol *41* is plainly a salmon and *42/3* is a sea-horse, but what are *31* and *39b*? They are related not only by their obscurity but by their position as two mediators on the right, the powerful side. It will be suggested in Chapter 7 that these are not actual animals but mythical creatures that function in Pictish cosmology, but that is for later!

The significance of the medial position of these water creatures is that they occur half-way through our vertical groups of 14 symbols and split all the sets in two. This accounts for the popularity of *41* and *31* at the primary level. What we have here is a hint of triadic relationships.

This transformation is represented in Table 5 below.

	3		*9*		*5*		*8*	
B	*44*		*40g*	*A*	*45*		*40e*	*Primary*
	6/7		*21*		*23*		*12*	*Level*
		41←				*31←*		
		→42/43				*→39b*		
	1		*19*		*4*		*17*	*Secondary*
D	*37*		*34*	*C*	*39d*		*38*	*Level*
	10		*46*		*15*		*14*	
	Left	*Centre*	*Right*		*Left*	*Centre*	*Right*	

Table 5 : The 28 symbols arranged in 4 sets of seven

The relationships may be made clearer by giving the primary sets descriptive names instead of numbers, cf Figure 3.

A	Double disc & Z-rod Serpent & Z-rod Notched rectangle & Z-rod 　　　　　'Elephant'	Crescent & V-rod Eagle Arch
B	Double disc Serpent Disc & notched rectangle 　　　　　Fish	Crescent Goose 'Tuning fork'

Table 6 : The 14 primary symbols

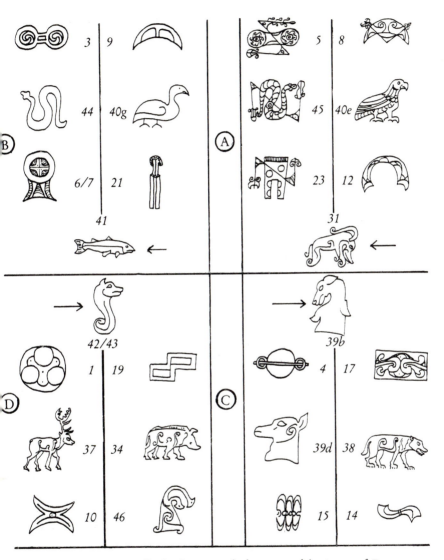

Figure 3 : The basic 28 symbols arranged in 4 sets of 7
(cf Table 5)

F

The common pattern to all these four sets is:-

Geometric		Geometric
Animal		Animal
Geometric		Geometric
	Animal	

Table 7 : The basic pattern of the four sets of symbols

If the frequency of pairing of symbols between these four sets is examined, we get the following table:-

	A	B	C
A	42	-	-
B	21	8	-
C	11	4	1
D	6	5	2
Totals	80	17	3

n = 170

Table 8 : The percentage of combinations between sets, cf Table 3a

It will be seen that not only are sets A and B present in practically every pair of symbols but also that these are the only sets to combine internally. However, set B is only a variant of set A (cf Table 3) so we can now state that set A is not simply the dominant set but that *it is the basic set of 7 symbols* that lie at the core of Pictish symbolism.

Set A is also unique in containing all the V- and Z-rods:

Z		V
Z		40e
Z		12
	31	

This basic set of seven symbols is internally articulated by three symbols: *8, 5* and *31*.

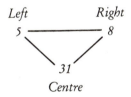

Together, these three symbols are present in 2/3 of all pairs as well as constituting 2/3 of the single symbols (i.e. those on damaged stones).

These conclusions are based solely on the statistical evidence as there are no other clues concerning the relative importance of the symbols. The fact that the symbols also fall neatly into corresponding groups: A/B & C/D can be no accident and so must reflect an underlying ordering.

Having discovered what appear to be the basic seven symbols we need to know how they interrelate with the other symbols. This can be done by grouping together all the right-hand symbols and all the left-hand symbols in two columns: one geometric, the other animal.

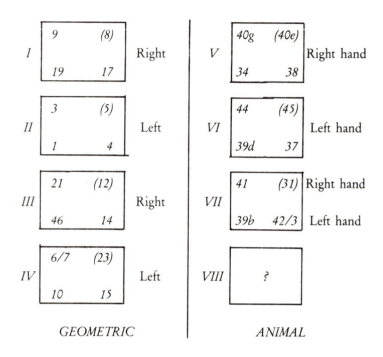

Table 9 : Sets of four symbols, cf Figure 4

In the above table the top right-hand symbols (bracketed) are the basic seven symbols. Because there is no set *VIII* it means that the alternation between right and left cannot be exact in the animal column and so set *VII* has to have one pair from the right and the other pair from the left : the intermediary symbols.

The frequency of symbol pairing in these seven sets is:

I	31	V	6
II	20	VI	7
III	9	VII	17
IV	9	VIII	-

Table 10 : Frequency of pairing of seven sets (in percent)

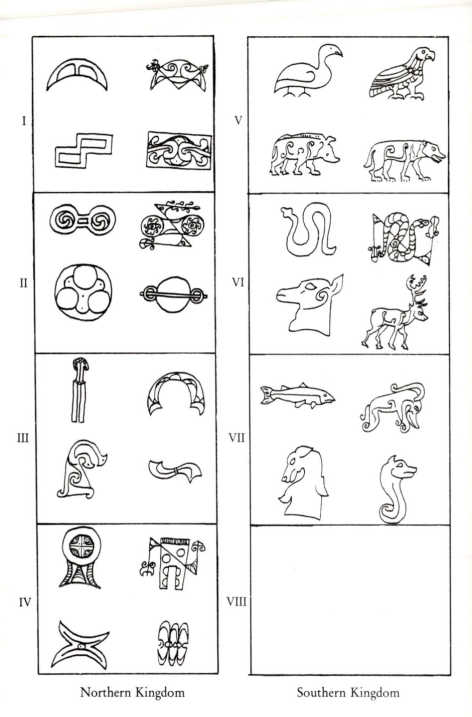

I

II

III

IV

V

VI

VII

VIII

Northern Kingdom

Southern Kingdom

Figure 4 : Sets of 4 symbols, cf Table 9

This particular arrangement of the 28 symbols into seven sets of four symbols, where each set contains one of the basic seven symbols, points us back to a *possible* original distribution of these designs in ancient Pictland. Every set contains two pairs of related symbols e.g. *8/9, 19/17, 40e/40g, 34/38,* etc. The powerful (i.e. statistically more frequent) pairs like *8/9* and *5/3* tend to have the same form with variations, like the rods, while the weaker pairs are only similar in function rather than in design. This division of the sets into two halves: strong and weak will be shown, in the next chapter, to be the standard Pictish pattern for marriage and alliances between lineages.

Table 10 indicates that the geometric sets become weaker statistically from *I* to *IV* while the converse is true of the animal symbols. So, if as seems possible, the geometric symbols are northern in origin, it would follow that in a *united* Pictland of seven provinces the Northern kingdom had four geometrical sets while the Southern kingdom had only three animal sets. If one reads the sets *I-VII* as running from north to south then the power centre of the North would be in the extreme north (Orkney?) while the Southern centre would be in the far south (the Mearns?). Bearing in mind the dualism of the Picts, this hypothetical Northern kingdom could also be divided in two, *viz* sets *I & II,* sets *III & IV,* with symbols *8 & 5* being the leading lights. The same division cannot be applied to the south because of the absence of set *VIII* but symbol *31* is still clearly the most important one there.

The reason why there is not a fourth Z-rod can be deduced from Table 9 and Figure 4, since it would have to have been joined with an animal in the missing set *VIII*. The only other symbol that could have had a V-rod would be symbol *12* and this does in fact occur *once*—design *13*—on a Class II stone, but it fails the test of being a symbol.

Why was there no set *VIII* in the South? The answer is that this set is just an artefact of Table 9, which is only a hypothetical arrangement of designs before the imposition of the mystic number 7 definitively limited the number of possible symbols. It is quite feasible that there *was* a balance between north and south such that they each had 16 designs before the symbols were decided upon. From the other designs of the Picts one can find four which *could* make up the missing set:

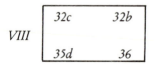

However, these designs are symbolically inappropriate *because* they are all domesticated animals: cattle, horse and hound, concerned with Pictish subsistence. Although the Celts might have ate horsemeat and probably dogs as well, these animals were chiefly used for hunting the boar and the stag for food—as the many lively hunting scenes on Class II and III stones testify.

All around the world totemic societies choose *wild* animals for their totems rather than tame ones; a common reason is that men tend to identify with their domesticated species which makes these animals less appropriate than wild species for differentiating *between* lineages. It is also often the case that lineages perform rituals for the increase of *natural* species but not for domesticates, since natural species are not under man's control like his own animals. Of course men wished for the fertility of their herds, but this was not the prerogative of a special lineage—everyone wanted their herds to increase. We find that the Picts did make small votive tablets with designs on them (primarily cattle) and as these are generally water-worn it looks as if they have been sanctified by throwing them into a river or the sea, often near to a Pictish fort. That these tablets were part of some fertility rite is confirmed by the fact that they are never combined with a symbol. (cf p.20).

Although set *VIII* is hypothetical, *36* only occurs once, while *35d* does not appear in Class I. As for *32b*, had it been a symbol then it should have been combined with a Z-rod to balance the distribution, cf Figure 5.

Three possible symbols, not accounted for, are *2, 11* and *18* which are similar to *13* in combining just once with another symbol and hence are temporarily rejected. As for the remaining designs: *16, 20, 22, 25-30* and *33*, not only are they unique but they are so lacking in artistic merit that they could have been made by anyone at any time. No. *35* is a lion but is purely Christian and not Pictish. These twenty designs have been omitted from the analysis because they fail to meet the test of being a symbol, besides which their significance is minimal, cf Figure 5.

Lastly there is one symbol—*24*—the mirror and comb, which is a very important symbol. However, it is not a lineage symbol like all the others but signifies another essential ingredient in lineage life—the giving of bridewealth or gifts to the bride's family. This special symbol is normally found beneath the pair of symbols that represent the lineages being united in alliance, it being usually placed next to the symbol that signifies the groom's lineage; its incorporation into the symbol system will be discussed in the next chapter.

Mirror and comb

24

Missing set VIII?

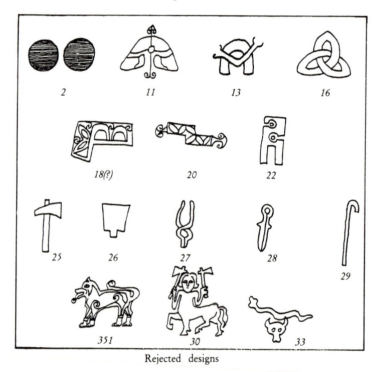

Rejected designs

Figure 5 : The remaining (non-lineage) designs

So far we have treated the symbols collectively, and no distinction has been made between symbols occuring on Class I and II stones, since we wished to present the widest possible survey of the Pictish symbol system. It will be found that the symbols on Class I stones conform very closely to the different arrangements that have been discussed so far, but the symbols on Class II stones deviate from these models because they have a more restricted symbol range. The following table indicates the *changes* that have taken place in Class II symbolism.

	3	*9*	*5*	*8*
B	† 44	‡40g	45	40e
	6	*21*	*23*	‡12
		41		*31*
	† 42/3		† 39b	
D	‡1	19	*4*	† 17
	‡37	‡34	† 39d	‡38
	10	*46*	† 15	‡14

Table 11 : Class II changes   ‡ - eliminated   † - weak

The number of animal symbols has been reduced to 8 while the geometric symbols are now 14 which comes to a total of 22 symbols, one third of which are marginal. Thus, in effect, Class II only makes use of half the available symbols while, moreover, even with its 22 symbols, the number of potential pairs is likewise reduced to a half of that possible with 28. Besides this, the actual number of paired symbols is half that of Class I while the number of stones is 2/5 of the Class I total. This halving of the options open to the Picts strongly suggests that their radius of interaction has correspondingly been narrowed to only a *quarter* of that in Class I times since options involve mutual pairing. This suggestion is strikingly confirmed by the tight geographical distribution of the Class II monuments, cf Maps 3 & 4.

If we now try to reconstruct groups of seven symbols for Class II on the lines of Table 11) we are forced into having just three sets:

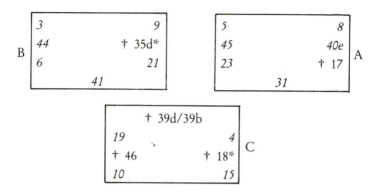

Table 12 : Class II regrouping   † new positions   * new symbol

(Note the introduction of two possible new symbols to replace the seven that have been lost in Class II times).

Set A contains 65 percent of all Class II pairs, B has 21 percent and C 14 percent, which means that A and B still control 86 percent of the total but the share of the triple alliance symbols—*5, 8* and *31*—has slumped to only one half the total. With slight modifications sets A and B are basically the same as in Class I but the secondary level has been drastically modified. Of course these sets do not have any independent existence for they are simply a convenient way to arrange the statistical data, yet despite this they can tell us more about the relative significance of the structure of the symbol system than, say, Table 3 which just lists the number of occurrences. These sets demonstrate the highly selective bias in the pairing of the symbols as well as their relationships in design that statistical frequencies alone fail to reveal. Thus had we simply compared the frequencies of occurrence of a particular symbol in Class I and II times and allowed for the differing totals, we would be little the wiser other than confirming the importance of *5, 8* and *31*. Taken in conjunction with the individual statistics, these sets enable us to detect the patterns that underlie the strong biases in the selection of pairs.

The changes in structure of the Class II symbol sets suggest that the triple alliance is no longer in complete control since, in the north, the symbols are tightly bunched together in discrete groupings while, to the south, the minor symbols have a greater degree of freedom of pairing than in Class I times. In detail, *5* is reduced to second place behind *8* and *31*, which means that *31* has greatly enhanced its importance at the expense of both *5* and *8*.

Hence in terms of the earlier suggestion that Southern Pictland was originally animal-oriented, the great concentration of Class II symbols in the south has simply strengthened the position of *31* over the other symbols. Yet, paradoxically enough, the animal symbols have been curtailed in the Class II period, although this counterbalanced by the disappearance of an important geometric symbol—*12*. All told, it seems that a shake-up has occurred to the dominant symbols that could reflect a weakening of the North in attempting to control the basically Southern Class II Picts; indeed, this whole period could have been a politically unstable one where no one symbol was clearly dominant as was the case in Class I times.

Naturally, the Picts had none of these tables in mind when they drew up their system of symbols, since they were only interested in recording the relevant pairs of symbols in the appropriate places. Yet the *outcome* of their many choices adds up to a very pronounced bias in their selection that can in no way be attributed to chance. Not only did the Picts have a limited number of symbols that were interrelated in design, but they also maintained a similar ratio of highly dominant symbols to others right throughout Pictland on both Class I and II monuments. Clearly these symbols had the same meaning everywhere, whatever it was, from which it follows that certain symbols were *necessary* in most districts. The statistics show that the symbols in the primary set A and B (above) were universal and abundant, although this does not imply that the sets had a collective and independent presence but they might have had.

This new look at the symbols has attempted to show that we can order the symbols into varying patterns that provide us with food for thought. This is not a solution to the Pictish problem but it is the basis for proof. Four more steps have to be taken to complete this exposition:

1) to explain why the symbols always occur in pairs—Chapter 5
2) to account for the actual geographical distribution of the stones—Chapter 6
3) to explain the meaning of the symbols—Chapter 7
4) to account for why the stones were erected—Chapter 1, Part II.

If all these steps can be successfully accomplished, as well as explaining the royal succession and the Pictish Oghams, then we will be well on the way to answering a difficult problem about one of Scotland's most enigmatic groups of inhabitants.

CHAPTER 5

The lineage basis for paired symbols

A major thesis throughout this discussion has been that symbols only occur in pairs, and this is actually built into the definition of a symbol itself; hence this necessity for having paired symbols needs to be demonstrated. If we set aside the special symbol *24* — the mirror and comb — besides the few designs that only appear once, the evidence shows that practically all the undamaged stones as well as many damaged stones just have paired symbols upon them. So the question remains 'Why two symbols?' The last chapter showed that the 14 main symbols were universally distributed over Pictland, from which it followed that the symbols designated a widely-held and common aspect of Pictish life. It will be maintained that *that* aspect can be none other than the lineage structure of the Picts themselves.

In the first centuries A.D. most tribes in Europe were unilineal i.e. they traced their descent and succession through either the male or female line. The Celts who then inhabited Britain were basically patrilineal where descent went through the male line. Even after the Anglo-Saxon conquest of England there was no change since they, too, were patrilineal. This bias is with us still since succession and descent is currently traced through the male line and patronymics are the rule, whereby the wife and children adopt the surname of the male. However, in Scotland women are legally entitled to retain their birth name although this is still based on the father's lineage. In Scandinavia and Slavic countries the

surnames (i.e. additional names, 1500 A.D., according to the
O.E.D.) were compound formations derived from the father's (and
sometimes the mother's) Christian name plus the suffix 'son' or
'daughter', e.g. Svensson or Svensdaughter. Such a system of
naming obviously blurred the lines of descent, since many men
could have been called by the popular Christian (actually pagan)
name of Sven and so there was no necessary kin relationship
between all the Svenssons. Thus, in Europe, there were two dual
naming systems:

1) Christian name plus father's surname (often occupational)
2) Christian name plus the Christian name of the father (or
   mother) together with the tag 'son' or 'daughter'.

Of these two systems, the former enables one to trace descent
more easily and was the one adopted by families that had power
and possessions to pass on, i.e. the nobility. This was also the
method employed by many of the early tribes of Scotland, since it
enabled them to identify their kin unambiguously as lineage
members who were duty-bound to support each other in blood
feuds up to the ninth degree of cousinhood, i.e. all descendants
from a common great-great-great-great-great-great-great grandfather!

The purpose of this discussion is to show that individuals are
universally known by a dual naming system that gives:

a) personal identity — the given name
b) lineage identity — the kin name

One result of the Scandinavian/Slavic naming system is that it
demands a recall of *all* the particular *marriages* that have taken
place if one wishes to trace descent, which means that this method
is more egalitarian since both sexes are accorded equal significance
in descent — so it is almost double unilinear descent or even
cognatic, like our present system![12]

These apparently trivially different modes of naming individuals
have a direct bearing on the Picts, as it is maintained that the two
tribes that eventually constituted the Picts were matrilineal, i.e.
descent went through women from a man to his sister's son. The
evidence for the Picts being matrilineal is that no Pictish king ever
succeeded to his father's throne until the very end of the Pictish
kingdom, besides Bede's testimony regarding the succession. Of
course it might be objected that if the Picts were Celts then surely
they should have been patrilineal like the Irish. However, it is
taken that the Picts were P-Celtic like the British and not similar
to the Q-Celtic Irish, besides which they could well have been
influenced by the indigenous Bronze/Iron Age population who,
most likely, were matrilineal since this could have been *the original*
mode of succession world-wide — but this is not proven! However,

most matrilineal societies live cheek by jowl with patrilineal
societies which do not differ one iota as regards environment,
ethnic composition or general culture, other than this one matter
of descent. So it is not so very extraordinary that the Picts could
have been matrilineal while all around them were patrilineal tribes
of the same ethnic group, since the whole question of descent is
merely one of emphasis. While there has been a historical tendency
for matrilineal tribes to go over to patrilinearity, there is no iron
law involved and some tribes may find that matrilinearity suits
their own purposes. Thus there is really no case for assuming that
the Picts were non-Celtic or even non-Indo-European simply
because the rulers (n.b.) adopted matrilineal succession. It cannot
be argued otherwise than that the royal succession was *not*
patrilineal, whatever the ultimate explanation is. Given the few
choices open to these tribes, the likelihood is that the Picts chose
matrilinearity since it is particularly suited to long-distance trading
peoples. Summing up, there is no indication whatever that the
Picts were patrilineal like the British or Irish; indeed this difference
might account for the lack of sympathy that is clearly displayed
between the Picts and the British, Scots and Angles. Although to
our minds these might seem inconsequential matters, they do affect
the rights of individuals that were of critical importance to the
people concerned, as one's rights hinged on the recognised
procedures for inheritance of office and power.

An absolute requirement for maintaining any unilineal system is
that marriages must be tightly regulated so that nobody can marry
a kinsman — the rule of exogamy. This means that the Picts had
three possibilities: a man could either marry—

1) his mother's brother's daughter (MBD for short)
2) his father's sister's daughter (FZD for short)
3) a complete stranger

All these three possibilities uphold the rule of exogamy, so the
Picts had to choose between them.[13]

These three possibilities are exactly the same for patrilineal
societies as well, because, in both cases, the cross-cousins (MBD
and FZD) can *never* be of the same kin as oneself, cf centre diagram in Fig. 6. It might be objected that if one is going to marry a
first cousin, then why cannot one marry one's parallel cousins
(FBD and MZD)? The reason is that parallel cousins are or may be
one's own kin, which the rule of exogamy expressly prohibits. For
example, in a matrilineal society a man's MZD is the same kin as
himself, while his FBD *could* be kin if his FB married his MZ.

The rule of exogamy (marrying non-kin) also avoids the sin of
incest, but its main purpose is to create interdependence between

different kin groups. While *we* count all four first cousins as equally close because of our bilateral kinship system, this is not the case in unilineal societies, as the cross-cousins belong to quite different kin groups since descent can only pass down *one* direct line—the male or the female. It will be recalled that the early Christian Church held that first cousins were too close to get married unless special dispensation was given. The reason had nothing to do with the allegedly bad effects of inbreeding, but more with the desire of the Chuch to gain control of the units of production and reproduction in society by making such marriages sinful *because* they were very popular! See the discussion in Goody (1983).

In tribal societies, one's life is regulated by kinship obligations and since one cannot marry kin it follows that households and settlements must contain members of *at least* two different kin groups. The question remains: who is one going to marry? Although marrying a total stranger solves the problem of exogamy it is not particularly desirable, since one knows nothing about them or their kin. In any case, who is going to go off into the unknown to seek a spouse when one would be unprotected by one's own kin—one's only true support? It is far better to marry someone you know—like your cross-cousin—because the two kin groups are already allied through marriage. Thus cross-cousin marriage is safe and it also cements an existing alliance.

MBD marriage can create a marriage system whereby permanent alliances are formed such that one lineage is always superior, thanks to an implicit rule that wife-givers are always superior to wife-receivers. Thus with four lineages: P, Q, R and S, then P will be superior to Q, Q to R, R to S because P gives wives to Q and Q gives wives to R, etc. Such a system makes P a perpetually superior lineage as long as it obtains wives from *outwith* the group of four, i.e. from a neighbouring kingdom. The alternative (FZD) system is more democratic in that it denies any lineage permanent authority, since they effectively marry in a circle whereby P marries into Q, Q into R etc., i.e. $P \to Q \to R \to S$, so that in this round P is superior to Q, Q to R etc. However in the next generation they must marry in the reverse order: $S \to R \to Q \to P \to S$ which means that R is superior to Q, Q to P, etc. — the exact opposite of what happened the previous generation. This reversal of marriage direction every generation is constant and sets up certain strains since it means that one is tied to two other lineages. Another feature of FZD marriage is that normally the minimum number of lineages involved will be four, whereas with MBD marriage the arrangement is open-ended but if there were only four lineages then both the first and fourth would still have to marry outside the group anyway, which thus extends the lineage involved to at least six.

Although matrilineal societies are not so common around the world nowadays, they very often have, interestingly enough, myths about the four original clan ancestors who founded their society. Such a four-fold division of society is quite common and with it goes a dualistic view of the universe such that the four clans are divided into moieties (or halves) with two clans in each half. This dualism divides everything into two opposing but complementary halves: men/women, good/bad, light/dark, left/right, etc. While most such societies associate men and (the) right — in both senses — with life, dominance and the order of things such as the sun, light and goodness, whereas women are linked to the moon, darkness and evil, there are exceptions. In parts of ancient Europe men were associated with the moon and goodness (of course) while women were linked with the sun and evil, cf. Needham: *Right and Left* p. 328. The only *certainty* is that men, who construct these dualistic systems, are always in the right!

To explain how FZD marriage works, it is necessary to give a kinship diagram: Figure 6a. Taking a four clan model marrying in a circle as the basis of the explanation, then women go as wives from lineage P to Q, Q to R etc., in the first generation, i.e. from left to right in the diagram, where lineage P is superior to Q, Q to R, etc. This arrangement, however, necessitates a reversal in the direction of wives in the second generation, besides a reversal of the power structure. In this simplified diagram (only one child of each sex is given) the males will be the heads of their lineages in their respective generations while their heirs will be their sisters' sons in the next generation. Should the marriage be virilocal (a wife lives with her husband's lineage), then the interesting consequence is that a man's heir lives as a child in a different village to his uncle; thus in the first generation Q's heir is with lineage R, in the next generation Q (who was brought up with R) finds his own heir back in lineage Q. More importantly it means that a man's grandson inherits his grandfather's title as head of his lineage.

Figure 6a may appear to be complicated, but careful examination will show that it is simply built up of several units of FZD marriages, cf centre figure. It is assumed that there are just four lineages marrying in a circle—hence lineage P is shown twice in order to reveal its linkages with lineages Q and S. The lineages are to be distinguished by the internal markings within the male and female symbols. It can be seen that each lineage in the figure comprises two identical FZD units and hence contains two sets of siblings and two sets of marriages. However, the links *between* lineages are just two sets of marriages on either side. While it is not necessary to draw four generations, it does help to show how these patterns are repeated every other generation. It can also be seen how lineages alternately give away their women to lineages on either side of them. As the marriage pattern is the same in any one generation, it means that women are given away as wives in the same direction around the circle of lineages; but this direction is reversed in the next generation—as the bottom figure indicates.

All this may seem very mechanical, but this is only a model of an ideal system and does not represent what happens in practice. To make a simple point: if there is no FZD available, then one may choose a second cousin who stands in the same classificatory relationship to Ego. However, the point of the model is just to illustrate the basic principles concerning the exchange of spouses and the alliances that are formed by marriage.

A shorthand way of accurately describing the lineage affiliations of all the people given in Figure 6a is to give each of them two symbols, one above the other, like P/Q where the upper symbol denotes the father's lineage and the bottom symbol the lineage of the mother. It follows that all siblings (brothers and sisters) have identical symbol pairs, since they are of equivalent standing in the lineage. Furthermore, if one looks down the male line from father to son we find that there is a repetition: P/Q, Q/P, P/Q, Q/P etc. This shows not only an identity between grandfather and grandson but also that father and son have reciprocal pairs: P/Q and Q/P. In other words, there is a merging of alternate generations and complete opposition between adjacent generations.

It is now possible to demonstrate that with a four lineage arrangement such as this, there are four reciprocal pairs of symbols which completely distinguish the members of the community:

Odd generations: 1, 3, 5, etc $\quad P/Q \quad Q/R \quad R/S \quad S/P$

Even generations: 2, 4, 6, etc $\quad Q/P \quad R/Q \quad S/R \quad P/S$

In terms of Figure 6a, it can be seen that the top symbols of the pairs in the above table indicate the directions in which brides are given in the odd-numbered generations: Odd — $P \rightarrow Q \rightarrow R \rightarrow S \rightarrow P$. The direction of bride-giving is completely reversed in the even-numbered generations: Even — $P \rightarrow S \rightarrow R \rightarrow Q \rightarrow P$.

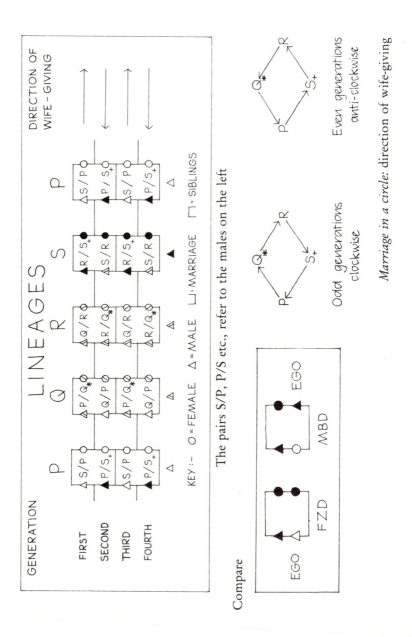

Figure 6a: Patrilateral cross-cousin (FZD) marriage

THE NETWORK OF KIN AND AFFINAL RELATIONS

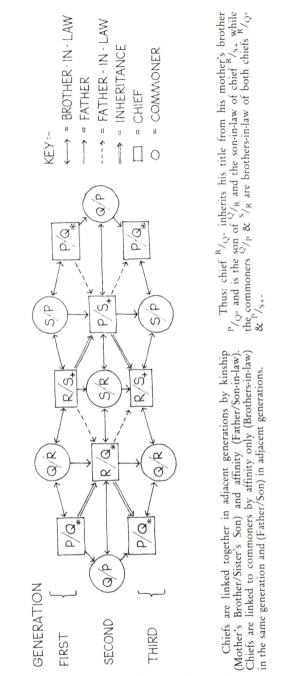

Chiefs are linked together in adjacent generations by kinship (Mother's Brother/Sister's Son) and affinity (Father/Son-in-law). Chiefs are linked to commoners by affinity only (Brothers-in-law) in the same generation and (Father/Son) in adjacent generations.

Thus: chief R/Q^* inherits his title from his mother's brother P/Q^* and is the son of Q/R and the son-in-law of chief R/S_+ while the commoners Q/P & S/R are brothers-in-law of both chiefs R/Q^* & P/S_+.

Figure 6b: Network arising from FZD marriages

However, given such a set of eight pairs of symbols there seems no obvious way of determining the relative status of the four symbols or lineages, nor which way a particular lineage must marry in any given generation so that the whole system does not collapse — a major weakness of FZD marriages, cf Needham: *Structure and Sentiment,* 1962, pp 101 *passim.* In order to explain this problem a further discussion of kinship is necessary.

Kinship diagrams do not pretend to reflect real life except in very general terms, since there could well be more than a dozen siblings, not the two given in the figure. Siblings are usually distinguished in terms of birth order, so we can take the diagram to summarise the actions of the eldest son and daughter, not the behaviour of all their siblings or their cousins — the children of their mother's younger sisters — all of whom are equal lineage members. Hence there is plenty of room for disagreements about succession and marriage.

Even in matrilineal societies, power is held by men, so it is more likely that the use of paired symbols will be used by men to proclaim their lineage identity. If the lower symbol really denotes a man's lineage then the upper symbol seems somewhat superfluous but, in fact, it is equally important as it is the lineage of his wife and so indicates where he should seek an alliance. Thus the two symbols also proclaim the alliance between two lineages in which the bride-giving lineage is placed above his own since it is superior in status. So while in a symbol pair $^P/_Q$, the symbol Q uniquely and unequivocally denotes a man's lineage derived through his mother, the symbol P has three levels of meaning:

1) the lineage of his father
2) the lineage of his wife
3) the superiority of lineage P, expressed by its position, in providing a man's father, wife and lineage ally.

In another sense, the pair $^P/_Q$ denotes the matrilineal *household* comprising members of the two lineages but where the children belong to the superior lineage P, a fact that enhances the position of the wife. The husband only comes into his own when he inherits his mother's brother's title as head of lineage Q. So this system of denoting a man's kinship links serves a number of purposes: the ranking of lineages, marriage choice, descent and succession — in an extraordinarily concise way.

To return to the problem of discovering the hierarchy among the four symbols P, Q, R, and S, it will be seen that there are two exogamous (outward-marrying) moieties in terms of marriage partners:

Moiety 1	S	Q
Moiety 2	R	P

Figure 6 shows that Q does not marry S nor does P marry R i.e. Q and S form one exogamous moiety while P and R form the other. All communities have leaders — either hereditary or elected — and it will be assumed that moiety 1 is the superior half with lineage Q (marked by *) as *the* chiefly lineage while S (marked by +) provides the sub-chiefs. This gives two sets of symbol pairs ($^P/_{Q*}$ and $^R/_{Q*}$) and ($^R/_{S+}$ and $^P/_{S+}$) which designate the four men who act as chiefs for the community, in the alternate generations. If we simply consider the odd-numbered generations, then the chief is $^P/_{Q*}$ and the sub-chief is $^R/_{S+}$ — indeed *this information is all we need to work out the entire kinship network and marriage arrangements:* $^P/_{Q*}$ marries the sister of $^S/_P$, the father of $^P/_{S+}$'s sister who marries $^S/_R$, son of $^R/_{S+}$; $^R/_{S+}$ marries the sister of $^Q/_R$, the father of $^R/_{Q*}$'s sister who marries $^Q/_P$, son of $^P/_{Q*}$

These intermarriages can be easily checked against Figure 6a and b.

But why are the chiefly lineages marked out by * and +? The answer goes back to a general rule that wife-givers are superior to wife-receivers. It will be seen that in alternate generations the chiefly lineages accept brides from lineages P and R, which technically makes them inferior. In order for the chiefs to maintain their status, they provide the wife-givers with substantial bride-wealth and this is indicated by the presence of * and +. In the case of the commoner lineages P and R, when they receive wives from Q and S they just acknowledge their inferiority and do not try to equalise by giving *significant* bridewealth payments, as this would challenge the authority structure.

Just to confirm the point that *just two pairs of symbols* are sufficient to provide enough information to reconstruct the entire kinship structure of a four lineage system, the argument will be recapitulated slightly differently.

Step 1: Given two pairs $^P/_{Q*}$ and $^R/_{S+}$ we know there must be two moieties:

S+	Q*	Moiety 1 — superior
P	R	Moiety 2 — inferior

Step 2: These two moieties will intermarry as follows:

$^R/_{S+}$ $^S/_P$ $^P/_{Q*}$ $^Q/_R$ one generation (e.g. odd)

$^S/_R$ $^P/_{S+}$ $^Q/_P$ $^R/_{Q*}$ alternate generation (e.g. even)

since only one* and one + are possible in any generation

Step 3: As S has received a wife from R, P a wife from S, Q a wife from P and R a wife from Q in one generation, it follows that the marriage circle is P→Q→R→S→P. In the alternate generation the wives flow in the opposite direction, cf Figure 6a.

In practise it would be expected that more than the minimum number of two pairs would be found to corroborate the sequences but there should be *at least* one pair in the home territory of each lineage, cf Table 14.

With this exposition behind us, it is now necessary to make a conceptual leap and state that these marriage and succession arrangements are those of the Picts, while the pairing of symbols coincides with the pairs of Pictish symbols found upon the Class I and II monuments. The kinship model is quite hypothetical, since we do not know the details of Pictish kinship, but its function is to provide us with a working model that can help us unravel the Pictish symbols and it is not to be taken as a finally true account. If it succeeds in explaining the symbol pairing, then it *might* possibly be correct, but that remains to be seen. In the context of a group of four intermarrying lineages it is proposed to call such groups *macro-pits* since each lineage (and its appropriate symbol) can be taken to represent one *pit* or a quarter of the community's land, it being generally accepted that the term *pit* is a parcel of land — according to the place-name evidence. The special marks used to distinguish the dominant lineages are symbol *24* (the mirror and comb) that stands for bridewealth payment, where * is the mirror and comb and + is just the plain mirror. As a non-lineage symbol, *24* is added to the bottom of the pair of symbols that denote a leader's lineage entitlements. As individuals they would have personal names, but they inherit a fixed set of titles, established within the macropit, at birth, that record the lineages of their parents. As there are only 28 lineages, it follows that some repetition of paired titles (the names of the lineages) will occur, but their significance is likely to be local and confined to the community in which they are found. Although major lineages are also likely to control many of the macropits, it does not necessarily follow that there was a centralized authority.

If the macropit is taken to be the basic unit of the Pictish community, then it can also be seen as a microcosm of Pictish society as a whole. The whole Pictish kingdom can be regarded as two major moieties:

X	W	Northern kingdom : superior
Y	Z	Southern kingdom : inferior

This pattern is repeated at every descending level: each kingdom consists of two halves while each of the four provinces — W, X, Y and Z — consists of two moieties, each of which contains two pairs of macropits. Translating this thorough-going dualism into symbol pairs, it gives, for the whole of Pictland, $4 \times 8 \times 8 = 256$ symbol pairs, which then should be the theoretical maximum number of symbol stones in Class I times. Just over a half of these stones have been found, while as for the dominant pairs (with * and +), that should come to a quarter of the maximum, i.e. 64 dominant pairs; some 2/3 of these have been discovered.

It might be thought that this dualistic system of 32 macropits spread over Pictland is far too neat to be realistic, but if the Picts were capable of devising a complicated symbol system then it would not tax their powers of invention to erect an administrative structure of tiers of authority based on the binary principle that underlies their symbolism. While such a structure is artificial, it would make good administrative sense in clearly demarcating the local authorities, besides providing a line of command from the top. Even our modern administrative divisions of Scotland into counties, regions or districts is as arbitrary as deciding on just 32 local centres of authority. In both cases the actual size of the population in each administrative unit will be different, but the *structure* remains the same and that is what is important. The following chapter will demonstrate that all the Class I symbol pairs can in fact be accommodated into exactly 32 macropits along the lines suggested above, and this astonishing coincidence is the best proof that it is correct.

Earlier, it was pointed out that it was possible to derive the full array of lineage combinations from just two symbol pairs, so why should the Picts erect any further stones, for they would surely be redundant? The answer is that both symbolism and natural languages need a certain level of redundancy to avoid the risk of misunderstanding. Such a possibility exists if the *pits* or settlements are situated close to each other on, say, a fertile strip of land, since the key signs (the dominant symbol pairs) could confuse because of their mutual near presence. In such cases, most or all the symbol pairs would have to be spelled out, with the consequence that in highly populated districts there would be almost complete sets of stones, whereas in sparsely populated regions there would only be a few stones. Thus a distribution map would (and does) reveal densely concentrated pockets of stones in clearly defined areas while elsewhere there are just some scatterings of stones in those less-favoured districts which ran little risk of causing confusion. Such an explanation *could* account for the 'missing' stones in the hypothetical total of 256. The tables in the next chapter can predict which are the symbol pairs that have gone astray, but it is not possible to account for why stones were or were not erected in particular places, since this is a matter of historical chance depending on the strength of the lineages at the time when the stones were erected.

If the Picts had adopted the kinship system presented in Figure 6, then it would provide a rational explanation of the pairing of symbols on stone, since the use of such permanent markers would reflect the ideal, *unchanging,* sets of symbols found within the community. Thus, far from commemorating specific individuals, the symbol pairs denoted those lineage links that all leaders, great and small, throughout the generations needed to possess to claim their rights. It would not be so surprising if the Picts really did tattoo their lineage members with their special symbols, for then a simple comparison with the perpetual symbol stones would prove one's claim absolutely. Such an indelible passport would cut down false claims as well as mobility, but whether this ingenious scheme for reducing feuds and promoting stability is true must wait until we find a perfectly preserved bog Pict!

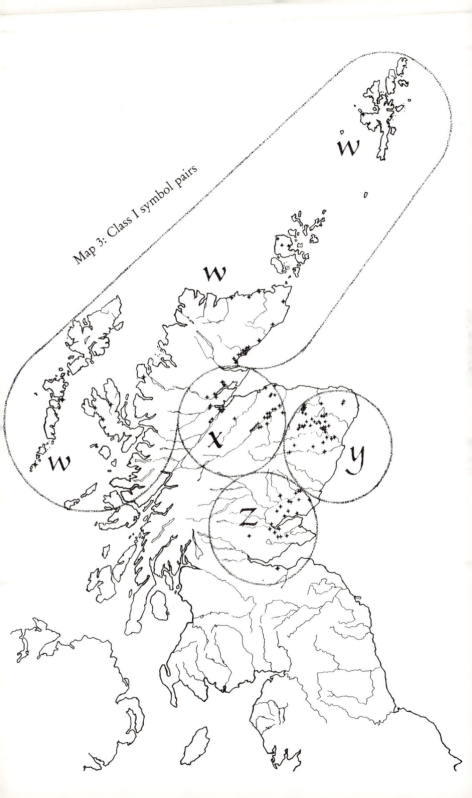

Map 3: Class I symbol pairs

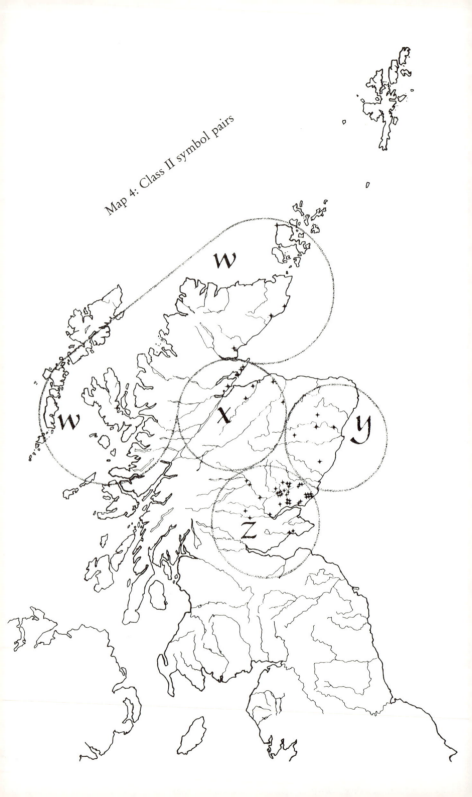

Map 4: Class II symbol pairs

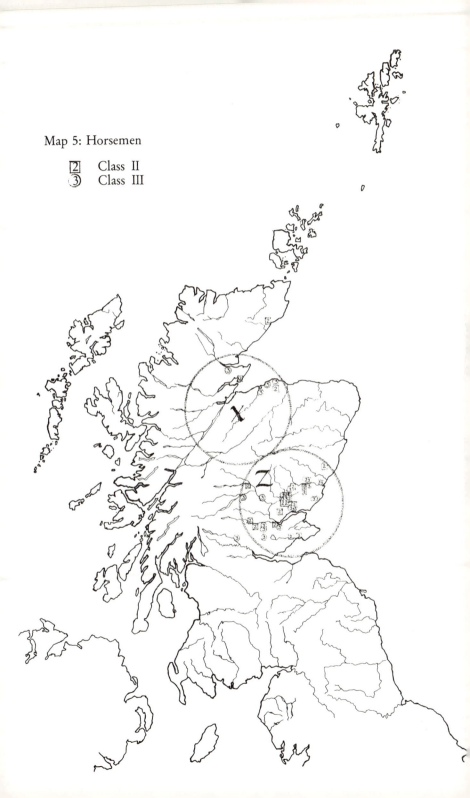

Map 5: Horsemen

☐2   Class II
③   Class III

Map 6: The distribution of *pit*-names

CHAPTER 6

Grouping and distribution of stones

This is the key chapter since it draws together the different strands of the dualistic hypothesis and puts it to the ultimate test: does it explain the actual physical distribution of the symbol stones? If the hypothesis can predict which symbols are paired and where they will be found, then this is the closest we can come to proving it correct, apart from discovering some old manuscript that explains the symbol system! Before pondering the evidence to be presented which, naturally, supports the hypothesis, it is worth considering what kinds of possible solution to the problem of the symbol stones there could be.

It is generally agreed that there has to be some rational solution and that the Picts were not being deliberately misleading in erecting such a widespread and well-executed series of monuments. It is also accepted that the symbol stones have reference to humans and not to spirits or gods, so the question is: how do the symbols relate to individual men and women? There can only be two answers:

1) the symbols are personal and refer to one individual at a time
2) the symbols denote specific categories of individuals

The first alternative was discussed in Chapter 3 and it was seen that this approach immediately runs into difficulties; for if the stones were funerary monuments of the type "Here lies A son of B" then the number of variations is extremely limited, very scarce and somewhat arbitrary. To escape from this dilemma, it was suggested that the symbols were the statuses held by particular persons, but if the Picts were so irrational as to just celebrate their status system we may as well give up in the face of this collective madness. No tribal society would ever go to all that trouble simply to honour the statuses of some *unnamed deceased* person — the idea is so unrealistic that it can only indicate a profound misunderstanding of the known facts of tribal life. In addition, besides the point that few of the stones are actually associated with burials, this proposal would make the symbol-combinations entirely a matter of chance, since individuals achieve their statuses by their own efforts, when and where they could. The greatest defect of the funerary monument idea is that as it is predicated on historical chance *it implicitly denies that there can ever be a systematic solution to the problem of the symbol stones.*

The second alternative holds out the promise that the symbols are arranged systematically according to categories of individuals. Which categories? In a tribal society like the Picts, the major categorical division was the lineage — the particular descent line to which every single individual belonged to. One's own lineage determined who were your kin, affines, allies and enemies. It may be hard for us to realise this today but, in tribal societies, one's lineage dictated who one obeyed, who one married, who one supported in battle, who one inherited from, and so on: most aspects of one's life were controlled by the lineage, in the shape of the lineage head. As such, a lineage is only a concept in the mind, for it comprised all the people (living and dead) who descended from either a male or female ancestor. Lineages, then, do not all live together, since one has to marry into a different lineage and this could mean leaving the main body of the lineage, but one always retains one's lineage membership. Thus one's lineage was what separated one from the rest of society (i.e. the other lineages) but it also provided mutual support from fellow members. In such societies there is no concept of individualism: all acts of individual lineage members reflected only to the glory or shame of the lineage. This notion can be found in Scottish history where the clan (a group of lineages *claiming* common descent) was the central rallying point, with the clan chief the object of honour. Heroes fought as individuals for glory in battle, but *only* as lineage members where their exploits would be celebrated in song and praise. The Dark Ages were renowned for their epic heroes — Beowulf, Roland, etc. — but they only fought for their liege lords to gain honour for their own lineage and people. Their praises were sung by and for their clans, since there was then no greater entity: the nation had not been invented. Indeed, the whole bardic tradition from Homer onwards was devoted to praising the lineage through recounting the exploits of its members. It was the bards who were the lineage's remembrancers: they formulated and promulgated the fame of the lineages; such boasting was the anvil on which reputations were forged in the Dark Ages and later.

The relevance of the above discussion to the Pictish symbol stones is that it was the lineage that was paramount in the Dark Ages. The quarrels between the Picts, a constantly noted feature, were inter-lineage rivalries just like those endemic to the Irish, British and Angles of the time. Before the rise of the nation state it is inconceivable that anyone would raise a monument to a *national* hero: one whose statuses were universally recognized and acknowledged. Even if the Picts formed a united kingdom, it was still composed of many lineages, and it would be incredible if they simply sat down to invent symbols recording statuses to place on somebody or other's grave. Had they really wished to record their dead, they could have borrowed the Irish Oghams or the Church's Latin to inscribe the traditional message. It is a curious fact that even after the Picts were long converted to Christianity, they *never once* inscribed a monument to their dead! The Class II and III stones bear witness to the fact that the sculptors were well acquainted with funeral stones elsewhere in Britain, so there was no reason why they should not have added an inscription if they wanted to.

Earlier it was argued that at the time of the erection of the Class I and II stones, the dualistic mode of thinking of the Picts caused them to divide their country into binary units of administration, from the kingdom at the top right down to the macropit level. Simply looking at the number of stones involved, it is clear that the two Class I kingdoms were twice as large as the Class II kingdom. Four blocs of 8 macropits are assigned to Class I and just two blocs of 8 macropits are given to Class II: this is illustrated in the synoptic table which gives the entire 48 macropits ordered geographically from north to south. The four Class I blocs have been given the generally accepted provincial names, while the two Class II blocs simply retain their kingdom locations.

The synoptic table 13 can be used to generate the 384 symbol pairs available in the 48 macropits since every macropit contains 8 possible symbol pairs:

S+	Q*
P	R

$$^S/_P, ^P/_{S+}, ^S/_R, ^R/_{S+}, ^Q/_P, ^P/_{Q*}, ^Q/_R, ^R/_{Q*}$$

This expansion is given in Tables 14 which are cross-referenced to the catalogue of stones: Table 2.[14] There are a number of single symbols on the damaged stones which are taken to have *once* formed a pair and so they have been incorporated in the Tables, but there can be no guarantee that these have been correctly assigned, of course! The main thing is that they *have to* appear in the correct geographical area. Although only 56 percent of these hypothetical pairs have been found so far, nevertheless 95 percent of the Pictish stones fit into this geographically oriented synoptic table. Any dubious pairs or pairs that have had to be omitted are mentioned at the foot of the relevant table. Most of the dozen omissions have uncertain identification or are just anomalous, as can be readily checked. Hence one can justifiably claim that *the synoptic table covers the entire range of symbol stones and places them in their correct geographical location.* Comparison should also be made with Maps 2 and 3 to see the precise areas involved.

Not surprisingly, the Pictish provincial names do not correspond to the late 19th century counties, for there is no reason to suppose that *Cat, Fidach,* etc. denoted *territory,* since it is more likely that they were the names of phratries or groups of lineages held together by common allegiances. Boundaries fluctuated widely over the centuries due to conquest, inheritance and changing patterns of alliance, although by the time of the Class I stones it is possible that the phratries had settled down into roughly discrete areas. The most important thing always was the *men* not the land: the strength of a lineage did not depend on its territory but on the number of armed warriors at its command. As basically a pastoralist people, the Picts were more concerned over rights to grazing than possession since property was held in common and not individually: hence grazing and watering rights were a matter between lineages, for they were most probably shared.

When we examine the distribution of symbol pairs[15] we find that those in *Cat* fit neatly into the synoptic table: most of those from the islands and Caithness fall into moiety i, while those from Sutherland mainly come under moiety ii. In *Fidach,* which stretches over four old counties, it is difficult to draw a north/south line since the boundaries are very complex around the Moray Firth, besides which the symbol stones here are some of the most anomalous in all Pictland. There is little doubt that *Ce* is Aberdeenshire but *Circind* is more complicated since one of its moieties is in Aberdeenshire while the other is in Angus! The reason for this split has to do with the actual timing and setting up of the stones and will be discussed in Part II. Summarising these geographical locations for Class I:

Cat	i :	Shetland, Orkney, Hebrides and Caithness
	ii :	Sutherland
Fidach	i ⎫ ii ⎬	Ross, Inverness, Moray and Banff
Ce	i ⎫ ii ⎬	Aberdeen
Circind	i :	Aberdeen
	ii :	Angus

TABLE 13: Synoptic table of macropits

I — NORTH	**CAT W***	12 1 / 17 8	8 14 / 17 7	8 41 / 17 40e	5 46 / 8 45	i
		8 4 / 46 12	7 23 / 15 8	17 21 / 8 41	31 45 / 8 10	ii
	FIDACH X*	40e 8 / 12 15	34 40e / 23 6	5 6 / 8 41	45 8 / 3 5	i
		23 8 / 6 12	8 12 / 31 23	? 41 / 40g 39b	4 1 / 8 44	ii
I — SOUTH	**CE Y***	6 12 / 40g 45	39b 38 / 5 17	41 14 / 4 12	54 41 / 3 45	i
		40e 8 / 23 3	17 9 / 8 1	8 41 / 5 31	31 45 / 8 5	ii
	CIRCIND Z*	31 1 / 12 8	5 6 / 8 4	31 8 / 23 5	21 8 / 31 10	i
		8 12 / 4 31	21 44 / 8 39d	41 5 / 44 3	45 5 / 8 46	ii
II	**NORTH W, X, Y+**	31 10 / 3 17	8 3 / 15 44	8 41 / 5 35d	8 45 / 31 21	i
		41 40e / 31 44	8 5 / 6 46	8 31 / 5 23	8 19 / 5 4	ii
	SOUTH Z+	3 5 / 19 9	8 4 / 39d 23	8 18 / 5 31	39b 45 / 31 41	i
		8 5 / 31 3?	8 6 / 5 31	8 5 / 31 3	4 45 / 46 40e	ii

* cf Map 3   + cf Map 4

H

TABLE 14: Expansion of the macropits

[1] CAT cf Table 2a (Nos. 1-36) & Map 3

										Total	m/c
i	12 / 17	12/17 —	17/12+ (1)	12/8 (29)	8/12 (9)°	1/17 (35)	17/1 °	1/8 —	8/1 (33)°	5	1
	8 14 / 17 7	8/17 —	17/8 (6)°	8/7 (6)	7/8+ (5)	14/17 —	17/14 °	14/7 (17)	[7]/14* (16)	5	2
	8 41 / 17 40e	[8]/17 (12)	17/8 (22)°	[8]/40e (2)	40e/8+ (3)	41/17 (11)	17/41 °	41/40e —	40e/41 (31)°	6	1
	5 46 / 8 45	5/8 (34)	8/5+ (32)	5/45 —	45/5 °	46/8 —	8/46 (36)°	[46]/45 (7)	45/46 °	4	1
ii	8 4 / 46 12	8/46 (30)	[46]/8+ (19)	8/12 —	12/8+ (20)	4/46 —	46/4 °	[4]/12 (15)	12/4? (14)°	5	2
	7 23 / 15 8	7?/15 (10)	15/7+ (8)	7/8 —	8/7 °¹⁴	23/15 —	[15]/23* (21)	[23]/8 (15)	8/23 °	4	2
	17 21 / 8 41	17/8 (4)	8/17 (23)°	17/41 —	[41]/17? (28)°	21/8 (30)	[8]/21? (18)°	21/41 —	41/21* (24)	6	1
	31 45 / 8 10	31/8 —	8/31* (25)	31/10 —	10/31 °	45/8 —	8?/[45] (27)°	45/10 —	10/45* (26)	3	2
										38	12

N.B.—Numbers in round brackets refer to the stones in Table 2. Missing single symbols are in square brackets. Bridewealth is denoted by + for mirror, * for mirror and comb, ° for comb, ° for possible mirror and comb (m/c).

14 See end-note 14.

TABLE 14: Expansion of the macropits

[2] FIDACH cf Table 2a (Nos. 37-70) & Map 3

									Total m/c	
40e 8 / 12 15	40e/12 —	12/40e (40)°	40e/15 —	15/40e °	8/[12] (44)	12/8 °	8/15 —	15/8 (43)°	3	0
34 40e / 23 6	34/23 —	23/34 °	34?/[6] (46?)	6/34 (45)°	40e/23 (54)	23/40e °	40e/6 —	6/40e* (62)	4	1
5 6 / 8 41 (i)	5/8 (41)	8/5 (50)°	5/41 —	41/5 (37)°	6/8 —	8/6 (63)°	6/41 —	41/6* (49)	5	1
45 8 / 3 5	45/3 (48)	3/45 °	45/5 —	5/45 °	8/3 —	3/[8] (38?)°	8/[5] (52)	5/8 °	3	0
23 8 / 6 12	23/6 —	6/23 (55)°	23/12 —	12/23 °	8/6 —	[6]/8 (70)°	8/12 —	12?/8* (51)	3	1
8 12 / 31 23	8/31 (59)	31/[8] (60)°	8/23 (67)	23/8 (69)°	12/31 (65)	31/[12] (56)°	12/23 —	23/12* (47)	7	1
? 41 / 40g 39b (ii)	?/40g —	40g/? °	?/39b —	39b/? °	41/40g —	40g/41 (51)°	41/39b —	39b/41* (53)	2	1
4 1 / 8 44	4/8 —	8/4+ (61)	4/44 —	44/[4]+ (58)	1/8 (41)	8/1 °	1/[44] (64)	44/1 °	4	2
									37	7

Omitted: (39) 19?//8?/21?, (42) 5/5, (57) 1?/8/8, (66) 5/11, (68) 37/17?
Dubious: (38) 3/3?, (41) 1?/8, (46) 34?/3?

TABLE 14: Expansion of the macropits

[3] CE cf Table 2a (Nos. 71-119) & Map 3

										Total m/c	
i	6 12 / 40g 45	6/40g —	40g/6+ (78)	6/45 (103)	45/6 °	12/40g —	40g/[12] [142]°	12/[45] (83)	45/12* (82)	5	2
	39b 38 / 5 17	39b/5 (94)	5/[39b] (87)°	39b/17 —	17/39b °	38/5 [130]	5/38 °	38/17 —	17/38* (90)	4	1
	41 14 / 4 12	41/4 (112)	4/41 °	41/12 (91)	12/41 °	14/4 —	4/14 °	14/12 —	12/14* (119)	3	1
	45 41 / 3 44	45/3 —	3/45 (98)°	45/44 —	44/45 °	41/3 —	3/41 °	41/44 —	44/41 (119)°	2	0
ii	40e 8 / 23 3	40e/23 (71)	23/40e °	40e/3? [141]	3/40e (77)°	8/23 (120)	23/8* (118)	8/3 (100)	3/8 °	6	1
	17 9 / 8 1	17/8 (73)	8/17 °	17/1 —	1/17 °	9/8 —	8/9* (107)	9/1 (80)	1/9 °	3	1
	8 41 / 5 31	8/5 (79)	5/8+ (95)	8/31 (112)	31/8+ (93)	[41]/5 (74)	5/41* (109)	41/31 (96)	31/[41] (97)°	8	3
	31 45 / 8 5	31/8 (102)	8/31+ (76)	31/5 (113)	[5]/31+ (112)	45/8 —	8/45 (108)°	45/5 (103)	5/45+ (89)	7	3
										38	12

Omitted: (81) 40e/31.
Dubious: [41] 40e/3?, [142] 40g? These square brackets denote that these stones are in another area and consequently out of sequence.

TABLE 14: Expansion of the macropits

[4] CIRCIND cf Table 2a (Nos. 83-144) & Map 3

		31/12	12/31	31/8	8/31+	1/12	12/1	1/8	8/1	Total	m/c
i	31 / 12	—	[88]°	[110]	[122]	—	[75]°	[116]	°	5	1
	5 6 / 8 4	5/[8] (92)	8/5* [111]	5/[4] [84]	4/5+ [86]	6/8 [99]	8/6 [103]°	6/4 [72]	[4]6* [114]	8	3
	31 8 / 23 5	31/23 —	[23]/31+ [113]	31/5 [117]	5/31+ [121]	8/23 —	23/8 [120]°	8/5 [101]	5/[8] [105]°	6	2
	21 8 / 31 10	[21]/31 (133)	31/21+ [85]	21/10 —	10/21 [114]°	8/31 (132)	31/8 °	[8]/10 [99?]	10/8 °	5	1
	8 12 / 4 31	8/4 —	4/8+ (137)	8/31 —	31/8 °	12/4 —	4/12 °	12/31 (125)	31/[12] (131)°	3	1
ii	21 44 / 8 39d	21/8 (136)	[8]/21+ (135)	21/39d (138)	39d/21 °	44/8 —	8/44 °	44/39d —	39d/44 °	3	1
	41 5 / 44 3	41/44 (135)	44/41+ (138)	41/3 —	3/41 (135)°	5/44 —	44/5* (126)	5/3 —	[3]/5 [104]°	5	2
	45 5 / 8 46	45/8 —	8/45 °	45/46 —	[46]/45 (122)°	5/8 —	8/5 [144]°	5/46 —	46/5* (124)	3	1
										38	12

Omitted: (127) 37?/44+, (129) 21/2?, (140) 6/6, (143) 5/12.
Dubious: [99] 6/?/10. These square brackets indicate the stone is not in Circind territory.

TABLE 14: Expansion of the macropits

[5] NORTH II cf Table 2c (Nos. 1-20) & Map 4

										Total	m/c
i	31 10 / 3 17	—	3/31 (8)	31/17	17/31 (5)	10/3	3/10 (3)	10/17	17/10	3	0
	8 3 / 15 44	8/15	15/8 (2)	8/44	44/8	3/15	15/3	3/44 (5)	44/3	2	0
	8 41 / 5 35d	8/5	5/8 (7)	8/35d (3)	35d/8	41/5	5/41	41/35d	35d/41 (5)	3	0
	8 45 / 31 21	8/31 (1)	31/8 (12)	8/21 (6)	21/8 (11)	45/31 (6)	31/45	45/21	21/45 (6)	6	0
ii	41 40e / 31 44	41/31	31/41 (3)	41/44	44/41	40e/31 (9)	31/40e (1)	40e/44 (15)	44/40e	4	0
	8 5 / 6 46	8/6	6/8 (1)	8/46	46/8 (5)	5/6	6/5 (16)	5/46	46/5	3	0
	8 31 / 5 23	8/5 (12)	5/8 (10)	8/23	23/8	31/5 (13)	5/31 (12)	31/23	23/31* (17)	5	1
	8 19 / 5 4	8/5	5/8 (14)	8/4 (16)	4/8	[19]/5 (20)	5/19	19/4 (18)	4/19	4	0
										30	1

Omitted: (4) 40e/41, (3) 19/43, (10) 8/8, (19) 5-13.

TABLE 14: Expansion of the macropits

[6] SOUTH II cf Table 2a (Nos. 21-56) & Map 4

										Total	m/c
i	3 5 / 18 9	3/18 (23)	18/3 —	3/9 (32)	9/3 —	5/18 —	[18]/5* (33)	5/9* (44)	[9]/5 (48)	5	2
	8 4 / 39d 23	8/39d —	39d/8 (43)	8/23 —	23/8 —	4/39d —	39d/4 (37)	4/23 —	23/4 (21)	3	0
	8 18 / 5 31	8/5 (22)	5/[8] (28)	8/31 (34)	31/8 (30)	18/[5] (24)	5/[18] (25)	18/31 (39)	31/18 —	7	0
	39b 45 / 31 41	39b/31 (29)	31/39b —	39b/41 —	41/39b —	[45]/31 (41)	31/45 (38)	45/41 —	41/45+ (29)	4	1
	8 5 / 31 3?	8/31 (50)	31/[8] (52)	8/3? —	3?/[8] (45)	5/31 (50)	[31]/5 (49)	5/[3?] (46)	3?/[5] (47)	7	0
	8 6 / 5 31	8/5 (27)	5/8 (53)	8/31 (52)	31/8 —	[6]/5 (40)	5/6 —	6/31 (31)	31/6 —	5	0
ii	8 5 / 31 3	8/31 (56)	31/[8] (57)	8/3 —	3/8 (52)	5/31 (56)	31/5 (35)	5/3 —	3/5* (42)	6	1
	4 45 / 46 40e	4/46 (36)	46/4 —	4/40e —	40e/4 —	45/46 (54)	[46]/45 (51)	45/40e (45)	40e/45 —	4	0
										41	4

Omitted: (26) 19/9.

When we come to Class II times, there are still two kingdoms, technically, but the major presence of stones is in the province of *Circind*, i.e. Angus. In early Class I times, *Ce* and *Circind* formed the southern kingdom and were not sharply differentiated, but by Class II times the Mounth had become a barrier and *the* boundary between the Northern and Southern kingdoms. This new political boundary left the three provinces of *Cat*, *Ce* and *Fidach* to constitute the 'Northern' kingdom, while *Circind* effectively was the 'Southern' and leading kingdom. At some unspecified later date, following the traditional bifurcation of kingdoms into moieties, the main (Southern) kingdom was split into four provinces: the northern moiety was known as *Circind* and *Fotla* while the southern half became *Fortriu* and *Fib*. However, as the Class II stones demonstrate, these divisions were not important in those days as *Circind* was dominant and the 'Northern' kingdom dispersed and weak. What is fascinating about this transition is that it is the origin of the myth about the seven Pictish provinces that historians have handed down to us but which is contradicted by the symbol stones!

Before examining the detailed composition of the synoptic table it should be stressed that the statistical probability that six sets of eight different macropits should, *by chance,* actually incorporate nearly all the symbol pairs ever found and in their correct geographical locations is so infinitesimally small that the possibility that the table is basically incorrect is ruled out. Even allowing for a few minor imperfections in this schema, the fact that macropits not only explain the meaning of the symbol pairs but also account for their particular combinations in limited geographical areas practically proves the dualistic hypothesis to be true. It has to be granted that the synoptic table is *post hoc,* since there was no way of predicting which symbols (lineages) were to be found where, but could macropits be pure invention? After all, the simplest way of constucting a macropit is to just put two symbol pairs together thus: $^S/_P$ and $^Q/_R$ gives

S	Q
P	R

This would mean that 96 such pairs would be needed to complete a synoptic table covering all the pairs, so how does it happen that our smaller schema accounts for more than twice that number of pairs *in the right place?* Given that there are over 700 possible different combinations of the 28 symbols — double the number the synoptic table provides — is it just coincidence that 48 macropits can give exactly the right combinations in just the right place? Of course it is conceivable that the synoptic table is only an ingenious construction but, then, why does it work? The fact that ¾ of the macropits account for more than a half of the *known* symbol pairs occurring in a particular place needs some explaining away if it is thought wrong. As these tables are the central proof of the dualistic hypothesis they must be scrutinised with care, but they cannot be wished away by saying there is no independent proof — the stones *are* the proof![16]

It may repay us to just look at some of the implications of the macropit idea. As has been noted above, the macropits have distinct geographical locations. Perhaps the most puzzling collection of macropits is the one that falls under *Cat i : viz* Shetland, Orkney, the Hebrides and Caithness. How can they come under a single category?

Let us consider just the first two macropits (Table 14) in terms of their location (Table 2).

12	1
17	8

There are 8 possible pairs but only 5 have been found.

If these pairs are listed in sequence we get:

1) *12/17*	missing		
2) *17/12+*	(1)	Sandness (Shetland)	lost
3) *12/8*	(29)	Little Ferry Links (Sutherland)	
4) *8/12*	(9)	Thurso (Caithness)	lost
5) *1/7*	(35)	Benbecula (Hebrides)	
6) *17/1*	missing		
7) *1/8*	missing		
8) *8/1*	(33)	Dunvegan (Hebrides)	

Possibly 1) was in Shetland while 6) and 7) were in the Hebrides.

8	*14*
17	*7*

Again there are 8 possible pairs but only 5 have been found.

1)	*8/17*	missing	
2)	*17/8*	(6)	St Peters (Orkney)
3)	*8/7*	(6)	St Peters (Orkney)
4)	*7/8+*	(5)	St Andrews (Orkney)
5)	*14/17*	missing	
6)	*17/14*	missing	
7)	*14/7*	(17)	Kintradwell 1 (Sutherland)
8)	*(7)/14**	(16)	Kintradwell 2 (Sutherland)

Possibly 1) was in Orkney while 5) and 6) were in Caithness or Sutherland.

Perhaps the first thing to observe is that we have six missing stones. There are three possibilities: the stones are lost (like 1 and 9), they have not been found or they were never there! If the last case were to be true, it would be impossible to prove, of course! The non-existence of the symbol stones postulated here can only be for one of two reasons: i) the stones were never erected because there were already sufficient stones to indicate the macropit, ii) my assumptions are false. It is interesting, then, that the chances of the macropit hypothesis being wrong are just 1:4, but only as regards the 'missing' stones! For, on the other hand, when one considers the chances that the particular symbol pairings *that we do know about* happen to be precisely where they are, it does suggest that there is an underlying pattern to the placement of the symbol stones. It does not follow that the combinations of symbols suggested for these macropits is absolutely correct, but it is an indication of what to expect, when we discover more stones, as we surely will. *This* will be the real test of the hypothesis, since it offers the possibility of being checked! Hence, despite the small chance that I may be wrong, surely it is worth suspending judgment until we have found a dozen or so more symbol stones, to see whether or not they agree with the principles put forward? Unless an alternative 'closed' solution can be found, we will be condemned to a quite meaningless array of symbol stones—the case, alas, hitherto.

What the two macropits, discussed above, show is that each moiety of the macropits, themselves, have a specific geographical boundary, yet it suggest that there are links between the Northern and Western Isles and Caithness and Sutherland. This may be confirmed by looking at the distribution of the other stones listed under *Cat.*

In terms of specific areas, it can be seen that Orkney is dominated by lineage *8* but also had three other lineages: *17, 7* and *40e.* The Hebrides (taken as a whole) were again dominated by *8* but also had lineages *5, 1* and *17.* Shetland (sadly only represented by a single lost stone) seems closely linked to the Mainland (Caithness and Sutherland by lineages *12* and *17.* The common factor in all these cases seems to be lineage *17* (later to be associated with weapon-making).

Map 4 shows the distribution of the Cat macropits, represented by the area W, which also corresponds to the greatest density of brochs, cf Map 2. This is, perhaps, no coincidence—as was suggested at the end of Chapter 1.

Unlike the other 'provinces' in Table 13 which are fairly closely bounded, Cat seems to be rather unwieldy and widespread but this is an illusion of the map. One could sail from Shetland to Golspie far quicker than it would take to walk from Thurso to Golspie! What united Cat was the sea.

Of course the macropit is a conceptual entity, like the lineage, which only summarises the organization of a group of four intermarrying lineages and has no concrete existence other than the symbol stones themselves. Naturally we do not know if the Picts ever recognized the existence of the macropit but, at least, it provides us with a convenient tool to analyse their pairing of symbols. It is of interest to note that *each* province in the synoptic table contains 16 different symbols as the basis for its 8 macropits, which, in terms of a possible original set of 32 lineages in ancient Pictland, shows that each province only contained half the total. Moreover, the combined total of *different* symbols for the Northern and Southern kingdoms (Class I) and the Class II kingdom is only 22:— 8 are animal and 14 are geometric symbols while, oddly enough, the number of *similar* symbols for these three blocs are half that: 4 animal and 7 geometric symbols. These are certainly numbers to conjure with but their implication will be left open at this stage, except to remark that these coincidences are again hardly likely to be chance.

Returning to the synoptic table, it will be seen that *every macropit in Class I and II times is different,* although there are some strong similarities due to the presence of the three commonest symbols: *5, 8* and *31*. Six times out of ten when *8* is present in a Class I macropit it is accompanied by *5* and/or *31*, but this proportion rises to nine out of ten in Class II. The significance of this is that *5* and *31* are dependent on *8* in Class I times and so exert little independent influence, but in Class II alliances all three symbols have become interdependent. In other words, from a position of absolute dominance in Class I times, symbol *8* has descended to being only *primus inter pares* in the period of Class II.

The following table summarizes the expansion of the macropits:

	Area	Symbol pairs		Mirror and comb		No. omitted from Tables	Sequence Nos : Tables
		No. found	percent of maximum [64]	No. found	percent of maximum [32]		
I	Cat	38	59	12	37	0	1-36
	Fidach	31	48	7	19	5	37-70
	Ce	38	59	12	37	1	71-119
	Circind	38	59	12	37	5	83-137
	Total	145	57	43	34	11	
II	North	30	47	1	3	4	1-20
	South	41	64	4	13	1	21-56
	Total	71	55	5	8	5	
	Total I&II	216	56	48	25	16	

Table 15

It will be seen that the highest success ratio is 64 per cent and the lowest is 47 per cent — both in Class II macropits. The number of mirror and comb (*+) symbols is moderate in Class I but very low in Class II, which gives rise to the suspicion that either bridewealth was frowned on by Christians or else it was no longer relevant in the new tribal hierarchy. There are some 8 per cent of the symbol stones that have *not* been incorporated into the tables because most of them are uncertainly identified — roughly one stone per moiety.

Not only do the macropits generate the current symbol pairs; they also segregate the two forms of bridewealth (+ mirror, * mirror and comb) into two distinct groupings (Table 14, columns 2 and 4, columns 6 and 8), which may be grades of sub-chiefs and chiefs. This additional constraint on symbol formation makes the comprehensiveness of the macropit notion all the more surprising since not only does it show which symbol pairs are missing but it also indicates if they should have the bridewealth symbol or not. It would appear that we are likely to have overlooked symbol *24* upon a number of existing stones, unless it was not always necessary to have four such stones but just the basic two.

The distribution map 3 of Class I stones suggests that there were four blocs of Picts whose sizes were roughly equal, having a radius of some 35 miles, covering some 2,000 square miles of *land*. If only half the land is agriculturally useful, then with a generally accepted density of population of 10 persons per square mile, this would give a total of 40,000 people. Assuming that each of the hypothetical 256 symbol pairs represented a settlement, then each community would have some 150 people or 28 households with an average of 5 members. Such communities are large enough to form a viable dual organization and also to provide "two *seven*-bench boats from every 20 houses" — if the Picts followed the practice of the Scots. Obviously some settlements would be larger but if one considers a macropit as a single entity, then this comprises some 200 households — 1,200 people — who are kin related and who could provide more than a dozen boats with 200 warriors. The implication is that *each* of the four blocs (or provinces) had at their command over 100 boats and nearly 2,000 warriors to man them. It will be seen that ¾ of the stones in the Northern kingdom are by the sea coast while none of the stones in the Southern kingdom are near the sea, which is very odd! At all events it meant that the Northern Picts could easily command 200 boats and 3,000 warriors to raid the south and enforce their will without fear of retaliation. The above figures are quite tentative and are given only to indicate the scale of the probable superiority of the Northern navy: the source of their power.

In Class II times there is an *apparently* equal distribution of Christians in the Northern and Southern kingdoms, each with 64 symbol pairs hypothetically. In the Southern kingdom (essentially *Circind*) there has been little change from Class I times as regards symbol pairs — 8 macropits; the only difference is that they all have become Christian! However, in the North the symbol pairs are often grouped together on one stone, which suggests that there were probably only 30 Christian settlements there and since the other Picts had not gone away, it means that the Christians only formed 10 per cent of the Northern population. The same conclusion is reached if we look at the number of symbol stones per 100 square miles: south of the Mounth there are six times as many Class II stones as there are to the north of the Mounth. Hence there seems to have been a complete polarisation between North and South by Class II times.

The simplest explanation of the above difference is that the Northern Picts remained pagan. There is a possibility that two rival Christian churches existed and that the northern church renounced all sculptures; but this is unlikely, for even in Class III times there are (apart from plain crosses) few signs of Christian activity in the north. Taking one category of Class III stones — those with horsemen, cf Map 5 — we find these occur where Class II horsemen are found, e.g. in the Moray Firth area, which has most of the Class II and III stones north of the Mounth. The dearth of Christian stones to the north, where the bulk of the Picts lived, can only indicate that when the overall kingship passed to the south in Class II times, the northerners retained their pagan ways and their Class I arrangements.

Although Class III stones have no symbols upon them and would thus seem to be irrelevant to the discussion, they do provide us with some interesting comparative data. They are difficult to deal with if we use ECMS, since they crop up from Shetland to Galloway and number over 300, but over 100 are mere fragments and 50 are just simple crosses, while almost 100 have various figures of men and beasts engraved on them. Half the stones are in traditional Pictland and the rest are scattered round Scotland. One third of the stones are in private hands or museums, while one half are concentrated in eight religious sites, each containing an average of 20 stones. Here, the new Class III (p.17) will be meant from now onwards.

A comparison of the figure sculptures on Class II and III stones reveals some startling similarities apart from the common use of interlace patterns on the crosses. The two types of figure: men and beasts, are found in roughly equal numbers. The men-like figures include warriors, horsemen, clerics, angels and laymen, while the beasts are normal species like horses, dogs, cows, boars etc., but they also have some fantastic beasts or monsters. Much play has been made of the monsters but they are *really* insignificant, amounting to 13 per cent of Class II and 6 per cent of Class III, and they are concentrated around Meigle and St Vigeans — a product of the lively imagination of some Class II sculptor no doubt! A comparison of the different motifs is given in Table 16:

Motif	Class II		Class III	
	No.	percent	No.	percent
Beasts	42	35 (40)	64	37 (39)
Men	22	18 (21)	40	23 (24)
Horsemen	28	23 (27)	39	23 (24)
Clerics, etc	13	11 (12)	20	12 (12)
Monsters	16	13 (0)	10	6 (0)
Total	121		173	

Table 16: Design Motifs

It can be seen that the proportions of the different motifs are very similar except for the monsters. If we discard the monsters as a particular local anomaly, then the percentage figures *given in brackets* show the near identity between motifs in Class II and III, which shows that they are closely linked.

The above Table 16 only indicates the number of *stones* that bear these motifs. Hence there are 42 Class II stones with an animal motif, but no distinction is made as to which animal or how many are to be found. The motifs may occur singly but often they are combined with many other motifs, and some 21 different permutations exist which it would be tedious to give. What the table clearly shows is the equal balance between men and beasts — monsters excepted.

One motif that deserves special mention is the 'horseman', since it is the only one that constantly figures as being central and important to the composition of the sculpture. There are 28 Class II horsemen and 30 Class III horsemen motifs in Pictland, while the actual number of horsemen on a stone can vary from one to six, as Tables 2 show. A discussion of this motif will be taken up later, but it should be noted that the Class II and III horsemen *are not far from each other,* cf Map 5.

Nearly ¾ of the Scottish sculptured stones lie in traditional Pictland, while many of the remainder are found at the religious centres of Govan, Iona and Whithorn. Besides the close links between Class II and III in terms of the cross design, interlace and motifs, it all adds up to the suggestion that Pictland is the real heartland of sculptured stones in Scotland.

We can summarise the true relations between the three classes of stones thus:

Class I   { Symbols
    II { Symbols   and   Cross with figures }
    III   Cross with figures }

Class II really seems to be an intermediary type between Class I and III in terms of design but not necessarily in terms of time.

The following table summarises the frequencies of the various sculptured stones by counties:

Group	County	I	II	III	Total	Total
	Shetland	1	0	2	3	
	Orkney	5	0	2	7	
W	Hebrides	5	1	2	8	52
	Caithness	6	3	1	9	
	Sutherland	17	1	7	25	
	Ross	6	5	5	16	
X	Inverness	12	0	0	12	48
	Moray	7	2	3	12	
	Banff	7	1	0	8	
Y	Aberdeen	50	4	1	55	55
	Angus	10	23	29	62	
Z	Perth	7	13	29	49	128
	Fife	6	2	9	17	
	Total	139	55	90	284	284

Table 17: Frequencies of Pictish stones by county

The above table 17 shows that groups W, X and Y are roughly equal in total numbers while group Z has almost half of the total.

Analysing how the different classes are distributed between the four regional groups (in %) we find:

Group	I	II	III
W	24	9	16
X	23	15	9
Y	36	7	1
Z	17	69	74
Total	100	100	100

Table 18: Regional distribution of Class I-III in %

Class II : Elgin   (Table 2C:14)

If one now looks at what percentage of the *total* number of stones fall into these categories:

Group	I	II	III	Total
W	12	2	5	19
X	11	3	3	17
Y	18	1	0	19
Z	8	13	24	45
Total	49	19	32	100

Table 19: Percentage of stones by regions

These two tables show that Class I are basically in groups W, X and Y, while Class II and III are mainly in group Z — a well-known fact — but Table 19 indicates that the number of Class I stones in the north is balanced by an equal number of Class II and III stones in the south.

Next, only the distribution of *Christian* monuments will be looked at:

Group	II	III	Total percent
W	3	10	13
X	6	6	12
Y	3	1	4
Z	26	46	72

Table 20: Percentage of Christian stones by regions

So ¾ of all Christian stones are tightly packed into group Z while ¾ of the non-Christian stones are in the other areas W, X and Y. These ratios suggest that the centre of Christianity began in the south and stayed there while the other groups stayed pagan.

Class II : Brodie (Table 2C:13)   I

Group	Pagan	Christian	Ratio : Pagan/Christian	
W	34	19	1.8 : 1	
X	32	16	2 : 1	4 : 1
Y	50	5	10 : 1	
Z	23	105	0.2 : 1	

Table 21: Ratio of Pagan/Christian stones

The difference between the northern groups and the southern one in terms of this Pagan/Christian ratio is 20 : 1 on average but reaches 50 : 1 on either side of the Mounth between groups Y and Z.

The above tables omit fragmentary Class III stones since they would be useless to reckon with, but it should be noted that half the Class III north of the Mounth are simple plain crosses without sculptured figures and that they, too, could have been from any age. If one discarded the plain crosses as not being *proven* Pictish then the Pagan/Christian ratio in the north shoots up to 8 : 1 which implies that the north is *forty* times more pagan than south of the Mounth! The conclusion thus seems inescapable that the north was fundamentally pagan, and this is reinforced by the fact that all the multiple symbol stones in Class II are in the north, as if huddled together against the pagans, besides which at least a quarter of these few symbol stones have been broken.

These conclusions have been reached simply on the grounds of the distribution of the sculptured stones of the three classes as shown in the many tables given above. It has emerged that these classes of stones are closely related either by design or distribution and can be regarded as unity within Pictland, if one leaves aside the fragments of Class III that are devoid of figures.

The reasons for Christianity's lack of success in the north will be discussed in Part II together with an analysis of the Class III interlace patterns and their derivations, cf Chapter 4.

Summarising the findings, an attempt has been made to show that there *is* a systematic solution to the grouping and distribution of the symbol pairs. It is maintained that the Pictish social structure was divided into a series of moieties extending right down to the household itself. This division of the tribes naturally affected their geopolitical divisions as well, and this is reflected in the location of the symbol stones. The synoptic Table 13 and maps support these geographical divisions besides the quasi-existence of the macropits. The schema also suggest there was a *maximum* number of macropits and that we have found more than half of them! In other words, there was an upper limit of permissible stones (though we do not know if they were all made), so what we have is *not* a small number at all, and that means that we do not have to explain away the two hundred symbol stones as just belonging to a very tiny, privileged elite!

Two possible consequences of the distribution of stones were touched upon: 1) the naval strength of the Northern kingdom, 2) the failure of Christianity in the north. Naturally these suggestions are highly tentative and are only offered as possible factors in the transition between Class I and II times, politically speaking.

Finally it was shown how the three different classes of stones are *remarkably* similar in many ways.

CHAPTER 7

The meaning of the symbols

Human societies are human creations designed to regulate and protect their members from the hazards of existence, and until a few centuries ago they were all organized on a tribal basis. Tribes are basically large families of interrelated kin who are united by language and customs *in opposition to* other tribes that exist around them. Whether or not these other tribes were recognized as being human, and not a set of wild animals, depended very much on the coincidence of culture because being 'human' meant being 'like us'. The very recent 20th century European notion that *all* men are humans, and thus have equal rights, is far from being universally accepted — not even in Europe. Hence it is not really surprising that a millenium ago the different tribes that populated the world then regarded each other with great distrust and often contempt.

The biggest barrier to our attempts to understand the past is the imposition of our 'enlightened' views of mankind upon societies that are utterly different in attitudes to our own. It is here that social anthropology can be very helpful, since it can suggest how tribal societies operated in the past, because it has made detailed studies of such societies all around the world. However there is a danger if one tries to identify a past society with a contemporary one just on the basis of archaeological artefacts, as the possibilities are so enormous. All anthropology can do is to hint at some of the variations that occur in tribal social organization while pointing out that there are common limiting factors in man's attempt to construct society. Thus there are only a few ways of defining membership of a tribe and these are normally based on kinship, i.e. on the evidence of some imputed biological link between the members. Most tribal societies are unilineal in kinship so that descent and inheritance either passes down the father's line (from father to son) or the mother's line (from mother's brother to sister's son). The main alternative kinship system is where descent may be traced through both lines. This simplistic account of a highly complex subject is merely a reminder about the importance of the lineage and the fact that choices are limited.

Given that our biology presents us with two complementary sexes, this fact is often used as the basis of a way of thinking that divides the world in two: male and female. It may be embedded in the language itself — the very tool of thought — and can be illustrated in all modern Indo-European languages. For example even in English, where gender is insignificant, the sun is male while the moon is female, as are boats. The lateral symmetry of our bodies also provides a universal distinction between the left hand and the right hand that is often incorporated into many peoples' thinking as are other oppositions such as day/night, summer/winter, light/dark, good/bad, black/white etc. Indeed Lévi-Strauss has argued that binary oppositions are the foundation of *all* thinking and this is clearly seen in tribal societies where dualism permeates much of their thought *and* social organization.[17]

Once having 'chosen' a descent system, kinship then dictates membership of the society and who marries whom, who succeeds whom, thus dividing the society into two, unequal halves: our kin and the others — both of which are locked into interdependence since kinsmen are forbidden to marry each other because of the incest prohibition. Incest is the sin of having sexual intercourse with a member of one's own kin, and as kinship itself depends on the system adopted it means that a man's father's brother's daughter would commonly be out of bounds. This does not apply in a matrilineal society except in the case where a man's father's brother married the man's mother's sister. What happens if incest does take place? The offence is thought to anger the ancestors (or the gods) who will then send misfortune to the guilty pair. Here, then, is an example of a social rule whose infringement causes mystical punishment while, in addition, should this offence become publicly known, it could result in the pair being executed.

Contrariwise, if people suffer misfortune it is often assumed that there must be a causal explanation, e.g. having sinned, or neglecting the ancestors. It is almost universally believed that men deserve only good fortune and that they can only be denied this by their own or other's shortcomings. The notion that one's sufferings are due to chance is not acceptable to people who live in a highly personalized world of men and mystical powers. Such powers could be magic wielded by fellow tribesmen, witchcraft, or the mystical actions of ancestors, spirits or gods who keep the tribesmen under constant surveillance. These unseen forces act to maintain the morality of the tribe by affirming the society's rules. As for other tribes, it does not matter what they believe in, unless, in the inevitable warfare between neighbouring tribes, they conquer one with the aid of their mystical powers — in which case it might be prudent to adopt these victorious powers oneself. The point is that tribal man attributes his success in any undertaking not to his own efforts alone, but to the goodwill of the mystical powers that surround him. This psychological dependency upon external forces is a commonplace in most societies, but takes different forms. As it is the culture which provides these mystical powers and details their actions in relation to men's activities, there is no real reason for doubting their existence, for they make sense of the world in which men live, suffer and die.

This long prelude to the discussion of the meaning of the symbols is to indicate how best we might incorporate the few facts we know about the Picts into a tribal setting. We are going to assume that the Picts were Indo-European, spoke P-Celtic and had a matrilineal kinship system, since there is no positive evidence against this view and much that suggests that this is the case. The Indo-Europeans were dualistic in thinking (cf their gender divisions, their division of time) and were mainly patrilineal sun-worshippers (the sun being male). However as the Picts were matrilineal, it logically followed that they would make the moon the object of their devotions, like many calendrically-minded peoples. Thus if the moon was good, then the sun must be bad — as some other Europeans believed. Now the argument takes a surprising twist: while the patrilineal British and Irish could happily associate their ancestors with men, the sun and all that was just and right, the Picts were logically compelled to associate their ancestors with women, the sun and all that was bad and unjust, since men, who are always in the right, were linked with the moon and justice!

These cosmological considerations had further complications for these tribes. It would be quite feasible for the patrilineal Celts to worship powerful male gods (possibly ancestral founders) who acted as severe upholders of tribal lore, but this would be difficult for the Picts since fathers were indulgent figures and it was the matrilineal side that was authoritarian and repressive. So while the patrilineal Celts could accept father-like, stern gods it meant the

Picts could choose between fearful goddesses or some bisexual figures (the mother's brother), or reject both and opt for watchful ancestors. The significance of these two different attitudes would become highlighted with the introduction of an alien religion — Christianity.

Christianity was an offshoot of the Jewish tribal religion and was naturally heavily influenced by the pastoralist tribes of Palestine. It preached a universal doctrine that a powerful God (Jehovah) sent his only son to redeem all mankind from its sins. Such a message would be perfectly acceptable to the patrilineal Celts as it made sense, but it would pose problems for the matrilineal Picts since fathers had no authority while sons belonged to their mothers' lineages and could not be delegated any responsibility except from their mother's brother. Thus to the Picts, Christianity must have seemed very alien and it would only be by switching to patrilinearity that the Christian message would begin to ring true. This changeover is not difficult, having happened on countless occasions when men desire their sons to inherit their position and wealth; but it causes basic changes in the cosmology such that the Picts would have to switch round the sun and moon, the ancestors and magic from one category to another, from bad to good. The upshot would then be that there would be little difference between the Picts and the Scots as fellow Christians apart from their dialects — everything distinctively Pictish would fall away and they would fade away as separate people.

However, it was suggested in the previous chapter that the Picts, north of the Mounth, did not accept Christianity except for a few discrete areas and for good reason, since it undermined their cosmology and demanded a radically different social organization. Possibly the Class II monuments were a temporary compromise, tolerated by the Church for a little while, before insisting that patrilinearity was the only permissible arrangement sanctioned by the Bible. Hence first-generation converts might be allowed to continue some of their old tribal ways but no further. The conversion of the king would ensure that his leading men followed suit, but they might have valiantly held on to their traditional alliances since these are not created overnight. There seems to have been a fairly widespread conversion to Christianity in the south in Class II times, but even there the small number of stones suggests that the practice of erecting such monuments ceased after a couple of generations. This cessation was likely to be reinforced when the kings themselves went over to patrilinearity, because lineage alliances became meaningless when descent only went through the male line, because *it did not matter* who one married in another kin group since they did not inherit and were now in a dependent relationship. Thus a gulf is likely to have been created between the Northern and Southern Picts by Christianity in its destruction of the peculiarly Pictish cosmology in the south where the Picts were hardly to be distinguished from the Scots. This estrangement among the Picts may have strengthened the determination of the Northern Picts to resist the conversion to Christianity, as the few monuments there testify. Hence Kenneth MacAlpin's alleged slaughter of the Pictish nobility may have just referred to the pagan northerners and recusant southerners!

How did the Picts see their world? One can begin by looking at seven reasonably undisputed postulates: *men* are *right* and *good* (a universal feature), the *crescent and V-rod* (the common symbol *8*) are to do with the *moon*, *chiefship* (dominance) and being *wife-givers* (that confers additional status). On this basis one can construct a list of some 28 paired items to do with other features of Pictish society: the North was originally the most powerful part of Pictland, the Picts were matrilineal and practised patrilateral cross-cousin marriage (FZD), the symbols refer to men's ability in mystical powers in magic and witchcraft while alluding to the ordering of society with the geometric symbols in control.

The list of binary oppositions in Table 22 is a possible reconstruction.

All the items on the right are considered to be desirable, powerful and correct for the continuance of the society, while those on the left are either reluctantly necessary, weak or dangerous. There is no absolute one-to-one relationship between the items in the columns but some *may* be related, e.g. the ancestors and illness, women and witchcraft, the sun and illness, etc.

There is no proof, other than the symbol stones themselves, that the Picts had such a binary classification, and so the above model is only offered as a possible entrée into their mode of thinking which, in its turn, may help us to understand the symbols. To the charge that this is just speculation and therefore inadmissible for serious discussion, it should be pointed out that the function of all models (which are *not*, of course, theories) is to explain the data by an informed guess. Models cannot, logically, be disproved, since they are just imposed on the data and are independent of the data. The sole purpose of a model is to suggest a way of making sense of the data, and once a model has shown that it is capable of some understanding, it can then be discarded and a better model provided. Only when the model is used to provide hypotheses does it turn into a deductive theory. As progress in understanding occurs by breaking the mould of received wisdom, it is hoped that the above model may contribute

Left	Right	Physical features
South	North	
Sun	Moon	
Earth	Heavens	
Rivers	Rain (clouds)	
Lakes	Sea	
Forest	Open arable land	
Nature	Culture	Moral values
Wild	Controlled	
Anomalous	Classified	
Odd	Even	
Bad	Good	
Unlucky	Lucky	
Illness	Health	
Sterility	Fertility	
Death	Life	
Female	Male	Society
Wife-receivers	Wife-givers	
Incest	Marriage (with FZD)	
Ancestors	Magic	
Witchcraft	Divination	
Mystical power	Political power	
Junior	Senior	
Subject	Chief	
Gift-receiver	Gift-giver	
Animal symbol	Geometric symbol	
Z-rod	V-rod	
Hunting	Cattle-keeping	

Table 22: Binary oppositions

to a better appreciation of the Pictish symbols by looking at them in a new way.

It has been argued that the Pictish symbols *must* reflect the concerns of the society: so if the pairings of symbols are related to the alliances between lineages, then it follows that each symbol must say something distinctive about each lineage. Since the symbols are either animal or geometric in design, what can this tell us? Of course a lineage with an animal symbol might have a special relationship with that animal, but what kind of relationship? What possible link can we find between a goose, a sea-horse and the 'elephant'? When one considers the actual size of a sea-horse in comparison, say, with a wild boar, then it seems a pretty weak emblem to choose! However, if they are only *totemic* symbols then size does not matter, for it is the contrast and similarity *between two totems* that is important, because it is the subtle differences between this pair that reflect real differences between the two lineages that are represented by their emblems. Thus we should compare the following pairs of totemic symbols: the sea-horse *(42/43)* with the Pictish beast *(39b)*; the goose *(40g)* with the eagle *(40e)*; the boar *(34)* with the wolf *(38)*; the fish *(41)* with the 'elephant' *(31)*; the snake *(44)* with the snake & Z-rod *(45)*; the deer *(37)* with the deer's head *(39d)*. These totemic pairs are of course the basis for Figure 3 which is statistically ordered.

So if lineage M chooses a goose and lineage N chooses an eagle they are really saying that the two lineages are basically similar (both totems are birds) but they differ inasmuch as the eagle is a carnivorous predator that soars in the sky while the goose is a vegetarian living on water. These contrasts in animal behaviour should reflect differences between the lineages, e.g. lineage N may be hunters while lineage M are agriculturalists. We do not know the significant features which the Picts employed to differentiate pairs of lineages, but this is the standard way in which totems are devised and it should be stressed that *totems are invented* to serve contrasting features between similar lineages. Clearly, the natural environment provides many items that can serve as totems but not all are chosen, and those that are do not necessarily imply a special relationship with that item, e.g. a deer or the sun, but it is quite likely that the object is invested with significance as it was selected for an important reason, which we can only guess at.

The 12 animal symbols thus reduce to 6 pairs of mutually differentiated lineages; whether these pairs are likewise significantly different between each other according to some overall plan is not easy to say, but there probably is one. The same argument applies to the 16 geometric symbols, for they can be arranged in 8 pairs: crescent *(9)* and crescent and V-rod *(8)* ; disc and rectangle *(6/7)* and rectangle and Z-rod *(23)* etc., cf Figure 3. Here the similarities and differences are hard to discern since these artificial geometric designs are not clearly based on recognizable objects and, again, we do not know what are the significant features. Nevertheless the disc (1) and the disc with handles *(4)* are as similar as the goose and eagle are, while the stepped rectangle *(19)* and the rectangle *(17)* are as close as the deer is to the deer's head. What is interesting about all these contrasting pairs is that they rarely form a symbol pair on the stones — as if they were too closely related, already!

So the 28 basic Pictish symbols can be divided into 14 pairs of differentiated lineages: 8 geometric symbol and 6 animal symbol pairs as shown in Figure 3. It might be thought that, in the ideal case, there should be 7 such pairs apiece for the animals and geometric symbols, but this would not allow for a balance between four groups, nor even between two groups as there *are* only 12 animal symbols. Figure 3 is balanced and it does indicate that the parallel between contrasting pairs can be fairly easily drawn, apart from the bottom line. It should be possible for anyone with a lively mind to draw at least a dozen similarities and differences between these contrasting pairs, but at this stage it does not seem profitable to list these in detail: it is sufficient to show that despite the numerous possibilities that exist, such an arrangement is both plausible to the eye and is supported by the statistical occurrence of these symbols.

We are now in a position to give interpretations to the symbols in the upper half of Figure 2.

LEFT-HAND SIDE		RIGHT-HAND SIDE	
M	N	M	N
Sun	Sun and Z-rod	Moon	Moon and V-rod
Serpent	Serpent and Z-rod	Goose	Eagle
House	Fortress and Z-rod	Lightning	Rainbow
Sea-horse	Beast (head)	Salmon	Beast (flying)

Table 23: Interpretation of symbols

There are obvious similarities between columns M and N on each side but also contrasts between the two sides: Moon/Sun, Bird/Serpent, Lightning/House, Salmon/Sea-horse in columns M, while there are others in columns N.

These meanings now have to be justified by appearance and symbolic reference to the dualistic model given earlier. While it is acceptable that the crescent *(9)* is the moon and good, why should its opposite, the sun *(3)*, have two conjoined discs? It will be recalled that the sun was assigned a generally maleficent role, but it has a good and a bad side that are linked to show both these aspects.

The opposition bird/serpent is a well-known motif that needs no special comment. As for the house concept *(6/7)*, this is very similar to the Pictish house at Buckquoy, excavated by Anna Ritchie, and consists of a circular room with two rectangular leg-like structures. Symbol *(23)* is basically a house-like structure which with the addition of the Z-rod (to be discussed later) is turned into a fortress. Forked lightning *(21)* would be especially dangerous to thatched roofed houses. The torc-like symbol *(12)* looks like a rainbow which heralds rain from heaven, as does lightning. The importance of rain and water is connected to the bottom line where all the four animals are associated with water, which acts as a mediator between the left hand side and the right:

Earth ← Water → Heaven

These four animals act as intermediaries between the four groups of symbols in Figure 2. In terms of the binary opposition model of Table 23, the salmon *(41)* is classified with the sea, the so-called sea horse *(42/43)* is in rivers, the 'flying elephant' is to do with rain, while the beast *(39b)* is a possible loch monster. However, the intermediary role of these animals is brought out by the fact that salmon swim up rivers, sea-horses are found in the sea, there are sea monsters besides loch monsters, while the 'flying' or 'swimming' elephant could be connected with storms at sea as well as on land. It is precisely because these are *anomalous* creatures that they can carry out their roles as mediators. Actually, of course, we are talking about the *roles* of the lineages who had adopted these totem emblems: that is what the symbols mean.

How does one discover the roles of the lineages? Obviously one must use the information that the symbols provide, but the key is not actually a proper symbol at all: it is the V and Z-rod. Since, as far as we know, the Picts had no gods or temples, then their only control over events must have been mystical and/or appeal to the ancestors : this is what the rods were to indicate. It has already been maintained that the lineages were ranked but the question is — what principle decided the ranking? An instructive parallel to draw with the Picts is the case of the Trobrianders (made famous by Malinowski) for they had four matrilineal clans and practised magic.

Simply on frequency grounds, the V-rod must rank higher than the Z-rods, since there is only one V-rod but three Z-rods. The actual V-rod may have originally been a divining rod used for discovering water and other hidden things. So lineage *8* could be skilled foretellers of the future: the rising and setting of the moon (the most important celestial body), the days and months of the calendrical year — even perhaps eclipses. As their sights were firmly fixed on the heavens, it is possible they had rain and storm magic, even the power to control the tides and the sea. Such claims are the strongest possible magic: weather magic. It was precisely that claim which the leading clan in the Trobriand Islands used to dominate the other clans. On the other hand, the Z-rods are to be associated with the ancestors — the matrilineage. Thomas may be right in suggesting that the Z-rod is a broken spear representing the dead, but it is not a dead *person* — it is *the* dead, i.e. deceased lineage members : the ancestors! Hence Z-rod lineages could call on their ancestors for aid in special cases, e.g. lineage *5* might summon help to counteract the evil effects of the sun, lineage *43* might be able to ward off illness and death, lineage *23* might be able to protect houses and fortresses from fire, attack or other threats.

In the Trobriand Islands, political dominance was achieved by three main things that only chiefs had:

1) possession of the all-powerful weather magic: creating fear
2) generous gift giving : creating dependency
3) command of a fleet to bring back goods: creating wealth

Magic, in the form of spells, was inherited by a man from his mother's brother and such spells were a closely-guarded secret and much fought over, since they could enhance one's personal reputation and following. The parallel between this matrilineal, sea-borne trading society and the Orkneys is irresistible.[18]

The protective role of the V and Z-rod lineages is seen in the fact that over 92 per cent of all the macropits in Class I and II times have either a V or a Z-rod or both. It could well be that revision of the synoptic Table 13 in the light of more discovered stones might show that *every* macropit had a V and Z-rod set of lineages to protect it.

Those symbols that are contrast pairs with those with the V and Z-rods could well be cadet branches who did not have such powerful magic. Many of the animal symbols could represent fertility magic concerning these creatures but, more likely, it is something else like: fleetness of foot (deer), cunning (wolf) and strength (boar).

The association of lineage strength with mystical power would mean that certain alliances between lineages with strong powers: *5/8, 8/31* and *31/5* would have been almost irresistible in strength and this might account for their relative frequency in comparison with other combinations. In the face of this overwhelming dominance, the other lineages may have been forced into dependence by these three main lineages who might have attempted to convert this power into authority — a permanent kingship. However to pass from the charismatic leadership that magic provides, into a legal-rational form of kingship, would need some type of legitimation. One can see *the erection of the symbol stones* as being the first step towards permanent authority being established. The most decisive step in legitimating later Pictish kingship came from the authority of the Christian church whose single symbol, the cross, also derived its power from heaven.

If the symbols stand for the lineages with mystical power, then by transference the symbols themselves will partake of this power, as will the stones on which they are carved. It follows that the actual size of the symbol is immaterial since it does not affect its power; also the stones are likely to be regarded with awe — hence so many of them survived. Magical properties are attributed to the stones and various practices grew up, but whether they had any connection with the original custom it is hard to know: for example, the Class II stone at Fowlis Wester was rubbed all over with animal grease annually until the turn of the last century! It is also interesting to note in passing that the symbols are not inscribed on prehistoric standing stones but may be found in caves that are to be found along the sea-shore, and mainly comprise symbols associated here with water!

As a coda to the argument, one may recall that in Adomnan's hagiography of Columba it is related that Broichan, magus to king Bridei (554-84), threatened he would prevent Columba making his journey up Loch Ness to Bridei's court. For, declaims Broichan, "I can make the winds unfavourable to the voyage and cause a great darkness to envelop thee in its shade." Adomnan remarks, quite innocently, that it really is not so surprising that these magi are sometimes allowed by God to raise tempests and agitate the sea! This account is not reliable history, but it does show what contemporary Christians thought about the mystical powers of the Picts. No mention is made of any gods. What is fascinating about this story is that the chief weapon used by the Picts against the Christian missionary was weather magic — their most powerful and feared magic!

Finally, to round off this chapter, some composite models will be put forward that combine the binary oppositions mentioned above with the statistical frequencies of the symbols. These models provide a set of interpretations which throw light on the possible interrelations between the lineages in a novel way that should give much food for thought.

Model 1

The following Table 24 combines elements taken from Tables 4 and 22 with regard to the ordering of the symbols with the binary opposites. The object is to see whether this line-up of different attributes and symbols makes intuitive sense or has to be rejected.

EARTH INLAND WATER SOUTH ODD		HEAVEN SEA NORTH EVEN	
— Junior Female Witches Left	Alliances + 24 Senior Male Ancestors Right	— Junior Female Magic Left	Alliances + 24 Senior Male Divination Right
3 44 6/7 42/3 1 37 10	5 45 23 39b 4 39d 15	9 40g 21 41 19 34 46	8 40e 12 31 17 38 14
Left	Right	Left	Right

Table 24: Model 1

It is interesting that *all* the lineages in the right-hand columns engage in mirror and comb *(24)* wife exchanges, mainly *between each other,* and account for 4/5 of the lineages so involved. This indicates that it is only the senior lineages that customarily engage in this practice. Only half the junior lineages participate, mainly with the senior lineages, which leaves a mere 4 per cent of these alliances among the left-hand lineages. This significant result reinforces the dominance of the right-hand, senior lineages.

It might well be asked what is the reason for having all these totemic duos? What is the importance of the lesser lineages? In the case of set A (Table 5), then the function of set B is to provide suitable alliance partners for set A. If, then, members of set B are just cadet branches of their corresponding lineages in set A, it means that these alliances fostered an extremely tight interlinkage between all seven members of set A. Of course, being a cadet branch of a main lineage means that one cannot intermarry, e.g. 40e/40g, 12/21, 44/45. Where totemic duos do intermarry, it means that they are far removed from each other in kinship. There is also the interesting aspect of a group of A set lineages who do not intermarry, *viz* 5, 23 and 45. All three are Z-rod symbols and this suggests that they formed some kind of phratry who could not intermarry for some reason — the common Z-rod? As it happens, there is a single exception here: 5/45 does exist — is this then a special case? A careful examination of other non-allied lineages might reveal more such phratries.

There may be an equation in Table 24 between junior and female with senior and male in the case of symbols 3/5, 9/8, 44/45 and 6/23, where the *rods* may denote the superiority of the lineages in the right-hand columns due to their control over the ancestors and divination. It follows that the lineages in the left-hand columns would use magic and witchcraft, e.g. 9 might employ magic to prevent any irregularities in the moon's behaviour while 3 could employ witchcraft to counter the baleful nature of the sun.

The major division on the left of Table 24 is the association with Earth, Inland Water, South and Odd: this could even be argued for in terms of the prevalence in inland regions, by rivers, in the southern sectors, of these symbols (lineages) which display an odd number of attributes — single: 1, 39b and 39d; triple: Z-rod, 4 and 15. The opposing division on the right have a predeliction towards the sky, the coast, and the north and to have even-sided characteristics.

The previous discussion on pp. 128-130 only offered interpretations of the 14 major symbols (sets A and B, Table 5) and it is now time to consider the others. Firstly, I would like to make a distinction between the primary and secondary level symbols (Table 5) and call them the *political and practical* lineages. The reason is that sets A and B dominate the symbol pairing and are clearly the authorities with political power. Sets C and D do not have such power, as is obvious by their almost complete dependence on sets A and B to form alliances. Such dependency indicates that they had some useful function in society: what better than being practical—in a word: craftsmen!

The general argument has been that the symbols represent the mystical powers of the lineages. Now, magic is the power to do things, and those societies who believe in magic attribute all success to possessing the right magic: spells and techniques. Such spells are closely-guarded secrets, since they are the source of that lineage's power in society: their monopoly over certain spheres of activity and their ability to produce the goods. There are many technical

Class II : Shandwick   (Table 2C:8)

secrets needed in craftsmanship, and apprentices are often sworn to secrecy, cf. the mediaeval guilds and even modern computer firms!

Bearing this in mind, it is possible that the secondary level of symbols are simply craftsmen and other skilled people. Referring to Figure 2 and the geometric symbols, consider them in their dualistic pairings, e.g. *17* and *19*. No. *17* looks like a shield and could be a weaponsmith's symbol, while *19* could be a forge, being a stepped rectangle. Similarly, *4* (a large pot) might represent the potter's skill, while *1* (a disc) could be three pots in a circular oven! Thus *17* and *4* are crucial skills for a community, while their complementary lineages have skills in firing the furnaces.

While craftsmen were necessary, they were dependent upon orders from the authorities, and hence lacked political power since they only had the necessary magic and skill to carry out their specialised tasks. As tradesmen they only controlled (through magic) *inanimate things:* iron, bronze, gold, silver, wood, stone, clay and leather — all these skills being represented geometrically. These practical lineages did not have the magic to control the *really* important aspects of life — the weather, ancestors and men — as did the political lineages. Likewise, the practical animal lineage symbols may have been magical control over the *wild*-animals: wolves, boars and deer.

This division into political and practical lineages accounts for the overwhelming number of alliances between the authorities themselves (70%), their lesser alliances with the practical lineages (26%), and the near absence (4%) of alliances between the practical lineages. Interestingly enough, it is only lineages 4 and 7 (the potter and the weaponsmith?) who intermarry other members of the practical class, and these two lineages account for ⅓ of all the alliances between the political and practical lineages, hence they must have been important to Pictish society if they could exert that degree of independence.

These observations are reinforced by some points made earlier on in connection with Tables 3 and 5:

1) set B as a cadet branch of set A merely serves to strengthen alliance ties between members of set A and has little other purpose.

2) sets C and D as the practical lineages also have just a supportive role: they seldom self-combine or even ally themselves with each other.

Returning to Table 24, it is noticeable, however, that the junior (cadet) lineages in the right-hand columns patronise those in the left-hand columns. The most 'popular' junior lineages are *3, 6* and

41: all in the primary level, they have captured more than half of all alliances between junior and senior. This is not so surprising really, since their seniors are *5, 23* and *31:* some of the most powerful lineages in set A.

Summing up, the primary level symbols are dominant because they had wide-sweeping mystical powers that *affected the whole community,* while the others merely provided useful services. Thus while every community needed to have many different leaders in their enterprises, they did not require more than a few craftsmen, since one could always *trade* goods but not leaders! These symbols, it should be recalled, represented the statuses of the lineages, and not individuals.

Model 2

Table 25 below sets out a scenario of the *type* of overall division of mystical power that we might, one day, establish. *This is a demonstration model only* and is not to be regarded as correct in detail or ascription. It is built up from details given in previous discussions. Like the succeeding model in Table 26, it is meant to stimulate our thinking by suggesting possible roles for the different lineages whose relative power is reflected in their symbols' frequency of occurrence.[19]

WITCHCRAFT	ANCESTORS	MAGIC	DIVINATION
3 v. bad influence of sun	*5* p. good influence of sun	*9* v. irregularity of moon	*8* p. good influence of eclipse
44 p. safety of soul	*45* v. ill-will of ancestors	*40g* p. increase of fowls	*40e* v. predators
6 v. attacks on household	*23* p. protection of fortresses	*21* v. attacks of lightning	*12* p. rain
42 p. safety of water creatures	*39d* v. land monsters	*41* p. increase of fish	*31* v. storms
1 v. failure of kilns	*4* p. success with pottery	*19* v. failure of furnaces	*17* p. success of weapons
37 p. increase of deer	*39d* v. failure of deer hunt	*34* p. increase of swine	*38* v. wolves
10 v. mystic attack on metals	*15* p. success in metal working	*46* v. failure in smelting	*14* p. success in artistry

v. = versus   p. = pro

Table 25: Model 2

Whatever the actual claims of mystical expertise that the lineages might have made, it has to be remembered that by the time the symbol stones were erected, the political pecking order had long been established. For example, if lineage *31* did have power over storms, then the fact that they became stronger in Class II times is not directly due to a deterioration in the weather! Political ascendency is due more to cunning and force of arms than it is to magic. Nevertheless, in order to command a following, one must have certain attributes. Hence if mystical powers enabled a lineage to establish themselves as leaders *in the past*, then one can capitalise on this accepted role and attempt to reach the commanding heights of the society through ordinary means. The above suggestions are to account for the success of certain lineages and the failure of others in the political sphere.

Some of the mystical powers ascribed in the table may seem trivial and even ludicrous in their specificity, but they did serve a function. We do not know anything about Pictish ritual but it is likely they could have had many ceremonies — great and small — like many other societies who recognize the powers of the different lineages in rituals that are designed to highlight their particular claims to be a *necessary* part of society. In totemic societies, the responsibility for the successful maintenance of *all* those activities necessary to existence was strictly divided up amongst the totemic lineages, and could not be encroached upon. Periodic ceremonies were performed by the different lineages *on behalf of the entire society.* Even should their remit be extremely small (e.g. my suggestion that *19* safeguarded the metal forges from failure), they *could* claim that their contribution was vital to society since nobody else was allowed to perform the necessary magic. It is important to stress the holistic nature of Table 25, for even though it may be wrong in detail it should be correct in principle, for the Picts, as a totemic society, are likely to have assigned responsibility to the various lineages, which reflects a scale of mystical power. What we need to do is to match up the political power (frequency of symbols) with the likely scale of the relative importance of the different types of magic employed. The above attempt is only a first try at making a match.

Model 3

The polar diagram of Table 26 attempts to group certain dualistic elements together into their respective quadrants in order to suggest further hypotheses about how the Picts conceived their world. Naturally this can be no more than a thought-experiment based upon the symbols, but there is an inflexibility in dualism which demands that if one item falls in one sphere then its complement *must* occur in the other sphere.

Starting with the simple opposition of sun and moon, Z-rod and V-rod, female and male, ancestors and divination, we can begin to build up Table 26, since females and ancestors go together (even male ancestors are female!) while the sun and the Z-rod also fall into the southern quadrant since they are both associated with death. By extension one may add evil, left, odd and inferior here since they *cannot* be added to the other quadrant which is a male preserve where all is goodness and light. The reason why all symbolic systems are similar to this is because they are invented by men for the express purpose of vindicating themselves and being in the right!

Some animal symbols are included: birds and serpents are placed in opposing quadrants as are the two sets of mediating symbols (cf. Fig. 2). It is to be noted that *40e* (the eagle) is near Heaven while *40g* (the goose) is near the Sea, *44* (the serpent) is near Earth while *45* (serpent and Z-rod) is near Inland waters. The case of the mediating symbols is interesting. *31* ('swimming elephant') is near Heaven, *41* (the salmon) is in the Sea, *39b* (the truncated beast) is on or near Earth while *42/3* (Hippocampus) is in Inland water. These mediating symbols may *pass* between their two elements: *31* may fly or swim as may *41* (when it leaps), while the other two, *42/3* and *39b*, are half-animal and half-fish that can be in either element.

It does not follow that all the items within a quadrant are equally interconnected, but they might be. If we take an example from the southern quadrant, we do not know if the ancestors are connected to the sun but the following set suggests that they may be:

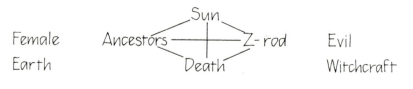

By contrast in the other quadrant we find:

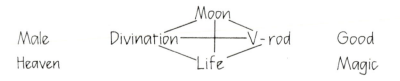

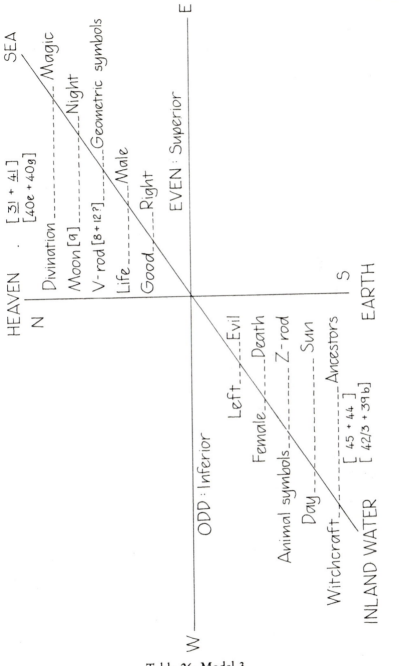

HEAVEN . [3ɪ + 4ɪ]
[40e + 40g]

N

Divination

Moon [9]

V-rod [8 + 12?]

Life

Good

Magic

Night

Geometric symbols

Male

Right

SEA

EVEN : Superior

E

S

EARTH

ODD : Inferior

Left

Female

Animal symbols

Day

Witchcraft

Evil

Death

Z-rod

Sun

Ancestors

[45 + 44]

[42/3 + 39b]

W

INLAND WATER

Table 26: Model 3

The latter even hints that moon divination (of eclipses?) was necessary to life! Such thought-experiments as these are designed to *reach* the truth; they do not pretend to be it. If they produce hypotheses like the above about the ancestors and the sun or the importance of lunar prediction, then we can search for other evidence to prove or disprove this. Our major problem, hitherto, has been that we have not known where to begin in trying to understand Pictish belief and thought. The above method may help us to start asking questions: this is the first step! A comparative search in the literature on contemporary tribes might offer some corroborative evidence about the symbols: the only genuine Pictish documents!

The three models given above are devices for extracting from the symbols more information than their mere appearances can tell us. Yet even this would not have been at all possible without the careful analysis of the frequencies of these symbols made in previous chapters. Better models can be devised after these have been studied and found wanting — that is the point of models: they are *not* themselves theories but they can be turned into theories!

It is hoped that the fact has now been firmly established that symbols *only occur* in pairs and that this dualism is *the* basic characteristic of Pictish thinking. It has also been demonstrated that the 28 symbols occur as discrete totemic duos whereby the two symbols are similar in function but have slightly different appearances.

If the Picts were dualistic, then it means that they categorized their conceptual world in a series of binary opposites of a type shown in Table 22. The binary pair given there are some of the commonest found in dualistic societies around the world. While there can be little disagreement about the majority of them, there is always room for doubt that they are in the correct columns. These are my guess and others are welcome to try changing them around but, as they will discover, there are inherent limits on what can be altered.

My interpretation of the symbols rests on their *presumed* intention in a Dark Age society which cannot have been much different to that of its contemporaries, about whom we know a great deal by comparison. The biggest difference from all their neighbours was the peculiar Pictish mode of royal succession, and this must have needed a powerful ideology to sustain it against the scorn of their fellow Celts and the Church. It follows that the Pictish belief system *must* have differed radically from their contemporaries in some important ways. If, as most people agree, the Picts were matrilineal, then this would pose problems for the men to justify their held authority. Clearly, lineages had to be sharply distinguished because of the dangers of incest — an ever-present fear to all societies — but it was even more important to matrilineal societies where it is harder to keep track of descent. The simple practice of tattooing one's lineage mark (on the wrists or shoulders of girls and on the chests of boys) is a widespread solution to this particular problem. While the Picts may have tattooed themselves, it does not follow that they used identical designs to those found on the stones. Indeed that seems doubtful, as the symbols were most likely tailor-made to rationalize the system of alliances. If that was the case, then what did the symbols represent? It had to be some distinctive feature of their society.

The symbols obviously did not represent their gods and spirits (if they ever had them) since they referred to humans. But what characteristic of human society was that important then? It could not be status *per se*, as has already been discussed, but it could be *power*. The question is, how did the lineages acquire and hold on to their power? My answer is that they had various forms of mystic power in their ideology: power of witchcraft, power of the ancestors, power of magic and power of divination — all common features to Dark Age societies. These mystical powers would not all be of equal potency or importance to society; our task is to decide which rank ordering the Picts employed to grade these powers.

This 'reduction' of the symbol to mystical powers may strike many modern readers as quite implausible, simply because they will (rightly, in my opinion) argue that magic does not exist. However, we have to remember that we are dealing with the beliefs of a people who lived over a millennium ago. The Picts were *never* in a position to doubt the existence of the mystical forces that surrounded them (none of their contemporaries doubted either) because this belief provided them with their *core* explanation of the world and all its mysterious activities. This was their only way of exerting any mastery over their world. It may have been misguided but what other way was open to them until Christianity offered an alternative? Even had they believed in capricious gods and spirits then, yet again their only way of coping would be to combat the spirits' own mystical powers by other mystical powers under human control.

There can be little doubt that the Picts held some notions of mystical power, and so the major question is whether they encapsulated these beliefs in the symbols. My reason for making this link is that the symbols are paired in such a way (representing marriage alliances) that they confirm the political dominance of set A (Table 3) and *maintain it in power for ever!* After all, that was the whole point of erecting the stones in the first place. The frequency distribution of symbols shows how *absolutely* set A controlled all the various alliances in order to ensure their own succession to power all over Pictland. This control of all political power must have had an ideological base in their belief structure — *something* had to explain the dominance of set A. As most people know, the ultimate legitimation of most kingships, the world over, has always been of a religious kind: the sacred world that religion creates also sanctifies the temporal world order. The same is true for societies like the Trobriands where magic is the main ideology: the possession of powerful magic guarantees one's right to rule. Such a belief is no more naive than that of the divine right of kings which was sponsored by the Christian church.

My argument boils down to equating political power with the possession of awe-inspiring mystical powers, represented by symbols, which effectively maintained that political regime until that ideology was undermined by an alternative, alien doctrine.

Our task, therefore, is to seek for the correspondences between on the one hand, the mystical powers that maintained authority, and on the other, the symbols. The rank order of the symbols has already been established in terms of frequencies, and so the logical step is to match this with a list of all the mystical powers from the most awe-inspiring to the least important. Such an ordering is given in Table 25, where the right-hand columns take precedence (i.e. Divination and the Ancestors) over the lesser left-hand columns (Magic and Witchcraft). These do range from the most powerful claims of control that man can ever make, in divination over the weather and general threats to society, down to the minor claims of witchcraft. There is quite a striking resemblance between some of these powers and the appearances of the symbols. Of course symbols are only conventional, widely-recognized, signs that stand for something else. There are not universally agreed ways of representing mystical powers, any more than written words in different languages are similar when referring to a common, *real* object. Our difficulty in seeing the relationship between a symbol and the power it stands for is because we do not know the convention the Picts used. Table 25 attempts to provide a possible key.

The association of mystical and political power with the symbol frequencies is more straightforward for sets A and B than it is at the bottom of the scale. Hence the secondary level interpretation is as weak as their power, but that does not matter since they were not that important and so these more fanciful associations do not invalidate the main argument. However it should be remembered that the refusal of a lineage to carry out its assigned role constituted a political sanction that had to be taken into account. For this reason, the very act of encompassing all the minor lineages into a net of alliances with set A and B ensured a compliance to carry out one's duties, since these minor lineages would be the fathers to the next set of rulers! Such an offer would be hard to refuse.

These mystical powers lay at the root of much in-fighting among the Picts because of their ambiguous nature. A refusal to conduct rituals was an act of defiance while, on the other hand, these powers could be turned against one's foes — causing storms, drought or lightning to strike them! This dual aspect to mystical powers meant that one could either use them for the good of the whole community or to wreak vengeance on people. This benevolent/malevolent aspect of mystical power is typical in most dualistic cosmologies and accounts for the ambivalence that exists between men and the gods and powers which they have created. This is the reason for giving the sun and moon their ambiguous nature in Pictish thought. It is unusual in Europe to associate the sun with women, but then it is equally unusual to have matrilineages. Symbol *8* is the most dominant (common) symbol and is clearly not the sun because it looks like a crescent moon! There can be little doubt that the moon is the *key* heavenly body for the Picts, and since men are always in political command they had to control the moon! The corollary follows, as night the day. This single complication makes Table 22 also unusual since it confounds many well-established associations found elsewhere between women and the moon; otherwise many dualities are unchanged in position and correspond to those normally found.

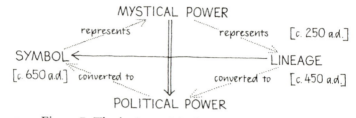

Figure 7: The basic model of the symbol stones

KEY

1. *Basically mystical power is transformed into political power.*
2. The lineages claiming this mystical power convert it into political power (right-hand side).
3. The 'powers-that-be' then create a set of symbols that represent and reproduce the rank-ordered mystical powers and lineages to be used on the symbol stones (left-hand side).
4. The 'mystification' in this simple equation is the 'obvious' identification of the symbol with the lineage.

COMMENT

1. The dates (given in brackets) are suggested periods when the steps in the transformation process took place.
2. The politically-motivated alliances between lineages were commemorated on stone in the form of paired symbols. In essence these alliances affirmed the unification of their 'powers' and confirmed the dominance of the major lineages. The political manoeuvring accounts for the skewed nature of the symbol combinations.
3. Although later Picts recognized the symbols as being associated with the lineages they may well have forgotten the real basis of the association: mystical power.
4. After 850 A.D. the precise totemic relationship between the lineages would be forgotten, as indeed would the connection between the symbols and their lineages, since political control had passed to the Scots who did not subscribe to the Pictish notions of mystical power.
5. To regard the symbol stones as curious, even mysterious, *artistic* memorials to the dead completely overlooks their true significance, since they were of vital importance to the Picts who erected them. Since the use of symbols was made redundant more than a thousand years ago, it is unsurprising that we know little about them, for they went out of fashion as Bede (our chief source of information) was compiling his great work.

This exercise in explaining the symbols has not been *that* simple since, otherwise, it would have been done long ago, but it has been reasonably consistent in its main premises throughout. Whether or not I have correctly associated *every* symbol with its imputed power is not of great essence, since the main thing has been to give the overall sense that these 28 symbols are part of that total system of belief which maintained the political structure of the Picts.

No attempt has been made to account for all the designs that have been rejected as non-symbols, since they fall outside the symbolic system, neither have the few anomalies that remain received an explanation. After all, there is no categorical imperative to explain every single design, despite Anderson's *obiter dictum!* In my opinion, these exceptions to my definition of a symbol are quite irrelevant to our general understanding of the system of symbolism which the Picts created.

In attempting this first comprehensive statement ever to explain the symbols and their distribution, I have had to take a pioneering stance without the benefit of previous guidelines. Despite the errors that are bound to exist in such a detailed work, I hope that I have established a viable and verifiable explanation.

The succeeding chapters in Part II are not contingent in any way on the correctness or otherwise of the findings here. They are simply provocative forays into well-known historical and linguistic matters; should they be found incorrect they, likewise, do not impugn the conclusions reached here on the symbols. The main reason for venturing into this separate area of discourse is to suggest to historians and linguists that the bases for some of their assumptions *may be* wrong! For should my hypotheses about the symbols be found acceptable, then it means that some recasting of whole sections of Pictish studies is called for.

The royal genealogies are highly problematical, but my suggestion about the alliances and the number of lineages involved might clarify some of the issues.

As for the debate about Sueno's stone and that about the Oghams, I think we have been barking up the wrong stones! Both are really about magical numbers.

Christianity is the crucial factor in the demise of Pictish culture, since its world view is poles apart from the mystical beliefs of the Picts who set up the symbol stones.

Part Two

TWO OF A TRADE SELDOM AGREE !

What is, is not; what is not, is.

Zen saying

CHAPTER 1

The historical Pictish kingdoms

Our knowledge of the kings of Pictland and those of Dalriada derives from a series of king-lists compiled in the 12th century on the basis of annals, doubtless kept by various religious houses. These annals are brief notes recording the obits of kings and other significant events—mainly battles. They begin in the 6th century A.D. where the first record of a Pictish king is in 579 A.D., but no layman is mentioned before 650. Not surprisingly, the Scottish kings are given an earlier mention, since these annals were composed on Scottish territory. [21]

The Pictish king-lists often attempt to trace the ancestors of the kings back to the Christian beginning, i.e. Adam, hence there are frequent mythical introductions. Thus List P (in M. Anderson's account) begins with Cruithne and his seven sons whose names are those of the seven Pictish regions that, traditionally, were accepted as comprising the whole of Pictland. This is followed by six more kings—making a total of 14 kings so far. Next come 14 pairs of kings called Brude: named 'Brude X, Brude Ur-X'. There are some 28 more kings before we reach Galam (505-525 A.D.) who is just 7 kings away from the first independently vouchsafed Pictish king: Bridei, son of Maelchon (554-584). The fact that the founding ancestor of this Bridei lived 77 reigns earlier is a tribute to the art of the historiographer: to arrange meaningful patterns of the past! Until Galam's reign we may safely assume that all these kings are quite mythical.

There is no guarantee that Galam is not also mythical, but he makes a convenient starting-point for a genealogy of the Pictish kings; since it puts them on a par with the first Scottish king—Fergus (c.502). Hence we can have dual genealogies for the Picts and Scots from 500 until 850 A.D. It is not particularly difficult to construct a genealogy for the Scots, since they were patrilineal whereby brother succeeds brother and sons succeed their fathers. The Picts are more complicated, for although brothers succeeded each other, no son succeeds his father until the very end of the Pictish line: the general rule is that a man succeeds to his mother's brother's position. That is to say, the Picts were matrilineal—if we accept Bede's testimony. If this is the case, it gives rise to problems of presentation.

Genealogies have been produced by some scholars who accept the matrilineal descent system of the Picts, e.g. M. O. Anderson tries to put the whole of the historical genealogy into a single lineage framework. Kirby, on the other hand, assumes that there were two major lineages—one in the north, the other in the south of Pictland. This particular genealogy only goes down to 763 A.D. and hence misses out a century at the end.

The major drawback to Anderson's analysis is to assume that matrilineal descent is like patrilineal succession where one line alone is sufficient to explain everything. In patrilineal societies women and *their* lineages are discarded as inessential, as succession goes directly from father to son, but in matrilineal societies there are two lineages involved: the father's and the mother's. The point is that a woman's brother is king but it is *her* son who succeeds; another lineage has to provide this woman with a husband and *he* is the father of the next king—that is why the Picts always mention his name. Not only that, this man is also the son of the previous king! Thus we have a tightly-knit group of men related through a woman: her brother, her husband and her son. The selection of husbands was not left to chance and normally it is decided by the rule of cross-cousin marriage. In order to show this we need to consider *at least* three lineages.

Kirby's genealogy is a move in the right direction by including two lines of descent, but it suffers from the fact that these lines are unrelated: there is no explanation where the fathers of the kings came from, neither does it account for the oscillation of power between North and South. There must be an explanation of these two points, and the answer is likely to be found in the marriage arrangements of the Picts since all royal marriages are highly regulated: they are *alliances* between countries—they are political alliances, not love affairs.

If the above point is granted about royal marriages (and this

Class II : Meigle 6   (Table 2C:32)

was the basis for the earlier discussion on symbols in Chapter 4) then both Anderson's and Kirby's genealogies have to be redrawn to take account of the father's lineage. It will be recalled that the combinations of the Pictish symbols was posited on the practice of patrilateral cross-cousin marriage (a man marries his father's sister's daughter) in a matrilineal society. Four symbols were used to represent the four lineages involved in the exchange. It is suggested that we also need four lineages to explain the royal descent lines.

The following genealogy (Figure 8) is based on the same system as given in Chapter 4, but it is assumed that there were only two royal lines: one in the North and one in the South. The royal lines provided the kings but they did not, could not, intermarry since that would exclude one or other from the succession, as no son could inherit the throne from his father. Hence it was necessary for there to be two 'buffer' lineages to provide fathers for the future kings. This genealogy provides a solution to this problem: there are four inter-marrying lineages Q, R, S, and P which are matrilineal and practise patrilateral (FZD) marriage. The two royal lineages are Q and S, but it is assumed that lineages Q and R are in the Northern kingdom while lineages S and P are in the Southern kingdom. However it should be noted that the lineages marry in a circle and that lineages Q and P intermarry, as do S and R, cf Fig. 6a.

In this genealogy there are six royal names which are shared by both lineages Q and S, while there are eight names that are only found in one or other lineage. These *fourteen* names are distributed as follows:

NAME	LINEAGE Q	LINEAGE S
Drest	4	3
Bridei	2	3
Gartnait	2	2
Ciniod	1	1
Galam	1	1
Nechton	1	1
Cailtram	1	-
Constantine	-	1
Elpin	2	-
Oengus	-	2
Talorc	-	3
Talorcan	1	-
Tarain	-	1
Uuen	-	1

Class III : Edderton (Table 2E:2)

K

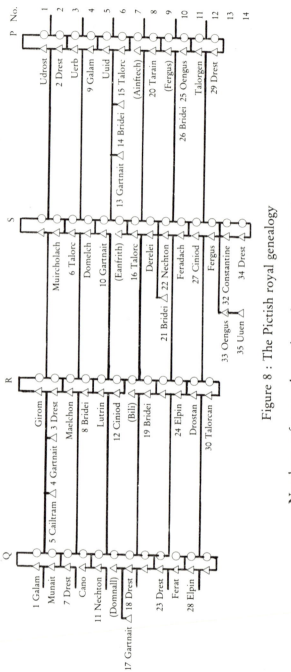

Figure 8 : The Pictish royal genealogy

Numbers refer to the order of succession. Brackets denote a foreigner

This list accounts for most of the Pictish kings, but it does omit a few problematical ones like Talorgen, son of Oengus, because if Drest (29) was also the son of Talorgen then this would be patrilineal succession! Neither was it easy to find a place for Canaul (31), son of Tarl'a, nor the bobtail of short reigning kings at the end of the lists, but these exceptions do not affect the main argument.

The *fourteen*-generation genealogy (Fig. 8) is not claimed to be historically accurate, but the span of 350 years gives it an average of 25 years per generation, which is quite acceptable for the time. It will be seen that in the two other lineages, R and P, (containing the names of both the fathers and sons of kings), all the names are *different* with the sole exception of Fergus. Interestingly enough, there are 14 fathers of kings named in the first 7 generations, and just 7 fathers in the next 6 generations (the 14th generation has non-Pictish succession, being patrilineal).

The purpose in drawing up this genealogy was to arrange it like a *macropit*, since this model was so powerful in explaining the symbol combinations and it seems most unlikely that the Picts had two different marriage systems.

The genealogy thus demonstrates that many kings *shared* their names (85% of the time) but the fathers and sons of kings did *not*. The simplest way of explaining this dichotomy is to postulate four lineages. Only the two royal lineages would have a vested interest in passing on their special names to their heirs.

The simple guiding principle in assigning kings to one or other of the royal lineages is that there was an alternation of overlordship between lineage Q and S, i.e. between North and South Pictland. The actual succession went first to uterine brothers, then to sisters' sons (real or classificatory), and this can be seen in the following list where B=brother, Z=sister, M=mother, S=son.

LINEAGE

1. B/B

Drest (3), Gartnait (4), Cailtram (5)	Q
Gartnait (13), Bridei (14), Talorc (15)	S
Gartnait (17), Drest (18)	Q
Bridei (21), Nechton (22)	S
Oengus (24), Bridei (26)	S
Constantine (32), Oengus (33)	S

2.MB/ZS

Drest (3) and (7)	Q
Gartnait (10) and (13)	S
Talorc (15) and (16)	S
Bridei (21) and (26)	S
Elpin (24) and (28)	Q

3. MMB/ZDS

Drest (18) and (23)	Q

4. MMMB/ZDSS

Talorc (6) and (15)	S
Bridei (14) and (21)	S
Oengus (25) and (33)	S

5. MMMMB/ZDDDS

Bridei (8) and (19)	Q
Drest (7) and (18)	Q

It will be seen that five of the commonest royal names *viz:* Bridei, Drest, Gartnait, Oengus and Talorc not only figure prominently in the adelphic succession but are themselves interlinked by direct lines of descent. However, those names which are common to *both* royal lineages are not related to each other in this genealogy!

Essentially, lineage Q has three basic names: Bridei, Drest and Elpin, while lineage S has four: Bridei, Gartnait, Oengus and Talorc. This leaves a couple of anomalies: Gartnait (4 and 17) and Drest (2 and 29), which seem too far apart in kinship terms and are also in the 'wrong' lineage. Perhaps they are misplaced—this is something that will have to be reconsidered.

The main point I wish to establish is that the name BRIDEI is *the* fundamental one which is shared by both royal lineages but which has two quite separate lines that are unrelated. We even find this point made in the mythical genealogies where there are 14 pairs of kings labelled Brude X and Brude Ur-X. Hence it is extremely interesting that Bridei (14 and 21) are related as MMMB/ZDDS while Bridei (21 and 26) are MB/ZS; this means that Bridei (14 and 26) are related as MMMMB/ZDDDS in lineage S. This is paralleled in lineage Q, for Bridei (8 and 19) are also related as MMMMB/ZDDDS—shades of Brude X and Brude Ur-X? Can this be sheer coincidence?

However, this *five*-generation difference seems a very remote kind of inheritance to have any practical significance. Well, of course, this kinship link is not directly related to succession every 125 years! One must remember that although the rules of succession were clear, it did not follow that every heir inherited the throne. What this data suggests is that the ZS of every Bridei was also called Bridei! However, there were many heirs and rival claimants, so the name Bridei only surfaces a few times. What is perhaps of greater significance is that this five-generation gap is probably related to the famous Murngin controversy (cf Lévi-Strauss, 1969) and to the similar breakdown of the historical Pictish genealogies after five generations due to the inherent fragility of their alliance system.

So the astonishing parallel of the two sets of royal Brideis in lineages Q and S may be a structural matter for we also have the fact that both Drest (7 and 18) and Talorc (6 and 16) are in this MMMMB/ZDDDS relationship. Indeed it is possible that Oengus (25) was 'succeeded' by his ZDDDS, for we know that Oengus (33) was ZDDDS to Oengus (25) but he had his son, Uuen, made king in a *patrilineal* fashion, contrary to custom. If one of the sisters of Oengus (33) had married the Scot, Alpin, who fathered Kenneth, then Kenneth would have a very respectable claim as ZDDDS of Oengus.(25)! Obviously this is speculation about structure but it must have happened something like this, for the dates are right *and* it occurred just when the Picts were changing the rules of succession which would have excluded the Scots.

Hence there are possibly as many as five cases of MMMMB/ZDDDS relationships and there could be more, for Gartnait (4 and 13), Nechton (11 and 22), Ciniod (12 and 27) and even Drest (18 and 29) are in the right generational sequence, even if they come in different lineages in *this* genealogy. Should this discovery be structurally significant, then, perhaps, my genealogy should be revised:

NORTH	SOUTH
Bridei (X)	Bridei (Ur-X)
Drest	Gartnait
Ciniod	Talorc
Nechton	Oengus

This would give us 7 basic names in 8 different areas—the sub-kingdoms of Table 13! Perhaps each name could be associated with one of the 7 principal symbols—the main lineages of the Picts. This might account for the well-nigh universal presence of symbol *8* (Bridei?). We have a long way to go before these identities can be established but it is a beginning.

The 'balance' between the numbers of kings coming from lineage Q (the North) and those from lineage S (the South) is roughly equal before 700 A.D., and this corresponds well with the equal number of Class I stones found in the two kingdoms (which divided along the Moray/Aberdeenshire border) and suggests that both kingdoms were politically equal in power. However, after 700 A.D. (when Southern Pictland became converted to Christianity) the 'balance' shifts dramatically so that twice as many kings came from lineage S than from lineage Q. Interestingly enough, the ratio of Class II stones north and south of the Mounth (the new border) is again *precisely* 1:2! There is absolutely no connection between the numbers of kings and symbol stones, but the ratios are significant in telling us about the balance of power between the lineages and kingdoms. However, what really counts is how long each lineage was in power. In Class II times (700-800 A.D.) lineage S seems to have held the reins for some 90 years!

Given that symbol stones were first erected in 683 A.D. and that Pictland, south of the Mounth, became Christian shortly afterwards and that lineage S dominated the 8th Century kingship, it is really surprising how few Class II stones were erected north of the Mounth. Half of these stones are multiple symbol stones that are found in discrete groups along the northern coast. Such a multiple form is rare in the south where the usual binary form is found well inland. Why, despite their apparent dominance, did not the Christian lineage S erect more stones in the north?

The answer to the above question is that the Northern kingdom probably remained pagan and did not welcome Christians, and so they were forced into small colonies as the multiple symbols suggest. The fact that lineage Q provided very few kings after 700 A.D. (as recorded by the Christian scribes) should not be interpreted as meaning that the Northern Picts had no kings—they simply did not reign over the South *as well*. My genealogy suggests how this bifurcation took place.

There are some historians, like Smyth, who suggest that the matrilineal hypothesis is a pure myth. It is fairly easy to show that the traditional arguments for matrilinearity are themselves suspect and that Anderson's single line genealogy is untenable, but that does not prove the case any more than does Smyth's elaborate explanation of the succession of the Pictish kings; for if the Picts were not matrilineal, they would *have to be* patrilineal like the Scots and Irish—as Smyth implies. Yet then we get the paradoxical situation that only some 8% of the Pictish kings had royal fathers but the Scots managed to get a 75% father/son succession. Were the Picts just unlucky?

The basic fallacy in reducing the king-lists to simply a haphazard collection of overlords is precisely the same as the widely-held view that the symbols are *just* Art or that the symbol stones are funerary monuments. What these attempts do is to individualize the data and make them unique—hence automatically precluding any chance of detecting a total pattern behind the data. This approach is quite legitimate if one prefers it, but is it justified when looking at tribal societies?

By contrast and by training, I take it as *axiomatic* that there are underlying patterns to be found. In fact, I believe there is a direct link between the symbol stones and the king-lists since they are both concerned with kinship and political power. Having shown in Part I that the symbols and symbol stones fall into distinct patterns, we have shown that there are also regularities in the king-lists—the five generational relationship, the 7 key names, etc. This suggests that these are not arbitrary sets of names since these patterns were *discovered* and not built into the genealogy. This is only a provisional demonstration model and it will have to be corrected by historians, but it will provide a working hypothesis that there is *more* to the king-lists than meets the eye!

Patrilateral cross-cousin marriage is inherently unstable, as social anthropologists invariably remind us, and hence it is not surprising that the system collapses by the fifth generation. There is just a possibility that the genealogy before Bridei, son of Bili, is only an attempt to show that the system *did* work in the past! At all events, by the 6th generation both the royal lineages are marrying outsiders, i.e. foreigners. This event has a knock-on effect since lineages R and P can no longer supply husbands in the old way and so even more foreign husbands are required in the 7th generation! It is conceivable that Bridei (son of Bili) did manage to stabilize the situation for a while, but eventually new Scots blood crept into the royal lines, especially into the Southern lineage C after the consolidation of the kingdom south of the Mounth during Bridei's reign.

Henderson comments that Bede made no criticism of Pictish marriage and therefore it must have been Christian. However, first cousin marriage was not approved, and so it is significant that this practice seems to have been abandoned after Ciniod (612-631) introduced foreigners as marriage partners and allies. Thus we know that Eanfrith (father of Talorcan, 635-657) married a Pictish princess and became a Christian, although he reverted to paganism when he later returned home. In a parallel lineage to Eanfrith we find Domnall marrying into the Pictish royal line and he must have been a Christian. So by the time that these foreign alliances were concluded, Christianity was established and there were no further cousin marriages—so Bede could have had no objection.

We can now come to a paradox: if Bridei, son of Bili, actually set up the Class I stones he did not have the Christian cross inscribed, so was he really a Christian? Apparently not, even if he did not marry his cross-cousin. My genealogy suggests that his mother was a pagan and that Christianity only flourished south of the Mounth. After the Northumbrian invasion of southern Pictland in 658, following Talorc's death in 657, the kings of Pictland were apparently the sons of the Scot, Domnall, until Bridei took over. The status of Christianity was clearly not that important in deciding matters between the two halves of the kingdom.

There was, it can be seen, an oscillation of power between the Northern and Southern kingdoms up to the 9th generation. After this time, there was a concentration of authority in the hands of lineage S in the south, with the likely eclipse of lineage P. This marks the transition from Class I (Bridei, son of Bili) to Class II (Nechton, son of Derelei). It is possible that north of the Mounth the Picts remained pagan, with lineages Q and R maintaining alliances (still Class I, of course). Yet it is equally likely that some members of lineages Q and R threw in their lot with lineage S in the south and formed an even tighter intermarrying clique of three lineages. By inheritance, some of the Christian Picts in the south could claim land in the Northern kingdom and they may have set up their Class II stones there—often bunched together for safety as the multiple symbols show.

Returning to the original task facing Bridei, son of Bili, he had to unite the pagan Picts against the pagan Northumbrians. There was little point in appealing to Christianity to unite the Picts; only their traditional method of alliance would do—not the new-fangled southern Christian marriages to foreigners. Bridei could claim descent from the Northern kingdom, while his father, a Briton, was at least ethnically related to the Picts—unlike the Scots and Northumbrians. That Bridei settled in the south after his defeat of the Northumbrians is not surprising, since he wished to keep what he had won; this was best done by being close to his enemies. However, Southern Pictland was a zone of Christian influence and soon we find Nechton (706-724) agreeing to the Roman Easter tables and even returning to a monastery! Perhaps it was Nechton, or more likely, Oengus (son of Fergus, 728-761) who was responsible for the Class II stones. This Christian resurgence seems to have had little impact north of the Mounth. If Bridei (son of Bili) had been a Christian, then surely he would also have caused Class II stones to be erected north of the Mounth? His ability to crush the Northumbrians *from the north* shows that he had the power to do so. Bridei also conquered the Orkneys in 682, but there is only one Class II stone there, yet a half dozen Class I stones. The previous year, there was a siege of Dunnottar, presumably by Bridei, which shows that he had probably spent the previous ten years subduing North Pictland from north to south. Some poorly executed Class I symbols have been found at Dunnottar. In 683, Dunadd in Dalriada was besieged and, although this is not necessarily connected with Bridei, there is also a single Class I symbol there on a rock. It is unlikely that this symbol is connected with Oengus' capture of Dunadd in 736—that is more possibly related to the Ogham inscription there. Oengus seems to have been well and truly a Class II person.

Single symbols such as these have always been a puzzle but perhaps they were only the marks of a conquering lineage, for they certainly cannot indicate alliances. It is surprising that the Picts did not seem to scratch graffiti very much—apart from in caves—so it seems that symbols were something very special.

Bridei's subjection of Northern Pictland from the very north to the south argues that he had a powerful fleet: this may have been *the* major force of the Northern Picts and the reason for their previous unification and strength in Pictland as a whole. Bridei's eventual settlement in Southern Pictland may have been due to a change in warfare whereby land battles were more decisive since coastal castles were again becoming impregnable to lightning sea-borne raids. Significantly enough, the major Scottish, British and Northumbrian strongholds were well inland, unlike the Pictish ones in the north. In other words, whereas naval supremacy could subdue most of the early Pictish settlements, it was not enough to defeat the land based armies of the enemies of the Picts. A corollary is found when another sea-borne power—the Norsemen— attacked, for they could easily subdue the Northern Picts as well as the other coastal settlements from Dublin to Lindisfarne. It appears that from 700 A.D. onwards, land battles were more decisive, and this might have contributed to the inability of the Northern Picts to influence matters further south. Apart from their logistic problems, it might have been impossible for the Northern Picts to muster enough men to oppose the tightly-knit and easily assembled armies in the south. To judge from the number of Class I stones in Aberdeenshire, it seems quite likely that they could attack south of the Mounth but they still do not appear to have been able to exert their will, possibly because of the growing alliance between the

Picts and the Scots—as the genealogies suggest. That a large number of Scots migrated into southern Pictland is documented by the name Fotla to the area where they settled. This combination of Christian communities could well have withstood the pagan incursions from the north—after all, what had the Northern Picts to gain? They had defeated the Northumbrians who were the major threat.

After 685 the Northern Picts were deserted by Bridei since he made his capital in the south, so what were they to do? They remained independent and stoically pagan against the spirit of the times. The evidence for this comes from the symbol stones and later history. If we assume that the population of Pictland in Bridei (son of Bili)'s time was equally divided between the Northern and Southern kingdoms, then this is corroborated by the distribution of Class I stones that he caused to be erected. Yet when we look at the distribution of Class II and III stones, we find that these Christian stones *in the same area* (though not now the same kingdoms) are totally different: 75% are in the south. This strongly suggests that there is a fundamental difference between the two kingdoms.

By Class II times, one can unequivocally state that the area south of the Mounth is totally Christian whereas there are only pockets of Christianity in the north. Since the north is four times larger than the south it follows that, proportionally speaking, it only contains 1/16th of the total number of *possible* Christian stones—had they been all Christians. Indeed, if one excludes all the undecorated Class III stones (which could have been put up at any time) and then considers that many of the Class II stones have multiple symbols, it really seems as if the Christian presence in the north was quite inconsiderable. In fact, there is little evidence that the Northern Picts were ever thoroughly Christianized until their Norse masters were converted in the year 1000 A.D. Hence, north of the Mounth could not be regarded as an integral part of the Pictish kingdom after 685 A.D., since it did not subscribe to the religion of the south. This may be reflected in the genealogies of the kings—as given here. Obviously the northern kings had a claim to the throne on traditional grounds, but they had to make good their claim—with force. This seems to have failed and the southern lineage remained triumphant until the advent of Kenneth MacAlpin.

It is well known that the Picts were frequently disputing the kingship and this is not surprising, given the number of possible claimants. The breakdown in the traditional succession had happened earlier than the blatant disregard shown by Constantine and his brother Oengus. At this point in time it was clear that

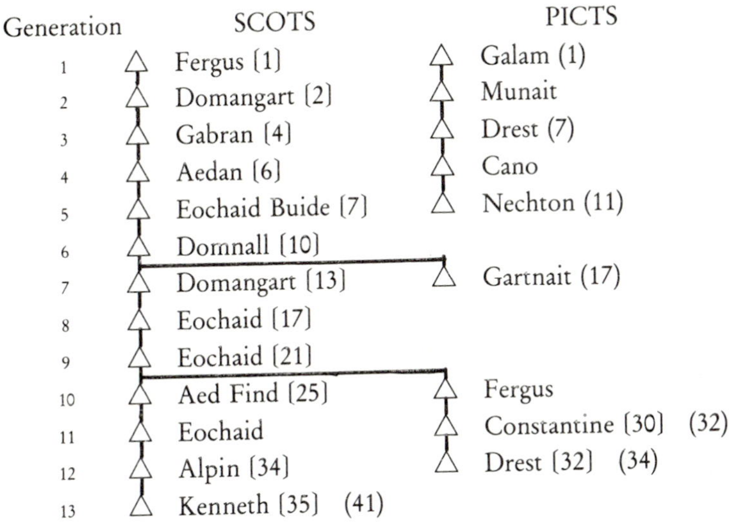

Generation	SCOTS	PICTS
1	Fergus [1]	Galam (1)
2	Domangart [2]	Munait
3	Gabran [4]	Drest (7)
4	Aedan [6]	Cano
5	Eochaid Buide [7]	Nechton (11)
6	Domnall [10]	
7	Domangart [13]	Gartnait (17)
8	Eochaid [17]	
9	Eochaid [21]	
10	Aed Find [25]	Fergus
11	Eochaid	Constantine [30] (32)
12	Alpin [34]	Drest [32] (34)
13	Kenneth [35] (41)	

Figure 9 : Partial genealogy of the Picts and the Scots

[..] Scots order of succession   (..) Picts order of succession

patriliny was beginning to overtake the matrilineal succession rules. Now since Constantine had a claim to the Scots throne as well—and even ruled as a Scots king—there was beginning a rapprochement of the Pictish and Scottish succession.

Clearly there was a personal advantage to reign over both kingdoms and to bequeath the kingship to the next in line—on the agnatic side! As is well-known, the Pictish kingship ends in a welter of confusing claims before Kenneth MacAlpin wins out. It is most likely that Kenneth had a claim to both the Pictish and Scottish throne, but he had to fight for it since there were more than enough Pictish contenders. However they were in a quandary, since they could only claim the Pictish throne through their mothers and could only lay claim to the Scottish throne through their fathers: did they have both? Obviously they not all did, so they could only muster *some* support for any joint claim. Kenneth was probably not best placed to make good his claim directly, but since he was a good soldier he won in the end. However, beating your enemies on the field of battle does not destroy all claims to the overall kingship: there is only one ineluctable argument—when there are no claimants! The next chapter suggests that this was the only alternative open to Kenneth.

The genealogy given here is not claimed to be absolutely

correct; it is only a suggestion that explains a number of points about the way the Picts could have married. What it demonstrates is that, despite its drawbacks, the ideal marriage system would have made sense of the matrilineal system that the Picts had adopted, for better or worse. The basic reason for this style of succession is where one has a trading society based on slavery: when that disappears, so does the rationale.

Only a partial genealogy of the Scots is given (Figure 9), to show the parallels with the Pictish one. For various reasons it does not match absolutely, but it indicates some of the interrelationships between the Picts and the Scots which begin with Domnall Brecc (628-642) *at the same time* as the southern kingdom allies itself with Eanfrith, the Northumbrian refugee. The combined genealogy shows how the succession to the two kingdoms overlaps.

There is little doubt that the Scots knew the order of succession among the Picts, and if they were ambitious enough they also knew how to arrange marriages to ensure that they could achieve a satisfactory political alliance. It was far more difficult for the Picts to make a similar deal when they had partially gone over to patrilineal succession with Constantine. It is at this point that carefully arranged marriages became very critical to the succession: in fact there *is* only one way in which both crowns can be united and that is by a Scots king marrying a Pictish royal princess. Hence the odds are stacked against a Pictish takeover of the Scottish crown since only a Scotsman can do that! No pure Pict could claim simultaneous descent in the male and female line. Their fate was effectively sealed by the incompatible descent systems and so their only alternative was to claim Pictish sovereignty and hence a fight to the death—which eventually came.

Finally, a few thoughts are offered on the possible identification of the lineages of the Pictish kings with the Pictish symbols.

The royal genealogy presented above (Figure 8) is based on the assumption that there were four intermarrying lineages P, Q, R, and S which, if thought of as a royal macropit divided into moieties, would look like this:—

S+	Q*	Moiety 1 : royals
P	R	Moiety 2 : lesser chiefs

Likewise the kingdoms can be ranked (p.75)

X	W	Northern kingdom : superior
Y	Z	Southern kingdom : inferior

Thus if the ruling lineages in the different provinces intermarried in Class I times it would produce the following division in Pictland:

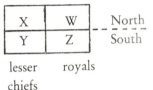

lesser   royals

chiefs

This arrangement would look like this geographically:

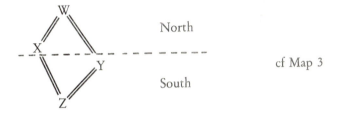

cf Map 3

and should be compared with marriage in a circle (Figure 6a):

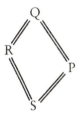

These diagrams indicate that the two royal lineages (Q and S) did not intermarry, since no son could succeed his father. They show that lineages Q and R are relatively close, as are lineages S and P, and also that there are links between the Northern and Southern kingdoms.

One possiblility is that P, Q, R and S are represented by the symbols *31, 8, 5* and *45.* In terms of spatial distribution and dualism (Table 4b) this would be:

5	*8*
45	*31*

North : geometric
South : animal

Left ⦙ Right

As a macropit marriage alliance system it would read:

45	*8*
31	*5*

royals
lesser chiefs

South ⦙North
Animal ⦙Geometric

In Class II times, the political boundary between the Northern and Southern kingdoms has shifted down to the Mounth, which suggests that the province Z (i.e. royal *45*) has become isolated. The Northern kingdom then consists of:

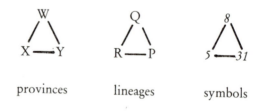

provinces   lineages   symbols

Such an arrangement for royal succession would work but it implies that province W, lineage Q and its symbol *8* is the only effective authority in the north. This triple alliance of *8, 5* and *31* would ensure that *8* retained the kingship, but if the Northern kingdom remained pagan (there being few Class II stones there) then an alternative lineage (e.g. *41*) might aspire to royal status instead of *45* to provide the fourth link in the marriage chain.

The situation in province Z (Circind) would be more critical since a single royal lineage cannot be self-sustaining *unless* it was patrilineal. The obvious solution would be to create three new provinces in the Southern kingdom to make up a royal macropit—this actually happened with the formation of Fotla, Fortriu and Fib. As for the provincial rulers, what better than simply replicating the old macropit and setting lineages *8, 5* and *31* in charge? These lineages would not be identical to those in the north but, rather, branches of the lineages brought south by Bridei (son of Bili) when he settled there. So again we find the triple alliance exerting its influence in the Southern Christian kingdom for these three symbols are predominant on the Class II stones and are especially associated with depictions of horsemen. A significant difference is that there are very few bridewealth symbols (24) on Class II stones, which suggests that the hierarchy is not so rigid and has become more flexible.

Hence in the Southern kingdom the once powerful lineage *8* is no longer supreme, and this might have tempted some of its members to try to persuade the king (lineage S) to go over to patrilinearity, for this would subtly allow them to regain a monopoly of power. Thus by offering potential wives to the royal Southern lineage they would disqualify themselves from the kingship *but*, at an appropriate time, when the new king's father, wife and sons were all from lineage *8*, with the blessing of the Church they might have succeeded in persuading the king to adopt patrilinearity. Once that was done, then lineage *8* would be in power for ever! An additional spur would be the prospect of uniting with the Northern kingdom, already ruled by lineage *8* in Class II times, so that a single Pictish kingdom would be on the cards. It is likely that some such Machiavellian design lay behind the shift to patrilinearity, rather than it being the personal whim of one monarch. At all events, the development of kingship in both kingdoms led to the same end: *one* kingly lineage.

The identification of the two royal lineages as being *8* and *45* can only be tentative. What is called for is a careful study of the size, style and location of these two designs, besides examining the non-symbolic designs on the Class II stones, especially the horsemen. A categorization of these two symbol in terms of their elaboration, on the lines suggested by Stevenson, may enable us to determine which members of a particular lineage were royals and which were commoners. It follows from the argument in Part I that there are only two royal lineages and these must have had their distinguishing symbols inscribed on the stones. However, these symbol pairs do not refer to individuals, so it means that we cannot associate a symbol stone with any particular king: the stones with royal symbols only indicate the royal alliances. Now the main object of the symbol stones was to order the alliances of the king's subordinates, and so it is possible that the royal houses were free to take up new alliances. The kings may have been polygynous and have had several sets of alliances besides the 'official' alliance since this would not upset the royal macropit arrangement upon which succession depended; because polygynous alliances are not hereditary and are only personal alliances of the king. This being so, such extra alliances would not be recorded on stone, and we are therefore unable to determine if the Picts were polygynous. Even had the Picts been polyandrous it would make no difference, since all the children born to a royal princess would belong to her lineage anyway, no matter who was the father.

To sum up, although we can assign symbols to the royal lineages, we cannot use the symbol stones to elucidate the Pictish royal genealogy, other than suggesting *where* royal alliances were first cemented. As it is likely that the royal court perambulated the kingdom and stayed at the royal demesnes, we might be able to locate these by royal alliance stones. Furthermore, it is probable that these would be the places where other alliances were made and so an examination of clusters of stones might reveal some interesting correspondences. A comparison of Tables 2 and 14 should indicate where to start looking.

The purpose of this digression has been to suggest that we can relate the Pictish genealogies with the symbol stones—a necessity if we are to make total sense of Pictish society. The subsequent chapters in Part II also aim to contribute to a holistic view of the Picts by bringing into focus certain aspects of Pictish society which have hitherto been treated independently. The full significance of these aspects can only be achieved by comparison with the symbol stones.

Class III : Sueno's Stone   (Table 2E:6)

CHAPTER 2

Sueno's Stone

Sueno's Stone is a Class III monument and is the largest of its type in Scotland, being 20 feet tall. It stands near Forres in Morayshire, the central area of Northern Pictland, not far from the old fortress at Burghead.[22] The stone is covered with carved figures in profuse numbers and is quite unlike any other monument. This uniqueness raises many questions: What do the scenes depicted represent? Who erected the stone and why? The common attribution to the Danish king Sueno (Sven) is most unlikely since he lived c. 1000 A.D. and this ascription was made in the 18th Century when *all* the Pictish monuments were called Danish! The carving and design is definitely Pictish and could be from the 9th or 10th century. There is little chance that it was put up by the Norsemen who were harrying the land at this time, neither is it likely to have been erected to commemorate their defeat by the Picts. The story it tells is far more sinister.

Apparently the stone had lain buried for many years but it was re-erected in the 18th century with the many-sculptured side facing east and with the cross towards the west. As the east face is the principal side of the monument, it will be examined first. Its proportions and composition are intricately balanced in a quite astonishing way.

The height of the monument is 7 times its average width, while each of the four major panels on the east face is divided in *exact* multiples of the width! As Figure 11 shows: Panel *A* is twice the width, Panel *B* three times the width while Panels *C* and *D* are equal to the width. It can also be seen that Panels *A* and *B* are subdivided in a regular way (in units 3/5 of the width, labelled *a*), with the exception of the middle section of the top panel (unit *b* is 4/5 of the width).

The ratio of these units a:b:w is 3:4:5—the dimensions of the famous Golden Triangle! Since these Golden numbers were used to map out the surface area of the stone it is not surprising that they also dictated the composition of the figures involved, cf Figures 10 and 11.

A brief description of the panel sections follows:

A1 : (badly weathered). 2 standing figures on either side of a central figure? Cf B1 below.

A2 : 2 horsemen above 3 others riding to the left.

A3 : 3 horsemen riding to the left.

B1 : 2 standing figures on either side of a crowned and kilted figure, holding up swords.

B2 : 2 sets of 4 warriors fighting.

B3 : 7 decapitated figures and their separated heads which lie above and below 2 pairs of fighting warriors. In the centre, a man with a staff faces a Celtic bell and 3 other men with staves on the other side. Below this is a man with raised sword who has decapitated one of the prisoners; behind him are three trumpeters.

B4 : 3 groups of 2 small horsemen are pursued to the left by 2 groups of 4 warriors.

C : beneath a semi-circular arch (a tent?) lie the decapitated bodies of 7 more men and their heads. All around them fight 8 pairs of warriors, the central bottom pair also depict a decapitation.

D1 : 4 warriors are pursued leftwards by 4 other warriors.

D2 : (now below the concrete base). This just repeats D1.

At the centre of the stone we find, presumably, its most important message: the seven decapitated men with their feet ranged up towards the left and the four figures around the bell *which is at the dead centre of the monument!* On the reverse side there is a gigantic cross and, curiously enough, the bell is exactly opposite the centre of the stem of the cross at the point where the decoration on the side panels of the stone divide. This is but one of a series of coincidences in the design—it was very well thought out! The ingenuity displayed in the construction of the overall design, quite apart from the sheer size of the monument (all 7 tons

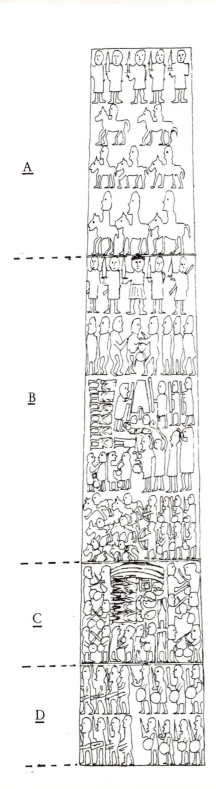

A

B

C

D

Figure 10 : Sueno's Stone

of it), indicates that it was a very important piece of propaganda. The question is—for whom?

The two repeated scenes of execution of seven prisoners was clearly meant as a warning of the fate awaiting the defeated army fleeing to the left if they should attempt another uprising. There now emerges a fascinating fact about these warring parties: their total numbers. Taking all the instances of conflict and dividing them into left and right factions (the left are circled in Figure 11a) while assigning all the triumphant figures to the right side— obviously—we obtain Figure 11b. As may be seen, the living left figures are just half the numbers of the victorious right. What is significant is that *these totals are precise multiples of seven!* The defeated side have 28 (7×4) plus 14 (7×2) dead, making a total of 42 (7×6) as opposed to the winners 56 (7×8). This makes a grand total of 98 figures or (7×14 or 7×2×2), which is a large number of 7's. [23]

The most likely explanation of Sueno's stone is that it relates the victory of the Christian Scots over the pagan Picts.

The two sets of 7 decapitated prisoners, their hands being bound, can only refer to the 7 royal Pictish lineages—one set from Northern Pictland (where the stone is erected) and one set from Southern Pictland (under a tent). The 5 triumphant warriors would be the Scots: the king of Dalriada (Kenneth) and his four henchmen from the southern provinces of S. Circind, Fotla, Fortriu and Fib.

Closer examination of the grouping of figures shows that the number 7 plays a crucial role in the actual composition. Thus there are:

(a) 7 sets of figures moving from the right-hand side to the left (*A*2, *A*3, *B*4, *D*1, *D*2)

(b) 14 figures retreating from the centre to the left (*B*4, *D*1, *D*2)

(c) 28 figures are in combat (*B*2, *B*3, *C*)

(d) 14 corpses (*B*1, *C*)

(e) the remaining two sets of upright figures (*A*1, *B*1) and two other sets (*B*3)

(f) 42 figures if those in (a) and (e) above are added together

(g) 42 figures of (b), (d) and the left-hand side of (c) are summed

(h) 14 more figures on the right-hand side than on the left— deriving from (c).

The other striking fact about the groups of figures involved is that they are *all* arranged in sets of 8 *except* for the two sets of 5

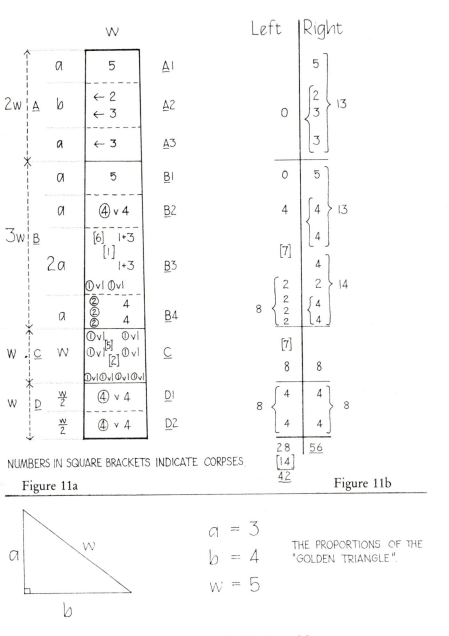

NUMBERS IN SQUARE BRACKETS INDICATE CORPSES.

Figure 11a

Figure 11b

THE PROPORTIONS OF THE "GOLDEN TRIANGLE".

$a = 3$
$b = 4$
$w = 5$

Figure 11 : Sueno's Stone—distribution of figures

(*A*1, *B*1) and the sets of 7 (*B*3, *C*). This suggests that these exceptions must be related to each other in some opposing way: triumph and defeat! In addition, these two opposing sides are similar in being dualistically organized.

This frequent use of pairs of figures is probably due to the dualistic division of authority in Pictland whereby every chief had his sub-chief. This pattern was also reflected in earlier days when the kingship alternated between the Northern and Southern kingdoms.

In order to make sense of the scenes depicted, we need to have some idea about how the Scots and Picts organized their military lines of command. If we assume that dual leadership was the order of the day, then, *on the basis* of the contenders shown on the stone, we can construct the following model of the two armies, of Fig 12.

It will be seen that the Scots army is equally balanced but that the Picts are not—the North has no infantry and the South no cavalry! This may well reflect the situation at the time of battle, but it is highly unlikely to have been the true case; but, remember, this stone is a piece of propaganda!

Panel *A* has the five Scots kings in overall triumph (also repeated in B1) while their victorious cavalry sweep all before them.

Panel *B* is the central one and clearly has the most important message. Again the five Scots kings (*B*1) watch the conflict between the sub-kings of the four Northern Pictish provinces (Cat, Fidach, Ce and N. Circind) and the four Scottish provinces (S. Circind, Fotla, Fortrui and Fib)—(*B*2). Panel *B*3 is the heart of Sueno's stone and depicts the execution of the Paramount king of Northern Pictland while his six confrères lie bound and beheaded.

This judicial execution is accompanied by the tolling of a bell and a fanfare of trumpets. The central position of the bell in the composition suggests that this was also a triumph for Christianity in putting down the pagan Picts. The four figures around the bell could be bishops holding their wands of office. The tongue of the bell can be seen hanging between a curious cut-away section in the bell which must have produced an odd clang. To the bottom left of the panel, two Pictish champions fight their Scottish counterparts. In panel *B*4, the small Pictish cavalry (on Shetland ponies?) are chased from the field by the Scottish infantry.

Panel *C* sees the Paramount king of Southern Pictland beheaded, with his six kings and sub-kings lying executed under a tent-like structure. All around, a battle rages between the champions and leaders of the Picts and the Scottish infantry.

Panel *D* shows the retreat of the remaining Pictish infantry *leaders* in the face of the victorious Scottish infantry, and parallels

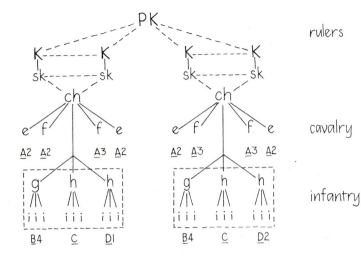

SCOTS

rulers

cavalry

infantry

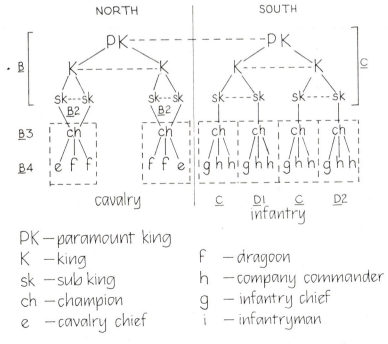

PICTS

NORTH | SOUTH

cavalry

infantry

PK — paramount king
K — king
sk — sub king
ch — champion
e — cavalry chief

f — dragoon
h — company commander
g — infantry chief
i — infantryman

Figure 12 : The Scots and Picts line of command

B4 where the cavalry is routed—thus indicating that panels C and D should be read together.

Despite the two execution scenes, this is no mere repetition of a single event, as the accompanying figures show. Since the stone was erected in the heartland of the Northern Picts, and as the central message is panel B, it follows that this scene relates to them. It may be that the Scots threw all their cavalry and some of their infantry against the Northern Picts who, strangely, have no infantry! Panel C is also curious in that the victims lie under an awning while only their chiefs battle away outside—without any cavalry.

Of course the odds were stacked against the defeated Picts, but how did it come about that they lost on their home ground? The answer lies with the arrival of a new force on the scene—the Norse! In 839, the Norsemen defeated the men of Fortriu and killed the Pictish king Eoganan (Uuen, son of Oengus, cf Fig.8)—the last recorded king of the Picts. This gave Kenneth MacAlpin his chance to move into the weakened Southern kingdom and take over as its legitimate ruler over the provinces of Fotla, Fortriu, Fib and Circind, and to set up his own vassal-kings in charge.

The threat of fresh Norse incursions might have encouraged the Picts to seek an alliance with the Scots against these invaders. As the Southern Picts were also Christian they could hope that the Scots would support them against the heathen Norse. A conference of all the Pictish and Scottish nobility to prepare a war plan could have taken place at Scone when—as legend has it—Kenneth caused all the Pictish nobility to be murdered at a banquet. Such could be the significance of Panel C, where the 7 Pictish lineage heads are executed under a tent while their retainers are fought off and driven away (Panel D). There was no Pictish cavalry or infantry present at a conference of course: this was no battle, just a slaughter. After this Kenneth was free to appoint four Scottish kings to Southern Pictland.

This event left only the pagan Northern Picts as the chief contenders to Kenneth's claim to sovereignty over the whole of Pictland. Kenneth could either bide his time and wait for another Norse attack upon the Northern Picts or, better still, encourage the Norse to make an invasion in return for certain considerations. If, then, the Norse attacked the fort at Burghead in 842 A.D. and started to harry the country, the Picts might well have asked Kenneth for help which he falsely promised. A pitched battle between the Northern Picts and the Norsemen could have resulted in the Pictish infantry being again massacred, while the Pictish leaders fled on horseback and fell into the trap as Kenneth's cavalry descended upon them. The pagan nobility are put to death and their remaining cavalry routed. Part of the package deal could be that Kenneth ceded his claim to Northern Pictland in return for no Norse attacks upon his southern kingdom! [24]

In whatever way the Northern Picts were defeated, it effectively ended their threat to Kenneth, since they fell into disarray after the Norse began to occupy their territory. Only Morayshire remained independent of the Scots for a few more centuries and culminated in Macbeth's seizure of the Scottish throne (1040-57). Because this area was still a potential threat, and to keep it in submission, Kenneth caused Sueno's stone to be erected at Forres as a reminder of what had happened—the complete extinction of the Pictish nobility. The fact that the stone was executed in a well-known style: Class II (without the pagan symbols) and replete with the mystical number 7, would not be lost upon the Picts. Such a use of a traditional Pictish way of proclaiming authoritative and politically-binding decisions would not be pure accident.

It is curious that the cross on the stone at present faces west since normally they are towards the east, but this might have been a mistake when the stone was re-erected later. It would make far better sense if the cross faced east because then the Scottish victory scene would face the Picts in the Moray Firth area while the rout of the Picts towards the left of the stone would point them towards the north—their homeland!

The reverse of the stone also has its message: there is the enormous interlaced cross which is without parallel in Pictish monumental sculpture. Under this Christian cross there is a curious scene in which two elongated figures, each supported by an acolyte, bend over a central person (alas, much defaced). These five figures are obviously engaged in some significant activity under the sign of the cross. The exaggerated size of the two major figures (both extremely tall and thin, apparently unclothed and having pigtails) could be supernatural agents, e.g. archangels. They stretch out their hands over the head of the central figure. Is this a blessing from on high or a coronation? Who but (the understandably defaced) king Kenneth could be the object of such devotion?

CHAPTER 3

Oghams and the language of the Picts

Some thirty examples of Ogham inscriptions have been discovered on all three Classes of Pictish monuments, as well as on plain stones and on bone knife-handles. These inscriptions have all been transliterated into Roman script but, unfortunately, the results are quite meaningless and have given rise to the belief that the Picts spoke some unknown tongue.

It is generally agreed that the Picts borrowed the Irish Ogham alphabet and used it for their own purposes from the 8th and 9th centuries A.D. Basically, there are some twenty letters, which consist of one to five strokes made at different angles to a medial line (*fleasg*) and they are read from the bottom, vertically upwards cf Fig.13. Unlike the Irish Oghams which follow set formulae and are generally memorials to the dead, the Pictish Oghams are variable in length and seem to contain no standard formulae. Half the Pictish Oghams occur on symbol stones and hence, if they really were funerary monuments, the use of Oghams would nicely complement the symbols. However, it has already been shown that the Pictish symbols serve other functions and since the Oghams display no obvious inscriptions like 'To X, set up by Y, his son', it is also likely that the Oghams are not funerary statements either.

The problem can be better explained by looking at the inscriptions themselves. Fig 14 shows all the major inscriptions—some fragmentary Oghams are omitted.[25] Although the Oghams are set out to be read from left to right (our convention), it should

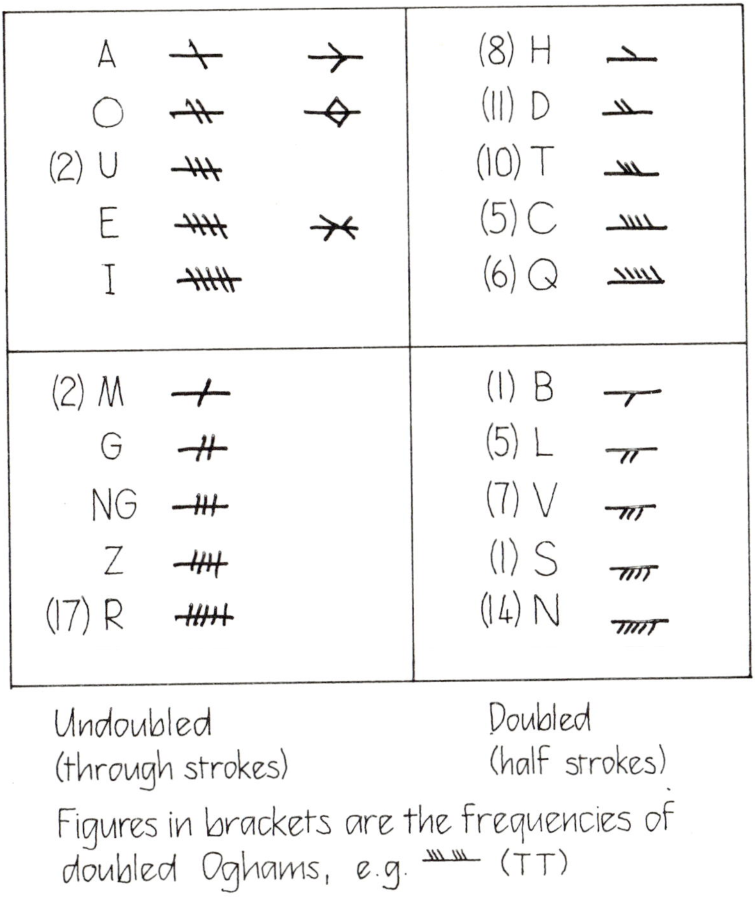
A
O
(2) U
E
I
(8) H
(11) D
(10) T
(5) C
(6) Q
(2) M
G
NG
Z
(17) R
(1) B
(5) L
(7) V
(1) S
(14) N
Undoubled
(through strokes)
Doubled
(half strokes)
Figures in brackets are the frequencies of
doubled Oghams, e.g. (TT)

Figure 13 : Pictish Oghams

be remembered that in fact they are read from bottom to top. Hence the page should be turned through a right-angle to gain a correct view, the left-hand side being at the bottom of the page. The translations of these Oghams are given in Table 28. It must be stressed that the renderings of these Oghams given here are only an attempt to give an overview of the inscriptions, since there are many difficulties in deciphering the strokes. This, then, is the kind of result that linguists have produced for us, even if some of the details are incorrect. It can be readily seen that the translations do not leave us any the wiser, give or take a few errors.

ABOYNE

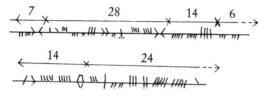

ALTYRE

AUQUHOLLIE

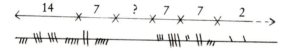

BIRSAY

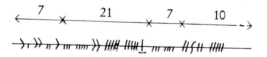

BRANDSBUTT

Figure 14 : The Ogham inscriptions [26]

BRESSAY

BRODIE

A

B

C

BUCKQUOY

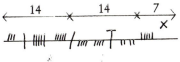

BURRIAN

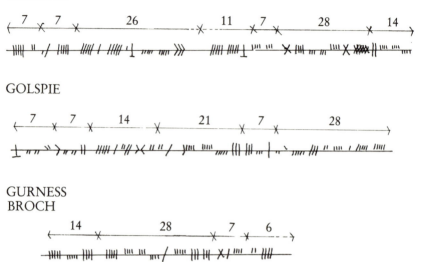

GOLSPIE

GURNESS
BROCH

INCHYRA

A

B

C

KEISS BAY

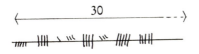

LATHERON

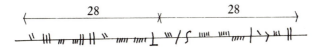

LOGIE
ELPHINSTONE

LUNNASTING

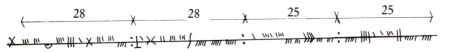

NEWTON

N.UIST

ST NINIANS

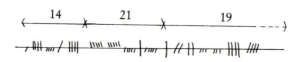

SCOONIE

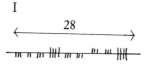

WEETING

I

II

Name	Ogham groups	strokes	strokes total	strokes above/below *fleasg*
ABOYNE	22	7,28,14,6→	55	27/42
	14	14,24→	38	34/24
ALTYRE	30	14,21,30→	65	43/43
AUQUHOLLIE	13	14,7,(?),7,7,2→	37	21/30
BIRSAY	15	7,21,7,10→	45	27/45
BRANDSBUTT	13	14,7,19→	40	31/33
BRESSAY	48	14,14:14,7,14,14:42,42	161	104/114
BRODIE A	7	10→,14	24	16/16
B	19	7,14,21,6→	48	28/36
C	16	14,20→,11→,5→	50	37/39
BUCKQUOY	12	14,14,7	35	23/22?
BURRIAN	31	7,7,26→,←11,7,28,14	100	79/77
GOLSPIE	34	7,7,14,21,7,28	84	61/49
GURNESS BROCH	16	14,28,7,6→	55	46/37
INCHYRA A	30	7,7,7,28,7,7,7,12→	82	71/48
B	16	14,48→	62	43/54
C	4	14	14	10/11
KEISS BAY	8	30→	30	25/23
LATHERON	20	28,28	56	35/35
LOGIE ELPHINSTONE	12	7,14	21	16/6
LUNNASTING	40	28:28:25:25	106	61/67
NEWTON	26	7,28,39→,7,14	95	51/84
N.UIST	11	14,21,3→	38	31/15
ST NINIANS	18	14,21,19→	54	33/44
SCOONIE	10	14,21	35	21/30
WEETING I	9	28	28	14/22
II	12	21,12→	33	20/26

Table 27 : The Ogham strokes

→ indicates an *incomplete* inscription

M

			References
*1	ABERNETHY	QMI	ECMS 309
2	ABOYNE	NEHHTVROBBACCENNEVV MAQQOTALLUORRH	ECMS 189
3	ALTYRE	AMMAQQTALLV LV BAHHRRASSUDDS	ECMS 136
4	AUQUHOLLIE	VUUNON ITEDOVOB B	ECMS 204
5	BIRSAY I	(M)ONNORRANRR	
*	II	BQI A B	
6	BRANDSBUTT	IRATADDOARENS	ECMS 506/7
7	BRESSAY	CRROSCC : NAHHTVVDDADDS : DATTRR : ANN	ECMS 8/9
		BENNISES : MEQQDDRROANN	
8	BRODIE A)	VON...ECCO..	ECMS 132/3
	B)	RGINNGCHQODTOSOMBS...	
	C)	EDDARRNONN... TTI... GNG..	
9	BUCKQUOY	(E)TMIQAVSALLC	PSAS 108, 221/
10	BURRIAN	IDBMIRRHANNURRACTKEVVCERROCCS	ECMS 24
*11	CUNNINGSBURGH I	IRU	ECMS 16
	II	.. EHTECONMORS	ECMS 16
		...DOV...DDRS	
	III	ETTECA...	RCAM : Orkn
		..V: DATTUA	Shetland no.113
		...RTT..	
*12	DUNADD	HCSD. T.. V. NH. T	Antiquity xxxix
		L....VQRRHMDNHQ	
13	GOLSPIE	ALLHHALLORREDDMAQQNUUVVHRRE.RR	ECMS 48/50
14	GURNESS BROCH	INEITTEMEN MATS	RCAM no.263
15	INCHYRA A)	ETTLIETRENOIDDORS	PSAS xcii, 33
		..UHTUOAGED...	
	B)	INEHHETESTIEQ... INNE	
16	KEISS BAY	NEHTETRI...	ECMS 28
17	LATHERON	DUV NODNNATMAQQNAHHTO...	PSAS xxxviiii, 5
18	LOGIE		
	ELPHINSTONE	CALTCHU	ECMS 176
19	LUNNASTING	ETTECUHETTS : AHEHHTTANNN : HCCVVEVV : NEHHTONS	ECMS 17
20	NEWTON	IDDARQNNNVORRENN IKU(A) IOSIE	ECMS 197/8
21	N. UIST	M..QUNTENAC..T	PSAS lxvi 56
22	ST NINIANS	(...) BESMEQQNANAMMOVVEZ	ECMS 18
23	SCOONIE	EDDARRNONN	ECMS 347
24	WEETING I	ULUCUVUTE	Antiquaries Jour
	II	GEDEVEM...DOS	xxxii,17
*25	WHITENESS	...VNDAR	PSAS lxxxi, 191-

Table 28 : OGHAMS: Transliterated
Triplets underlined (i.e. of the form: xyy)
* Omitted from further analysis because of their fragmentary state

The object of this chapter is to show that the Pictish Oghams were *not* used as an alphabet in the conventional sense but had quite a different purpose. The attempts by linguists to abstract words from the inscriptions will be discussed below.

It is very important to notice the geographical distribution of these Ogham inscriptions: with four exceptions (Inchyra, Abernethy, Scoonie and Weeting), *all* the Oghams are in the later Northern kingdom of Pictland, especially the Northern Isles (Orkney and Shetland). The significance of this is that it was a region where Christianity was least strong and where the sway of the post-685 southern Pictish kingdom was weakest. This was an area where belief in magic still held the symbol stones in high regard. Secondly, we are dealing with the use of Ogham scripts of differing periods (there are open and closed Oghams) upon differing classes of monuments. There is no proof that the Oghams were inscribed at the same time as the monuments were erected—they could all have been later. It should be remembered that less than 10% of all Pictish monuments have Oghams inscribed upon them.

In this Northern kingdom there is no clear evidence that the monuments of Class I, II and III follow a strict temporal sequence— they could all have been erected within 50 years of each other, *in any order!* The reason for this assertion is that the Northern kingdom probably remained pagan long after the area south of the Mounth had been converted to Christianity. While it seems fairly clear that the Picts erected the Class II stones, there is no reason to conclude that they were responsible for the Class III stones in the north—consider the similarities between the Class III stones in the Northern Isles and those at Whithorn in Dumfries! It is also interesting that bind Oghams are mainly found in the Northern Isles as well as up the Tay on Class III stones—this could have been a late development. Perhaps mainland Scotland used open Oghams in the Class I/II period whereas the islands took up the idea later: such an idea squares with the notion that Oghams first spread to the Inverness area from the west before they were used in the north and east. At all events, the use of Oghams was not universal and only seems to have served a limited purpose—for whatever reason. The Oghams might all have a common function, but this was quite distinct from the symbols which were already in use; the Oghams always take second place to the symbols and are usually badly executed, aesthetically speaking.

One point of entry into the meaning of the Oghams is to examine their use on artefacts: one spindle whorl (Buckquoy) and three knife handles (Broch of Gurness, N.Uist and Weeting). Obviously these inscriptions cannot have anything to do with funerary usages, but only with something that is everyday and commonplace. The interesting thing about these artefacts is that they are personal and portable. The spindle whorl is most likely to have been a female object, while the knives could have belonged to a male or female. In our age of personalized objects, we could assume that the obvious reason for writing on an object is to put one's name on it; but in the 8th century would one have gone to such lengths? Were there not other things more important than claiming possession? As these are objects used every day, would not the meaning of the Oghams also have a *useful* function? What is remarkable about these Ogham inscriptions is the number of strokes:

Buckquoy (spindle whorl)	5×7 = 35 strokes
N.Uist (knife handle)	6×7 = 42 strokes*
Broch of Gurness (knife handle)	8×7 = 56 strokes*
Weeting (knife handle) I	4×7 = 28 strokes
II	5×7 = 35 strokes*

The common denominator is 7, of course. Sequences of 7, 14 and 28 strokes can be found in these examples, but unfortunately three of these artefacts are damaged (marked*) and so the *final* total given here is a reconstruction. However, the point is established that there are *clear* groupings of strokes into 7's.

The argument can also be extended to the stone monuments, for we find that half the Ogham inscriptions consist of multiples of 7 strokes too! Again, alas, many inscriptions are damaged but not sufficiently to distort the general finding that there are distinctive patternings of strokes into 7's, cf Fig. 14. Indeed, it needs only the addition of one or two 'missing' Oghams to these stones in order for nearly every inscription to conform to this rule of 7. One justification for suggesting these amendments is the relative ease with which it can be done, besides having the support of the 'punctuated' inscriptions of Bressay and Lunnasting, cf Fig. 14.

A further common feature of these inscriptions is the use of triplets of strokes in the form xyy, where one Ogham (x) is followed by a pair of other Oghams (yy). This is clear in the transliterations, cf Table 28. The interesting point is that generally no cross-stroke (other than R:⫽⫽) is doubled, only the half-strokes (i.e. those not crossing the *fleasg*) are repeated, cf Figures 13 and 14.

The only argument that the Oghams are a written form of language[30] is that presented by linguists, *viz* the appearance of certain 'words', among the 300-odd Ogham characters that exist. These words are *maqq, cross, Naiton* and *Edern*. Their occurrence is as follows:

<u>*maqq*</u>

Class	Location	Letters	No. of strokes
II	Aboyne	MAQQO......	14
III	Altyre	AMMAQQ......	14
II	Golspie	...DMAQQ.....	14
II	Latheron	...TMAQQNAHHTO/	28

<u>*cross*</u>

III	Bressay	CRROSCC/	28
III	Burrian	..(C)ERROSCC/	28

<u>*Naiton*</u>

II	Aboyne	NEHHT....	14
III	Bressay	NAHHTV...	14
II	Latheron	..TMAQQNAHHTO/	28
	Lunnasting	NEHHT...	14

<u>*Edern*</u>

II	Brodie	} EDDAR(RN).....	14
II	Scoonie		

Table 29 : The Ogham 'words'

All these four 'words' contain a triad (xyy), besides which they are part of a string of 14 strokes when they *begin* an inscription but are a part of a 28 string when they *end* an inscription.

The 'abstraction' of *these* words from their context seems highly dubious when there are other sequences, e.g. ANN, ETT, ALL, etc. that could have been chosen. As can be seen, the particular 'words' that the linguists have singled out are *not* that unambiguous, and it may be doubted if they have made a case at all. Thus despite Wainwright's claim that there are easily recognized words, the fact is that they are *not* that easy to recognize. The four words given as evidence do not amount to much, since the other 85% of the Oghams tell us very little.

The curious fact that the only 'words' elicited by the linguists should always be embedded in sequences of either 14 or 28 strokes suggests that *numbers* are more important than letters! It is also rather odd that these inscriptions occur in one unbroken chain and with such a high proportion of triplets. These triplets xyy, xxy, xyx, yxx constitute ¾ of the Ogham sequences. It is the triplet xyy that is largely responsible for any pronounceability that the transliterations have, since the x is often a through stroke— generally a vowel. The significance of the triplets will be discussed later but, in the context of these Pictish Oghams being regarded as a written language, these triplets provide an insuperable barrier to translation. An inspection of Table 28 shows there are *far* too many consonants for the transliterations to be pronounced. Because the Picts made full use of the 'vowel' strokes, it is therefore inevitable that *some* triplets will create monosyllables that resemble *some* Irish monosyllables—just by chance—since there are a large number of monosyllables in Indo-European tongues. Even the famous MAQQ example only occurs four times and, as will be explained later, this may have been dictated by other consider- ations. It is, though, the very lack of polysyllables that is puzzling if this is a language. Even had Pictish been purely monosyllabic then one would have expected sequences of monosyllables, but they do not occur either.

As has been pointed out above, the four 'words' so far 'discovered'—two nouns and two names—are somewhat contrived considering that, at best, collectively they amount to less than 5% of possible monosyllables, had the inscriptions been written that way. To suggest that the finding of these 'words' in the currently- admitted mish-mash of letters is a great achievement makes one wonder whether linguists have not gravely prejudged the issue of the Oghams. Their simplistic assumption that Oghams = Language is understandable but not, therefore, excusable. Should they not have analysed the structure of the strokes, the sequences, the triplets and go on to show *whether or not* the Pictish Oghams could ever have been a written language? Simply to dismiss he Pictish engravers as incompetent in using the Oghams to represent their language (as does O'Rahilly, p.375) hardly helps to excuse our own incompetence in deciphering the inscriptions! [27]

If we depart radically from the linguistic approach and just consider the strokes, viewed vertically, it will be seen that the number of horizontal strokes (a peculiarity of Pictish Oghams) is roughly equal on either side of the medial line, while the downward-pointing strokes are commonest but the upward- pointing strokes are fewest and tend to occur on the left-hand side. Why this disparity?

The differences in these frequencies is related to the use of full strokes. *All* the half strokes point downwards. If one considers the frequently occurring triplet xyy then it usually begins with a through stroke (a vowel) followed by two (consonantal) half strokes. The only other through strokes used are M and R, which give upward strokes to the left. Naturally, the vowels should, correspondingly, give upward strokes on the right of the medial line, but they rarely do as they are mainly written horizontally. Thus it is as if upward strokes are badly thought of!

It is not possible to fully explain the significance of the direction of the strokes, since ⅔ of our inscriptions are damaged or incomplete. By and large, one can state that the numbers of strokes on either side of the medial line are unequal but there is a tendency for them to be either a multiple of 5 or 11. Perhaps, if direction is important, then the downward strokes are good, the horizontal ones neutral while the upward direction is bad—assuming the strokes have some predictive power which they might have, if the Oghams were calendrical.

I should like to hypothesize that the Oghams are indeed calendrical markers intended for the highly important task of working out the annual Pictish ritual calendar. Like other Celts (for I hold that the Picts were in fact P-Celts) they wished to know when to celebrate the beginning of Spring, Summer, Autumn and Winter—or, to give these quarter days their common (current) names, the time for the fire festivals of Bride, Beltane, Lammas and Hallowmass. Today these feast days are fixed on February 1, May 1, August 1 and November 1.

We know that the Celts used a 28-day lunar calendar, but this would not help them to work out the quarter days, since these depend on the sun's position at the solstices and equinoxes. Hence it is only by *counting* days, not moons, that one can arrive at the correct answer. This problem can be elucidated by considering the quarter days in relation to the sun's position by starting on November 1—the Celtic New Year's Day.

These four quarter days were the main Celtic festivals and were later taken over and incorporated into the Christian calendar—a system that was only fully accepted in Britain in the 18th Century for regulating the civil year! There are 91 days between each festival, with a 3-week period before and after each feast day; whether these intercalary dates had any significance is an open question, but they do enter into the computation of the calendar. The principal astronomical events of the year—the autumn equinox (heralding winter), the winter solstice (the turning point of the year), the spring equinox (announcing summer) and the summer solstice (marking the decline of the year) were noted, but not

Event	Date	Interval	
Hallowmass	November 1		
	November 22	49 { 21 days / 28	
Winter solstice	December 20		91 days
	January 10	42 { 21 / 21	
Bride	February 1		
	February 22	49 { 21 / 28	
Spring equinox	March 20		91 days
	April 10	42 { 21 / 21	
Beltane	May 1		
	May 22	49 { 21 / 28	
Summer solstice	June 20		91 days
	July 11	42 { 21 / 21	
Lammas	August 1		
	August 22	49 { 21 / 28	
Autumn equinox	September 20		91 days
	October 10	42 { 21 / 21	
Hallowmass	November 1		

Table 30 : The important calendrical events

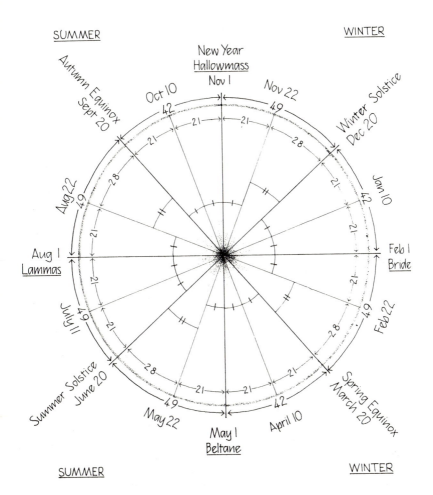

Figure 15 : The Pictish Calendar

celebrated as they were by the Norsemen. It is interesting that both the Celts and the Norse celebrated their festival with bonfire—though at different times.

There were exactly 49 days between the beginning of a festival and the next solstice/equinox while there were just 42 days between that astronomical event and the next festival. Thus the whole quarterly cycle is 49+42 = 91 days or $(7 \times 7) + (7 \times 6) = (7 \times 13)$ days. Hence their year was $4 \times (7 \times 13) = 28 \times 13 = 364$ days—just 30 hours out of true! Of course, this means that their calendar slips away from the sidereal year and needs periodical revision. Nowadays, people are no longer surprised at the sophistication of their remote ancestors with numbers and astronomical observations so there is no need to make a strong case that the Picts were quite as accomplished a mere millenium ago. It is true we have no extant Pictish calendar, but we still have the quarter days. This fixing of dates for ritual purposes has always been a universal feature of mankind, as has been the symbolic manipulation of numbers. There is no reason why we should deny the Picts mathematical skills, for it is hoped to show that the Oghams were indeed used as sophisticated calculators.

We have previously discussed the importance of the number 7 in Pictish thought with regard to the symbols where 7,14 and 28 figure prominently. While 28 is an important astronomical number for the lunar cycle it is not helpful for working out periods of 49 and 42 days—here one must resort to the lowest common multiple of 7.

To substantiate the numerical use of Oghams, it is necessary to try to present a complete a picture as possible of the Ogham inscriptions. As has been noted, there are 18 damaged inscriptions cf. Table 30 where the arrows denote possible missing strokes. These deficiencies are made up in Table 31, where a suggested addition of just *one* Ogham can bring most of these inscriptions to conform to the rule that the strokes should occur in sequences of multiples of 7. The astonishing thing about these amendments is how readily one can add the few strokes necessary to complete the sequence, without any forcing of the data. Even if these additions are rejected (and they are only 5% of the total) it is still surprising how well the inscriptions are capable of being sectioned into multiples of 7.

Name	strokes	total strokes	extra strokes needed
ABOYNE	7,28,14,7	56	+1
	42	42	+4
ALTYRE	14,21,35	70	+5
AUQUHOLLIE	14,7,7,7,7,7	49	+12 [+7+5]
BIRSAY	7,21,7,14	49	+4
BRANDSBUTT	14,7,21	42	+2
BRODIE A	14,14	28	+4
B	7,14,21,7	49	+1
C	14,21,14,7	56	+6 [+1+3+2]
BURRIAN	7,7,28,14,7,28,14	105	+5 [+2+3]
GURNESS BROCH	14,28,7,7	56	+1
INCHYRA A	7,7,7,28,7,7,7,14	84	+2
B	14,49	63	+1
KEISS BAY	35	35	+5
NEWTON	7,28,42,7,14	98	+3
N.UIST	14,21,7	42	+4
ST NINIANS	14,21,21	56	+2
WEETING II	21,14	35	+2

mean = 3

Table 31 : The 18 incomplete inscriptions with suggested additions underlined, cf Table 27

　　　The next question, is how do the Oghams help in determining the significant dates? If one looks first at the domestic Oghams, it will be seen that Buckquoy (spindle whorl) has a three-fold sequence: 14 + 14 + 7. For this to be used to calculate the length between festivals (91 days), one could postulate a three-fold division of the period:

1st	14 + 14 + 7 =	35
2nd	14 + 7 =	21
3rd	14 + 14 + 7 =	35
		91

The same line of reasoning would apply to Weeting II, i.e. 21 + 14 = 35. If we look at Aboyne and Newton (read backwards), they have the same format:

$$7 : 49 : 42$$

This translates as follows:

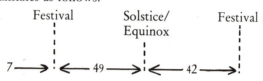

Here the sequence begins a week before the first festival.

The Bressay stone has the sequence: 28, 49, 42, 42. Again there is the 42 + 49 = 91 stroke element but there are longer pre- and post-warnings that are related to the astronomical markers.

There are many other ways of arranging this 91 day cycle, e.g.

a)   35 + 21 + 35
b)   35 + 56
c)   7 + (21 + 21) + (21 + 21)
d)   7 + (14 + 28) + (14 + 28)

All the above combinations are found in the Ogham inscriptions in one form or another, but it is clear that these inscriptions only had a limited span and remit, for none were annual calendars. This restricted scope is understandable, since it would have been difficult to keep track of every single day of the year when, in any case, it was only necessary to keep count of the 91 days between festivals. Even so, there had to be a way of counting the days since the Oghams could not be so used. The simplest ways of doing this are to make knots in a piece of string or to cut tally-marks on a piece of wood. Then a simple comparison with the inscription would place where one was in the ritual cycle. However, the Oghams had an additional property that knots and cuts lack—they could indicate, depending on the slant of the Ogham stroke, whether things would turn out well or otherwise on a particular day.

The function of these rare, and generally self-effacing, Ogham inscriptions would be to act as standards for calculating local festivals, for they could be copied by others onto wood or some portable item. It would seem likely that the Picts did have calendrical staves of wood (clog almanacks) like the later Christians to determine their holy days. So far none have been discovered, but it is noteworthy that a sixth of all the inscriptions are on portable objects!

With the exception of three stones: the Class I stone at Inchyra (Perthshire), the fragment from Abernethy (Perthshire) and the Class II stone at Scoonie (Fife), all the other Oghams are north of the Mounth in pagan territory, despite ¼ of them having a Christian cross upon them. The point is that in a pagan world the Ogham calendrical markers were their *only* calendars. The Christians, to the south, devised their own calendar of holy days. The Christian year was slightly different and stressed other dates, but it was not much different in principle except for the notorious problem of calculating Easter which had no fixed relation to the Spring equinox because it involved the full moon—as we all know to our cost!

Thus Oghams have a peculiar relevance to the Northern Picts in their remembering of their local festivals. Since Oghams were devised to be cut on wood originally, it seems most probable that this was their original use among the Picts and that it was later applied to stone. It is important to note that more than half the Ogham inscriptions do not occur on Pictish monuments at all while less than ⅓ are on symbol stones. Since the attempt to link the symbol stones with burials has been shown to be nebulous, it is even more unlikely that the Oghams could have anything to do with recording memorials to the dead. Attention should be drawn to the different ways in which the Ogham inscriptions are placed on the admitted Pictish stones. Class I Oghams tend to be boldly across the face of the stone, Class II Oghams are along the side of the symbol face while Class III Oghams tend to be along the edge of the slab. In other words, the Oghams are pushed into more and more insignificant places as one progresses through the series. If, as has been argued, these are written statements, then the Picts were being very discreet about the matter since, other than Class I stones, they gave absolutely no prominence to the Oghams. Besides which, most Oghams are executed in the most careless of styles that are quite incompatible with the high degree of skill shown on the rest of the monument. Never do we get an integrated Ogham inscription which is *part of the overall design* of the monument. Everthing argues for a later addition of these inscriptions to the Pictish monuments, and *hence* they have no relationship whatever with the purpose of these monuments. There seems no good reason, if Oghams were contemporary with the carving of the stones, why the Oghams were not equally well carved, for the Pictish masons were generally past masters at accomodating designs into their sculptures. It seems much more likely that the Oghams were inscribed on these stones because they were upright and there, by some local diviner for his own purpose, using the crudest of methods to inscribe his calculations.

In this discussion, no attention has been paid to the different styles of inscribing Oghams—open and closed forms—they have all been treated as one basic form. All the same there is a problem here if the Oghams stretch over many generations—how did they maintain consensus? This is a similar problem to the question of symbols. While it is easier to maintain that the symbols were limited in time, this is not possible with the Oghams since they seem *post hoc* and there are far fewer of them. As suggested above, perhaps there were wooden or bone exemplars that set the standard and maintained a certain consistency. This is one of the dangers of considering the whole *known* output of a particular entity, *viz* to assume that they form a complete unity of purpose. Hence trying to reconcile the various Ogham inscriptions assumes that they have an underlying identity—something that really has to be demonstrated rather than taken for granted. What my analysis has assumed is that the fundamental purpose of the Ogham inscriptions is to simply mark out days leading towards some important event. It is quite likely that there will be local variations and, indeed, there are few identical inscriptions and certainly no standard formulae.

My assumption about a core of meaning may be demonstrated by the universal presence of triplets. These are found in all styles of inscriptions. What, then, is the function of such triplets as xyy, yxx, etc? An analysis of the xyy triplet reveals the following frequency table:

		1	2	3	4	5	Totals x
	1,1,	-	1	4	3	5	13
	2,2	11	-	5	4	3	23
yy	3,3	7	4	-	6	1	18
	4,4	4	3	1	-	3	11
	5,5	16	5	2	8	-	31
	Totals	38	13	12	21	12	96

Table 32 : Frequency table of xyy triplets

The most revealing feature of this table is that the most frequent *total* numbers (i.e. the sum of x + y + y) are the prime numbers: 5, 7, and 11 since they, *alone*, account for 54% of all the triplets. The identical result is found if one adds in all the other triplets. It is clear from the above table that the commonest triplet is 1,5,5 (=11), while 5,5 is the commonest doubled Ogham. Perhaps it should be pointed out that the above table is biased in favour of prime numbers, since they amount to half the possible totals of x + y + y. Hence the triplets are a way of generating prime numbers, and this seems to have been its purpose.

The requirement that Ogham strokes should be grouped in multiples of 7 means additional strokes are normally needed to expand the triplets. This imposes a restraint on their use, since only six of the eight triplets containing 1 or 1,1 can form a simple 7—e.g. (4 + 1,1) + 1. All the other triplets (except 3 + 2,2) must be part of a 14 or higher stroke sequence. As Table 31 suggests, and as is found in practice, ⅓ of the sequences of strokes are in plain 7's while ⅓ are in 14's. Thus triplets are a good way of organizing basic sequences of 7 and 14 strokes. This structural constraint obviously affects the nature of the additional strokes that may be required, e.g. if we take (1,5,5) then there are just three strokes needed to make this a 14 stroke sequence: but there are four possibilities: 3, 2 + 1, 1 + 2, 1 + 1 + 1. Which combination will be chosen, and where it will be placed, are limited choices since e.g. (2+1) + (1+5+5) would give (2+1+1) + (5+5) which destroys the original triplet. Perhaps the paramount consideration in the correct choice depends on the overall direction of strokes on either side of the medial line.

The point being made above is that although Ogham building is complex it has, nevertheless, internal rules which governs its structure. The end result, while being outwardly calendrical, contains much subtle calculation. But why is it necessary to be so complicated if it is just a matter of counting 91 days? The answer is that this calendar, like the Chinese calendar, not only spells out the sequence of days but it also provides information about the character of each day - whether certain activities will prosper or not. [28]

Previous discussion has shown that prime numbers (especially) must have had an important role in the thinking of the dualistically-minded Picts. It will be recalled (Table 22) that odd numbers were assigned to the left, bad side and were unlucky, while the converse was true for even numbers. This characterization of numbers possessing lucky or unlucky properties is commonplace and, in fact, is still with us—consider the number 13!

Most societies attempt to predict the year's progress either through natural signs or by computation. Those that get involved in counting, inevitably come up against the curious properties of numbers. If we consider the first 100 numbers, then half are even (divisible by 2) while the other half are odd (indivisible by 2). Of the odd numbers, half are prime numbers (completely indivisible) and the other half are multiples of prime numbers and hence divisible. Naturally, most even numbers are formed by doubling up prime numbers and hence this makes prime numbers even more of a mystery since *they* cannot be divided yet they are constituents of most other numbers. It is this property of utter oddness that is likely to have convinced the Picts of the great mystical power of prime numbers.

Hence if 3 sets of strokes (xxy) add up to a prime number these 3 days may have extraordinary consequences—good or ill—the interpretation depending on the slant of the strokes. Thus the calendrical markings also serve predictive functions about the days: they act as divination tables. As with so many of these devices, they tend to become complicated and therefore *require* an expert to explain them! This justification has been met with before.

Figure 16 : The Newton Stone inscription

Note on the Newton Stone, Aberdeenshire

This famous stone bears both an Ogham inscription on its side and several rows of some unknown script on its face, cf Figure 16. The stone has been a constant puzzle to scholars as all attempts to decipher the special script have been in vain, yet it *must* have a meaning, possibly linked to the Ogham inscription. If we take another tack from the linguistic one and consider these these signs as numerical indicators, then a surprising order emerges.

Basically there are two types of sign in this special inscription; they may be characterized as either **λ** or Y whereby two prongs point down or up. For convenience's sake these two signs wll be denoted by A and U but they have no alphabetical connotation. There are 33 instances of these basic signs, plus 10 other signs that are 'neutral' inasmuch as they point equally up and down. These 10 signs will be called 'markers' and they are /, O, C, Θ and 卐

Southesk (p.15) lists 45 signs in all but I consider that his signs 28 and 29, taken together, form a U, while numbers 30 and 31 are an A. My 'translation' of these 7 basic signs is given in Figure 16.

If one simply gives the A and U sequences without the 'markers', then we get the following table:

A U U A

A U A U A A U A

A U A U

U A A A U A

A A U U

A U U A U U A

Table 33 : Newton inscription

If we place these 33 signs in three rows of 11 signs, we get:

(AUU)(AAU)AU(AAU)

(AAU)(AUU)A(AAU)A

(AAU)U(AUU)(AUU)A

This gives nine triplets: five (AAU) and four (AUU), which is a remarkably concise way of summarising the inscription: just two triplets that are symmetrical opposites.

The next step in the argument is to compare these signs with the Ogham inscription. In order to do this, it is necessary to convert the Oghams into U and A forms by calling all the odd-numbered strokes (1,3,5) A and the even strokes (2 and 4) U. If we then place both inscriptions side by side, reading from left to right we obtain:

Script	AUU	AAU	AU	AAU	AAU	AUU	A
Ogham	AUU	AAA	AA	AUU	AAU	AAU	U
		*	*	*		*	*

Script	AAU	A	AAU	U	AUU	AUU	A
Ogham	UAA	.	. AU	U	AA .	. . .	.
	*	*			*		

It is quite surprising how closely these two series agree, for only ¼ of the characters (*) are wrong. The gaps in the Ogham sequence are probably due to 'missing' strokes, cf Fig. 14.

Next one must look at the role of the 'markers'. Their numbered position in the sequence is given, cf Fig. 16.

Marker	Expansion of its position number	Number after marker	Expansion of this number
10	2×5	11	Prime
16	(4^2), 2×8	17	Prime
18	2×9	19	Prime
20	2×10	21	7×3
21	7×3	22	2×11
22	2×11	23	Prime
25	(5^2)	26	2×13
34	2×17	35	7×5
36	(6^2), 2×18	37	Prime
38	2×19	39	3×13

Table 34 : The Newton markers

The markers themselves are generally even numbers—2 × (5,8,9,10,11,17,18,19), and they include three squares: 4^2, 5^2 and 6^2. The only odd number is 7×3. What is remarkable is that half the numbers *following* the markers are prime numbers—11,17,19,23 and 37—while the rest are multiples of prime numbers: $7 \times (3,5)$, 11×2, $13 \times (2,3)$.

The conclusion is that the markers are evenly placed in the inscription, while the signs following them are not therefore just simply odd numbers but mainly prime numbers or multiples of primes not directly represented in the sequence, *viz* 3,5,7, and 13. There is no obvious reason why the markers should be placed *before* so many prime numbers, but it can hardly be a coincidence. This fact, though, lends credence to the division of the other signs into the two categories: A and U.

The closeness between the two sequences of A and U from the unknown script and the odd and even numbers from the Ogham script suggests that there is an identity of purpose here. Thus the downward prongs (A) and odd numbers may be lucky positions while the converse could be true of the upward prongs (U) and the even numbers. Perhaps prime numbers were extra-lucky—as might be the good luck swastika in position 25 (5^2)! The only reason for suggesting that downwards is lucky is that most Ogham strokes point downwards and diviners tend to be perpetual optimists. However there is a strong case to be made that the Picts *could* have been pessimists and they did not expect much good luck. This would make better symbolic sense if even numbers are good and on the right side—in that case U is an O.K. sign while prime numbers are doubly bad and odious. The swastika, despite it being an odd number, might retain its luckiness because it is 5×5.

The purpose of this note has been to suggest that there is some advantage in abandoning a strictly linguistic approach to the Newton stone in favour of a numerical solution. Naturally this method cannot produce a translation of the unknown script any more than it can with the Oghams or symbol stones, but it does more than hint that the Picts were keenly aware of the property of numbers, especially if they had mystical significance!

It is purely by accident that the Newton stone was looked at all, since the unknown script is daunting enough at the best of times, but because it was susceptible to counting signs it was included. While it is debatable whether some signs are A or U, there can be no doubt about the markers as they are quite clear and distinct. The unique sign θ (No. 22) is the central sign: there are 21 signs on either side of it. Here then is another instance of rule of 7. In fact, if one wished to find fault with the composer of this script, it would be with his use of sign 21 (i.e.7×3) as a marker. Had it been an A or U it could have been better—there would not have been the oddity of 7×3 in the marker column, nor the even number 2×11 in the other column. However, one cannot get the symbolism of numbers to agree with one's desires always.

The extreme closeness between the two different inscriptions on the Newton stone is quite remarkable—given the assumptions made. The other features which link the two scripts are the presence of triplets and the sequences of multiples of 7, besides the concern with prime numbers. All these points tie the two inscriptions very closely to each other, but they do not mutually explain each other.

In conclusion, we may say that the Newton stone simply demonstrates the importance to the Picts of numbers: prime numbers, the mystic number 7 and triplets. This importance can only relate to the mystic value imputed to numbers and, in this instance, to the days of the periods between festivals. [29]

CHAPTER 4

The role of Christianity and the symbol stones

There is no doubt whatever that Christianity played a major role in affecting the destiny of the Picts, but it is unclear how this took place.[30] There are conflicting reports about the successes of the various saints in converting the Picts to Christianity, for while it is most likely correct that missionaries such as Ninian and Columba did convert certain 'kings' of the Picts, we do not know the extent of their activities, nor their lasting success. Obviously the Picts were exposed to Christianity from the 5th century onwards, but the only evidence of significant gains comes in the 8th century with the Class II stones south of the Mounth. What was the situation in Class I times, especially in the north?

Christian missionaries saw their task as eradicating pagan beliefs and inculcating their new message, but they did so diplomatically by tolerating pagan beliefs to begin with. Their strategy was to seek to convert the chief or king first, in the hope that he would command his followers to accept the new religion. This method worked quite well with the normal patrilineal societies that Christian missionaries faced at the time, but there were problems with the Picts, since a king's conversion did not bind his successor — his sister's son — who would be brought up elsewhere. This might have puzzled the missionaries, because their technique of converting the king and his family did not automatically ensure that the *next* king would be Christian. The Pictish royal succession was also complicated by the alteration of overlordship between North and South Pictland, let alone the innumerable possible successors. The only sure way of converting the Picts would be to convert *all* the population — however, the early missionaries were individualistic. The Celtic church sponsored individual cells of Christians rather than the Roman version of one Church, and so the conversion proceeded piecemeal and rivalries were not suppressed. It is highly probable that until the 8th century (Class II times), Christianity in Pictland was pretty patchy and definitely unorganized. Like the early days of the conversion of the Vikings to Christianity, the Picts probably took out fire insurance and accepted the new religion alongside their old one! The succession rules probably militated against any continuing and abiding acceptance of Christianity.

What Christianity introduced was a new conception of the cosmological order, in which the Picts could extend their range of mystical agents to include a supreme god. Curiously enough, the notion of the crucifixion of Christ on a cross for man's sins does not seem to have been an important component of their Christianity, to judge from the absence of such representations in Scotland.

It is only the symbol of the cross that seems to have fired the imagination of the Picts: a new, powerful and universal symbol of magic (i.e. a device capable of influencing events) that was better than their old ones. Indeed the use of this device is still apparent even today in warding off evil.

Interestingly enough, no Pictish symbol resembles or incorporates the cross, even though the cross is purely symmetrical. We cannot be certain that the early missionaries used the sign of the cross as a symbol, but they undoubtedly had manuscripts of the Bible and other books that contained drawings of the cross. Symbols, such as the signs for the four apostles, were probably represented as being powerful in themselves: what is significant is the notion of symbols. Of course the Picts might have tattooed themselves with their lineage marks, but we cannot be certain of that. If, though, we assume — as we must — that the Picts invented their symbols in the 7th century, then Christian symbols might have acted as an inspiration. It is the existence of itinerant masons specializing in Christian monuments who could have supplied some suggestions. *One* skilled artist could have supplied the Picts with all the designs they needed to express their mystical beliefs about their lineages. It is not suggested that Christianity directly inspired the idea of symbols, but the existence of skilled masons may have had a lot to do with it. There would be, of course, skilled pagan craftsmen, but they may have been unversed in monumental sculpture: the techniques of metal-working and masonry are quite dissimilar. The outstanding feature about the Pictish symbol stones is that there are no practice pieces; they emerge fully mature from the start. Whoever carved these stones knew what he was about, and such skill does not come without a tradition of stone-carving.

Stones have played a significant role in Scottish prehistory from henges to monoliths, right down the millenia. Normally these stones are not incised with designs, but they have played an important role in the ritual life of the inhabitants of Scotland of old. Such standing stones have been attributed magical powers and this is why they have been left untouched. The addition of symbols (unique to Scotland), but discarding cup and ring marks, are a feature of Pictish times only. As found today, the Pictish symbol stones are usually single, ungrouped monuments that do not occur in henges. However, it is likely that originally they were not that isolated but occurred in related groupings. Thus while we never find a henge (or circle) of symbol stones, they sometimes are found geographically close to each other — as if they were related. It is the case that symbols have been found in henges but this is most likely the whim of a later landowner: had we found a henge of symbol stones we would have had quite a new problem on our hands.

An examination of the interlace patterning and the cross types and figures found on both Class II and III stones shows that they share many common features, i.e. they have a mutual repertoire. What is surprising about these Christian monuments is that *they are all individual in composition:* no two stones have the same designs and composition. The patterning and the figures have many parallels elsewhere: Wales, Ireland and Northumbria, where there are not only carved monuments but also illuminated books. It thus seems as if the masons and scribes had pattern books, but then both groups of craftsmen could have been monks, drawing on a common tradition. The main conclusion to be drawn is that these patterns were not unique to Pictland and hence are unlikely to have been created there, despite the possible existence of a good school of masons. On the other hand, the Pictish symbols are unique and are not derivative from Christian art: their only association with Christianity is their co-existence on Class II monuments.

This independence of the Pictish symbols certainly suggests that the Class I stones are a separate creation from the Class II stones. Actually, ⅔ of the Class II monuments have the symbols and the cross on *opposite* sides of the slab: this suggests that they were serving different functions. What is most surprising is the fact that most of these stones contain other figures: what was their purpose? These figures are hardly religious in intent. The most significant of these secular figures is the horseman — either hunting or in battle. We might surmise that this representation denotes the local king or chief who caused the erection of the stone. As for many of the animals, they only seem to serve a decorative function, apart from the monsters depicted on the stones from Meigle and St Vigeans. There are of course various depictions of angels, clerics and scenes from the Bible.

Interestingly enough, there is almost an equal degree of representation of men and beasts — a possible reflection on the status of animals in the Pictish world: both real and mythical creatures. By contrast it should be noted that Class I stones only have symbols upon them — there are no other figures. So what were these Class II and III stones telling their viewers? Obviously they were Christian while, additionally, the Class II stones said that such and such lineages were also Christian. We may also draw the conclusion that in Class III times this notification about lineages was no longer important or worth recording. It should be borne in mind that there were two versions of Christianity in Pictland: the Celtic and the Roman church. This may have something to do with the variations of the decorations of the stones.[31]

A question that one keeps returning to is: why there are so few Class II and III monuments north of the Mounth? It is well-known that the centre of Pictish power was south of the Mounth after 685 i.e. in Class II and III times, so it is to be expected that we will find the bulk of these stones here. However, why was this? Why had the north been abandoned? There are two possibilities:

a) the north remained basically pagan
b) the northern kingdom adopted, or kept to, the Celtic church in opposition to the Roman church in the south. The Celtic church might have set its face against graven images, including the cross.

If Class II stones are placed at the time of Nechton's acceptance of the Roman Easter dating, when it was important to stress the power of the cross, then since Iona could hold out until 724 A.D. it is possible that other areas resisted even longer. Maybe the Northern Picts were non-conformists! Hence the paucity of Christian monuments in the north could be a doctrinal matter about graven images. Although possible, this is an unlikely explanation. After all, why should the abandoned northern Picts adopt Christianity anyway? It is more likely they blatantly reaffirmed their belief in their old ways as against the southern Picts and their Scottish friends.

If Class III monuments began with Constantine (789-820) as joint ruler of the Picts and the Scots, there would be no need to put up lineage symbols any more since the old Class II alliances still stood; the Scots had no need of them. The invasion of southern Pictland by the Scots would be a disincentive to erecting monuments, even if this was a peaceful invasion, since the purpose of the stones was beginning to lack force. One good reason why Constantine should wish to undermine the Pictish succession would be to ensure that *his* family continued to rule over both the Picts and the Scots. The current system made such joint rule only possible once in a while, yet by banning the use of lineage symbols on the stones that *he put up*, Constantine could disavow their right of succession. As we know, Constantine was first succeeded by his brother Unuist as king of both the Picts and the Scots (though not simultaneously) and then Constantine's son Drest, before Unuist's son Uuen took over the kingship of the Picts alone. The ironic thing is that the kingship of the Scots went to Alpin in a collateral line while the Pictish kingship went in the patrilineal line! After this rejection of the normal rules of succession, the Pictish kingship was thrown into utter confusion with many claimants to the throne until Alpin's son, Kenneth, began his slow climb to the top.[32]

Although not inconceivable, it seems unlikely that Constantine would systematically eliminate his Pictish kinsfolk simply to ensure that *his* family would keep the kingship, when a mere change in the rules of succession could ensure this without bloodshed. Kenneth, on the other hand, would have no such scruples since the Picts were not his kin but his traditional enemies. Furthermore, if there had been a legislative change in the inheritance laws of the Picts to allow sons to succeed their fathers then Kenneth's chances of achieving the Pictish throne were doubly dashed. He could no longer make a claim through his mother's line while, in addition, the sons of *all* 14 main Pictish lineages would be a perpetual threat. Indeed, the patrilineal idea was catching on among the Picts, for Uuared (838-42) was succeeded by his three sons. Thus Kenneth was locked into a war of attrition against numerous claimants. The final solution would be to eliminate all these potential rivals once and for all: Sueno's stone with its depiction of the execution of 14 men (the main Pictish lineages) would be their most appropriate epitaph. The tales about the treachery of the Scots in killing off the Pictish nobility may have been no idle invention of the times. The irony is that if the Picts had bowed to pressure from their king and from the

Church to give up their 'backward' rules of succession, then they had betrayed themselves! It is a fact that Kenneth did destroy the Pictish nobility, though perhaps not so dramatically as the stories suggest, since they were never afterwards a force to contend with and neither did they succeed to the throne of the new Scotland. What these 9th century Picts did not realise, as did Bridei (son of Bili) when he consolidated the Pictish nation against the Northumbrians by causing the erection of the Class I stones, was the strength of their kinship system. It had its weaknesses but it could be a unifying factor! Such a change from matrilinearity to patrilinearity is not an uncommon occurrence around the world, so there is no cause for surprise. Unfortunately for the Picts, this changeover did not bring the benefits they expected — it might have done if they had been masters in their own house. As it was they had two aggressive, expansionist peoples wanting their territory and they were militarily crushed between the mill-wheels of the Scots and the Norse forces — possibly in collusion. In the late change to patrilinearity the Picts had not had time to develop a new system of alliances that would provide them with a fighting army. In the confusing state they were in about loyalties, they remained divided and could be picked off one by one. Nothing united them any longer, there was nothing distinctive about their culture left and so they just merged with the rest of the population — ruled by a Scots kings and *his* nobles.

The distribution of Class III monuments makes an interesting comment upon the state of Christianity and the rule of the late Pictish kings (including Kenneth). The two Shetland stones are typologically, in terms of designs, related to Whithorn in Dumfries rather than anywhere else. The remaining Class III stones in Orkney, Caithness and Sutherland are just plain crosses with no decoration whatever and hence are of unknown period. If one continues southwards and disregards the fragments of stones in Rosemarkie, Tarbet, Birnie, Burghead and Drainie, the remaining six stones are interesting in all having representations of men: half of them with horsemen, *viz* Edderton, Kincardine and Forres (Sueno's stone). South of the Mounth, again disregarding all plain crosses and undecorated fragments, more than ⅓ of the decorated stones have horsemen on them, cf Map 5.

Interestingly enough, over one half of the Class III stones are found in just six religious sites: St Andrews, Meigle, St Vigeans, Govan, Iona and Whithorn. This is, perhaps, to be expected since monastic sites *would* produce carved Christian monuments. The important point here is that these stones were erected by monks and not by the secular authorities.

If the two Shetland stones are assigned to Whithorn monks,

and all 11 plain crosses in the north are rejected together with the fragments, then we are only left with ten decorated Class III stones north of the Mounth. If the 17 Class II stones are also included, it means that there are only 27 Christian Pictish stones north of the Mounth — a sixth of all Christian stones. Contrariwise, $^5/_6$ of all Class I stones are to the north. This exact reversal of the proportions of pagan and Christian monuments north and south of the Mounth implies a complete contrast in beliefs in the two areas. If, additionally, one considers the depiction of horsemen on the Class II and III stones, then one finds that ¼ are to the north and ¾ are to the south the Mounth: these are likely to be indications of royal power. It suggests that the royal writ did not extend very far, since there is a thousand miles of coastline from Dunnottar to Skye.

In summary, it appears that the Picts were never again united after the efflorescence of the Class I symbol stones: north and south went their separate ways.

Conclusions

Bede seems to have regarded the Picts with only mild curiosity at some of their odd customs, for otherwise they did not appear very remarkable and were certainly not mysterious. How then did the Picts acquire this reputation for being a people of mystery? Part of the reason lies in the fact that they lost their sovereign independence in the 9th century and, whatever influence they still exerted during the subsequent consolidation of the Scottish kingdom, it had all but evaporated by the 11th century. Thereafter, knowledge of the Picts lapsed until they were rediscovered by the Victorians in that wave of national pride that swept across Scotland after Sir Walter Scott's revival of interest in the past. Mysteries appealed to the Romantic imagination, and so to find one on our own doorstep was an irresistible challenge!

It was historians like Skene, who wrote several books on the ancient Picts and Scots, and his contemporary, Stuart, who produced the first illustrated catalogue of Pictish monuments, who made the general public aware that there was an interesting problem to be solved. This popularisation was also carried forward by the newly-formed antiquarian societies that had received a boost with the establishment of archaeology as a scholarly and respectable discipline.

One cannot simply dismiss the earlier writers, for it is an indisputable fact that it was really the Victorian era that saw all those revolutionary advances in geology, biology, chemistry, archaeology and linguistics which are the pride of scholarship and our civilization. One of the glories of comparative philology was its discovery of the Indo-European language connection which opened up whole new areas of research. Hard on the heels of the final decipherment of Egyptian hieroglyphics came a surge of interest in cracking the codes of other forms of lost languages — cuneiform, ideograms, etc. It was inevitable that the Pictish symbols and Oghams came in for the same treatment.

Having set the Pictish ball rolling, what did Victorian scholarship achieve? Historians compared the various king-lists of the Picts and the Scots and tried to reconcile the discrepancies they found, in order to produce a reliable chronology. Little new material ever came to light, and so the reconstruction of Pictish history was still based on shaky foundations. The archaeologists, on the other hand, found new symbol stones and the occasional metal object but they discovered no graves, houses or settlements. They proceeded to classify the stones in their time-honoured fashion of sequences. The linguists were completely baffled. This can be seen in their wilder assertions that the Picts were Buddhists (Moore) or had a world-wide religious eclecticism from all Indo-European cultures (Southesk). The Oghams were translated on the assumption that they were similar in function to Irish Oghams, i.e. as funerary texts. Church-art historians sought to relate the symbols and motifs to religious manuscripts and sculptures elsewhere in Britain and Ireland. They made no headway with the symbols, but they did establish the fact that many of the designs found on Class II and III stones were commonplace elsewhere.

All these findings were skillfully brought together in *ECMS:* that block-buster of Pictish studies! What this volume achieved, among other things, was a consensus that *the symbols and the Oghams were a written language.* The common conviction of all scholars was that these stones must function like Roman and Christian headstones: commemorating the dead. Hence both symbol pairs and Oghams *must* be read in the conventional way: Here lies X, remembered by Y. These very understandable conclusions have been with us ever since and *not* to our advantage, as I have argued throughout.

This division of labour between historians, archaeologists, linguists and art historians continued unaltered up to Wainwright's conference in 1952. Although this meeting was a brave attempt to reconcile the differing views of these scholars, it did not tell us anything basically new. Thus, a half century after *ECMS,* we were little the wiser. One positive result of this conference, apart from the book *The Problem of the Picts,* was to encourage further meetings on the topic from time to time.

The position today is that some historians are engaged in a lively debate on the construction of the king-lists, using anthropological insights. One archaeologist, Anna Ritchie, has found the first identifiable Pictish dwelling-house and so has laid the basis for further discoveries. Linguists have given up symbols but they still think of Oghams as a language. Art historians still muse over the roots of Pictish art but are making little progress. Sporadic attempts have been made to interpret the symbols (Diack and Thomas) but these attempts are vitiated by being imprisoned in Victorian assumptions. Thus future advances seem to be in the hands of the historians and prehistorians.[33]

In chapters 3 and 4 (Part II), I have suggested some alternative solutions to the problem of the Oghams and Christian art. These suggestions, if partially accepted, should give linguists and art historians a further dimension to their studies. It would be helpful if linguists continued to explore the distribution of *pit*-names and the local geography, since we know insufficient about this naming system. There is still much research that needs to be done on the extra-symbolic Christian representations on the stones. Here again, art historians could look carefully at the territorial distributions of these different types of figure.[34]

Historians and prehistorians are both in grave difficulties with regard to the Picts, because of the paucity of the evidence. It is this grave lack of source material that has created 'the problem of the Picts' since the historians have little with which to speculate. However, this problem is an illusion that is tantamount to the 'problem of totemism' which plagued earlier thinkers, for it is a product of one's assumptions. Those scholars thought that totemism was a religion and they were quite baffled by it, not realizing that they had totally misunderstood the phenomenon, by classifying it wrongly. Their error was pointed out recently by Lévi-Strauss in a brilliant essay.

The comparable illusion that many historians suffer from is the belief that they have to use their traditional methods to understand the Picts, i.e. they are waiting for the documentary evidence to turn up. Their problem is that this evidence is not forthcoming. It is highly likely that these postulated records never existed among the Picts at all. For such reasons, some historians and prehistorians have turned to social anthropology to see if its insights can be helpful in understanding pre-literate people in the past.

There is a more serious cultural reason why Western historians have found it difficult to come to terms with societies that lack writing, for as Lévi-Strauss (1966:232) points out in his discussion of the modes of thought in 'savage' society: there is a fundamental antipathy between history and systems of classification, that has resulted in a 'totemic void' in our own civilization. Because we, Europeans, have elected to *explain ourselves by history,* such a mode of explanation is quite incompatible with understanding societies that classify things and beings by means of finite groups, i.e.

totemic classification. In other words, we are culturally blind to appreciating alternative ways of explaining things — we are, simply, ethnocentric with regard to knowledge.[35]

My position is that the Picts were, indeed, a totemic society and it was only after the Picts had merged with the Scots that they emerged into history and into that type of self-accounting that characterises our civilization. It is precisely at this point in time that *we* begin to recognize their historic presence. As they must have existed before this time, yet have no *written* records of their own and are only mentioned in passing by others, this previous existence becomes a problem for historians.

It is important to realise that as a history-less (totemic) society, the Picts could not comprehend history, and hence made no efforts to keep written records for posterity. For that matter, the Scots were little different until they became Christian (that most time-oriented religion which actually provides the historians with their chronologies!), and then, having absorbed the Picts, documents did indeed accrete around them — religious charters and records, and legal documents.

With an anthropological background, there is nothing particularly remarkable in the fact that societies lack history as we know it. Social anthropologists frequently work in time-less societies and they have built up a method to cope with this problem: they use the ethnographic present — a timeless sphere of rules and structures. In this way they can bring together their observations of social behaviour, along with the rules, myths and beliefs they discover, into a satisfactory whole. They are rarely interested in our type of history, since it hardly exists in the first place and would not, even if known, be very helpful in explaining the structure and function of the society they are examining.

It may be legitimately objected that this is all very well for societies that can be visited for several years but what about those societies in the past which *cannot* be physically visited? Obviously we cannot then employ the same techniques, but so long as we know something about the nature of that society we are able to make an informed guess. At present ethno-history (as it is called) is quite booming, while many historians (Laslett, Macfarlane, Thomas and Le Roy Ladurie) are using anthropological insights in a stimulating way.[36]

The main concrete evidence regarding the Picts, as my readers will be only too well aware, is the existence of the symbol stones. These stones were *not* erected as time-markers for the dead nor in any other chronological way, because they represented eternal truths, *ever valid*, about the lineages, their alliances and power. These statements were true *before* their material representation on imperishable stone and would remain *for ever,* since they were permanently present in the time-less collective consciousness. In Lévi-Strauss' telling phrase, one can regard the symbol stones as "machines for the suppression of time." They announced eternal verities, omnipresent and everlasting, since the Picts had no conception of a changing time.

In order to give an understanding of Pictish society, it is clearly necessary to make certain assumptions about the symbol pairing. The key premise is that the Picts were dualistic: all the known evidence supports this view. What I have done is to take this argument to its logical conclusion and posit that dualism is a constituent part of all Pictish thinking. The numerous examples adduced show the usefulness of this concept as an explanatory tool.

It is unlikely that we will find any further evidence about Pictish marriage customs, so my three assumptions (matrilineal descent, patrilateral cross-cousin marriage and marriage in a circle) will have to do to explain aristocratic families. All we are concerned about is the leading families (whose symbols are on the stones) and to postulate some set of ideal rules which correspond to the symbol pairings. That this system of marriage broke down after five generations is hardly surprising: it is quite typical (cf. Lévi-Strauss: 1969: 181 ff). Reality has little to do with ideal rules of kinship, which are almost designed to be broken! In a time-less world one is not so bound by tradition as might be imagined: changes can be rationalised as having always been the case! Paradoxically, it is easier to change the rules in a traditional society than it is in our more progressive society, for they just rationalise the changes as having always been the case! This is something that we could not get away with, because of all the historical records to prove that this was not so. The significant point here is that even if my three assumptions were to have been true when the symbol stones were first erected, it does not mean that this was the case always, for how was it possible for Constantine's sons to inherit the throne? Traditional society's denial that change has taken place is part of their time-lessness, because their belief entails a perfect creation that never alters.

The erection of the symbol stones as a permanent witness to eternal alliances was quite rational, since the Picts could not foresee a time when things might be different. Well, such a time did come when certain lineages wished to break out of the strait-jacket which the symbol stones enforce : this was only possible when Class III announced a break with symbol pairing. and hence with the old marriage rules and inheritance patterns. This is likely to be the time when there was a basic change in the descent rules from matrilinearity to patrilinearity which made marriage alliances redundant since they no longer affected succession. Such a radical change would not be lightly accommodated even in a time-less society, and it is at this point that new myths (history) are likely to be created. This can be seen in the Pictish king-lists (which are actually Scottish), where the transition from the old style of succession of Pictish kings to the Scottish patrilineal mode passes without comment! However by the time that Constantine had so changed the rules to allow his family to reign legitimately it was too late — they were to be the last of the Pictish kings!

Had Kenneth (who was probably quite oblivious to the true meaning of the symbol stones since they were irrelevant to his claims) *not* won the throne, then it is most likely that Constantine's successors would have smashed the symbol stones since they would have indicated a change in the rules. To the Scots the symbol stones were a monumental irrelevance, and by the time that they had established full control these old stones were both powerless and meaningless. So, ironically, we are probably indebted to the Scots for neglecting these stones, for a further century of Pictish rule would inevitably have meant that even more stones would have to have been destroyed in the interest of the 'traditional, unchanging' society.

The Scots could not have been unaware of the Pictish stones and that they proclaimed some sort of right over territories. When they took over, they tried to continue this tradition by putting up territorial markers over the king's hunting demesnes — all those crude Class III stones with horsemen on them who are hunting! The equally crude crosses on the stones indicated that the king was blessed by the Church — he therefore had the right to the land. What other explanation can there be for these appallingly executed monuments? They may not have been very good propaganda but they did function as warnings: Keep Off — Royal Property! These 'No hunting' signs are the first hints of that tendency towards the private ownership of things that patrilinearity breeds. Such signs are usually well away from villages and churches and hence are most unlikely to record the burial of someone who is now in that great hunting ground in the sky! There are, too, the purely Christian Class III monuments found near monastic centres, but that is a different kind of propaganda: Church Property — Be Respectful!

The most superb Class III monument is Sueno's stone: here the hunting is deadly serious — the killing of men. In 1813 the skeletons of eight (!) people were dug up, but it is unclear whether they had their skulls with them! The style of this huge stone is basically Class II without the symbols, and there can be no doubt that this is a gigantic 'Keep Out' sign which is the ultimate in

Dark Age propaganda. The Romans were also skilled in this art of frightening off people and, it must be said, the Christian church was not slow in using monuments for their own purposes — as witness the scenes on the Class II and III stones. If the Class III stones were erected, as I have suggested, c 830 A.D., then it is quite natural for Kenneth to have raised this stone in 842 after his victory over the Picts *and in such a manner* that the defeated Picts would recognise it as having the stamp of inexorable authority — a Class II stone without symbols! The subsequent stones were not really that important and could well be left to anybody who could wield a chisel. Their relative unimportance may be judged by their few numbers, but it is significant that many of these Class III stones stress the martial nature of the horsemen depicted: they are armed knights, not peaceful courtiers pursuing the stag! This is quite a contrast to the Class II horsemen who are generally following their liege lord. Perhaps a closer study of these horsemen is called for. Whenever Class III stones went up, they indicate an unruly society: the most likely period is that when the Scots were enforcing their rule on the Picts. Once that had been accomplished then *all* such monument-raising suddenly ceased.[37]

My association of the Pictish symbols with mystical powers is neither surprising nor unusual for 7th century Europe. After all, both runes and Oghams — indeed *any* writing — were credited with magical power at that time! The disappearance of the symbols in Class III times has more to do with the irrelevancy of lineage alliances and the growing magical power of the cross, than anything else. The magical frame of mind had not vanished — it *still* has not, for one can see plenty of examples all around us. In a totemic society, such as the Picts, it meant that certain lineages had hereditary mystical powers (transmitted through the mother's brother) which consisted of spells that affected everyone's well-being. In those days, as we know, cursing and blessing were commonplace and socially effective in keeping people in their place. Magic (essentially being the power of words) was an integral and integrative part of the social fabric.

Magic does not consist only of oral spells, for the written word was equally, if not more, powerful. The astonishing success of Christianity was, in no small measure, due to the fact that the Christians had a *written* book which certain wise men could read with remarkable consistency. This was, and is, an astounding early phenomenon that has been without parallel in proselytizing religions: Islam is the only other one to have followed this path. What chance had the remembrancers of tribal cultures (e.g. the bards) against this devastatingly persuasive religion? After all, the bards and the magi had to rely on their memories, besides having to trim their pronouncements to local political realities. The early Christians were fanatics who risked life and limb to spread the word of the Gospel: such bravery was impressive to every culture (especially Dark Age Europe) that prized bravery above all other human virtues! Heroes, in most cultures, are assured of bliss as their reward. The problem with the Christians was that they did not play the heroic game according to the accepted rules: warriors battling it out to the death! One could not defeat the missionaries by offering battle, since they would not accept the challenge. On the other hand, the local magicians or magi *could* pit their powers against the missionaries. We know of one such contest in Pictland but the result was a foregone conclusion since it was recorded by a Christian. Given the equally dubious powers of either magi or Christian saints to control events, we have to remain unsure of the outcome of other contests of strength. Obviously the Christians could not always have won!

The Pictish magi were obviously at a disadvantage when the Christians arrived to challenge their powers: what could they do — they had no sacred books! In addition, these Christians were receiving support from certain local kings — the missionaries had taken the obvious precaution of converting the king first! In these circumstances, some magi adopted Irish Oghams to show that they had some skills which the Christians did not. Unfortunately, these magi did not compile a book of wisdom but only inscribed a few Oghams on symbol stones and a few other objects to demonstrate their skill in prediction. As far as I can see, the Oghams appear to be calendrical prognostications — something that the magi, perhaps, had always practiced. To us this matter of the calendar is of slight importance since we have worked it out: however it took until the 18th century before Britain fell into line with the rest of Europe about the year! The Christian church had its own peculiar problem about working out Easter, of course, but at least that fitted in well, in principle, with the Pictish lunar calendar: this might account for the famous Easter controversy that raged in Scotland: two similar systems that gave different results![38]

Model 4 is built up by analogy to the Irish Celtic territorial calendar and incorporates traditional 'Scottish' customs, as well as placing royal Scone almost directly opposite the Irish coronation site at Tara where it follows the Celtic New Year. In addition, there are the four major *rites de passage*, the four royal symbols, and the four colour references, as well as the four kingdoms.

This model is designed to bring together various dualistic and quadripartite features that have been noted in this work and to relate these to the individual life-cycle from conception to death, as

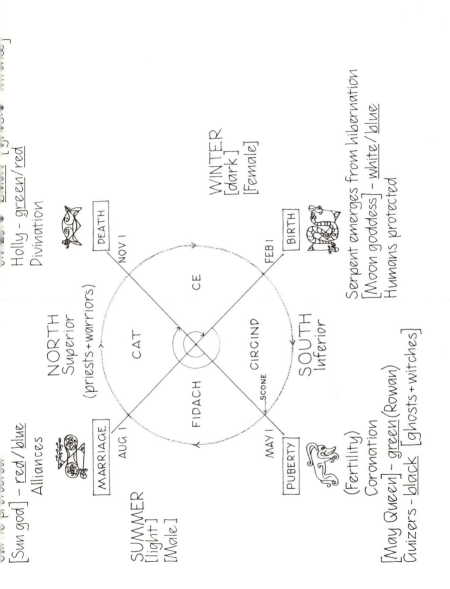

Figure 17: Model 4 — The symbolic Pictish year

reflected in the various stages of growth that are marked by rites of passage during the calendrical year.

The introduction of 'Scottish' folklore at the quarter days may seem trivial, but these customs *are* Celtic and may well be Pictish since the Picts did not vanish overnight! What is of particular interest is the masquerading that occurs on the eves of Beltane and Hallowmass, where people (mainly children) dress up as witches and ghosts.

There is one big question that I have not yet discussed: "Where do children come from in a matrilineal society?" Such societies generally deny any real physiological contribution from the husband in producing his wife's children. So what makes babies since women cannot have them by themselves? Matrilineal societies are forced to give some ideological reasons (implausible both to us and neighbouring patrilineal tribes) to account for why descent goes through women. The commonest solution is to suggest that the ancestors are reborn as children and that some mystical conception takes place as spirits seek to return to this world. This, then, explains why ancestors choose their own female kin to perform the task of bearing them — it is their duty! No incest occurs since no sexual intercourse takes place; but the lineage perpetuates itself, in more ways than one!

Such beliefs explain why ghosts (ancestors) are prominent at Beltane when newly-fertile women conceived, and why the ancestors are remembered at Hallowmass, the death of the Old Year. The fact that guizers smear their faces with ashes and soot is simply symbolic of the dead. Witches are also black but they are human and evil, for they vie with the ancestors *at the same time of the year* by trying to prevent conception and to cause death, so their co-appearance is not accidental.

Earlier, I argued that Z-rods stood for the ancestors and so it is significant that Z-rod symbols are present at marriage and birth rites — occasions associated, respectively, with the sun and moon but also with the protection of the cattle and human populations. As for Hallowe'en, we know that this is the major festival for predictions, and so the association with the V-rod and moon are not so surprising. At the opposite pole, Beltane seems more related to kingship — the May Queen and possible coronations of real monarchs.

The division of the Celtic year into summer and winter produces two sets of opposites: Summer — maleness, light, the sun, the Northern, superior (and geometrical) kingdom; Winter — femaleness, dark, the moon, the Southern, inferior (and animal) kingdom.

Colours might seem an oddity in this model but the three basic colours — white, black and red — are found closely associated with rituals, the world over. The blackness of the guizers has been explained already, but what about the other colours? Rowan is especially associated with Beltane, a time when it is *green*, but it produces red berries later in the year, just like holly which is associated with the New Year: these two particular bushes are thought to be very effective in warding off the attacks of witches. The colours associated with Bride are white and blue (the Virgin's colours) while Lammas employs red and blue.

Looking at these colours, we find that the Beltane/Hallowmass axis is green while the Lammas/Bride axis is blue; a point to note is that some societies, especially in the Far East, do not make a conceptual distinction between blue and green. It can be seen that the summer half of the year is associated with red, while the winter half is dominated by black and white. Perhaps red refers to the sun or even ritual sacrifice (of cattle in the autumn), while white refers to the moon in the black nights of the winter period. While the significance of colours in the Pictish world is obscure, we should not underestimate the importance of colours in tribal rituals for we can easily show how important a role they play in *most* such societies.

The four (Class I) kingdoms are placed in the model, like the four Celtic Irish kindoms, as a possible structure of the total Pictish kingdom where the two main centres of power in Cat and Circind are diametrically opposed. The model might even indicate the perambulations of the royal court from summer to winter.

All the above suggestions are made at the extreme limits of speculation about Pictish cosmology, and I only include them as a *jeu d'esprit* with which to end the book. We should reject no evidence that might help us to resolve the problem of the Picts. There are far too many binary oppositions here for this model to be pure fancy, and it does have a powerful internal logic. I present this more as a final puzzle: why does it even appear to be remotely possible? The facts are reasonably correct, so why are the associations that plausible? Anyway, it is nice to end with another conundrum.

In line with the modern 'total' history approach, I have tried to take the broadest perspective and weld together the main facts we know about the Picts. I am, however, no historian and there are so many gaps in our knowledge that I was unable to produce a flowing chronological narrative: instead we have a rather jerky presentation as I attempt to make good our deficiencies of knowledge before proceeding to the next point. My purpose has been to suggest answers to some difficult questions *by treating the symbol stones as documentary evidence.* This task has involved a thorough examination of the symbols in Part I. I hope to have convincingly demonstrated that the symbol stones represented political alliances in different parts of Pictland and that that can tell us something about the past we did not know before. This novel way of writing history carries with it all the usual risks when interpreting old documents.

This attempt at 'total' history *is* only an attempt, for it would need a skilled historian to do it proper justice. Perhaps someone will take up the challenge and use the symbol stones as that 'long-lost book' of the Picts we all have been waiting for! There is plenty of work yet to be done even if this new insight is confirmed, because I have only scratched the surface of what could be a profitable deep mine of information about the past.

Let me conclude by hoping that this analysis of the symbol stones will provide much food for thought and, subsequently, a lively debate.

Envoi

1. These thoughts about the Picts are offered as a *possible* explanation of the symbols and their meaning.[39]
2. At this distance in time and cultural development, there is no way of testing if this hypothesis is trustworthy other than the symbol stones themselves and the internal logic of the argument.
3. My 'solution' is an attempt to relate most of the known facts about the Picts into one synthesis which provides a plausible explanation of Pictish society.[40]
4. Although on this broad canvas I will have, inevitably, committed some small errors, I hope to have presented a reasonably coherent case that should only be challenged by an equally complete scenario.[41]
5. I do not deny that this is speculative but it *is* founded on solid evidence! In the circumstances, how else are we to make any progress except by guessing?[42]
6. I hope to have shown that there are no viable alternative explanations — at the time of publication, December 1984.[43]
7. My hope is that this outspoken book will provoke 'traditional' scholars to think again and reconsider their basic assumptions![44]

End Notes

Chapter 1

1. The best introduction to the subject is still Henderson: *The Picts*, while the recent reissue of Wainwright's *The Problem of the Picts* presents a scholarly assessment, which, if dated, does contain an extensive bibliography.

    Surprisingly, despite their comprehensiveness elsewhere, none of the major works on the Picts devotes more than 5% of the text to analysing the symbols.

2. A good archaeological and historical background is provided by G. & A. Ritchie: *Scotland* while Alcock (1980) gives a wide survey of the archaeological record that includes a full bibliography.

    The results of the 1982 Glasgow Conference on the Picts have just been published — J. G. P. Friell and W. G. Watson (eds): *Pictish studies* (1984). Although this volume came out while my book was in press, I have added appropriate comments at the end of Chapter 3 and in the end-notes. In a way, this volume is a natural successor to *The Problem of the Picts* conference, held 30 years previously, since it holds exactly the same presuppositions about the symbol stones (grave markers) and the Pictish Oghams (a non-Indo-European language).

3. Duncan's history of Scotland ably carries the story forward past the demise of the Pictish kingdom and so usefully gives us a hindsight into what became of the amalgamated

kingdoms. See also Smyth's history of Scotland — discussed briefly in note 35.

Chapter 2

4. Table 2 was first compiled in 1980 using all the public sources available: the Royal Commission, Ordnance Survey, *Proceedings of the Society of Antiquaries of Scotland, Discovery & Excavation in Scotland, The early Christian monuments of Scotland, Sculptured stones of Scotland* besides personal observation. While this list is *reasonably* accurate, it has not been possible to check the details on stones kept privately or those that have been lost. Unfortunately this listing does not guarantee access, since some stones are in private grounds while others are in 'closed' museums and churches. In addition, many stones standing in the open are now badly weathered, some having lost all traces of any inscription. Certain stones have an infuriating habit of disappearing and turning up elsewhere — others vanish entirely!
The case of the stones at Tillytarmont farm is a typical example of the problems. Up to 1982 the original stone recorded in *ECMS* still stood near the farmhouse but then it was uprooted and 'lost' for a while, although it surfaced in 1983. The other four stones had been found when the owner deliberately deep-ploughed and searched a peninsula lying between two rivers. They were kept at the nearby Dykehead farm but removed in 1983 to Whitehills (where the owner had retired) to decorate a garden wall! These large stones have *all* the set A symbols except 23 while one (81) is unique in being almost circular. Since this was not an archaeological investigation, we will never know why these stones were buried in the sub-soil.

5. The ordering of the stones along a roughly north/south axis is to bring neighbouring stones together in the table. A strictly alphabetic arrangement produces quite an arbitrary array of stones. I have retained the old shires for the administrative areas since these are better known than the new divisions, besides which they permit easier cross-reference to older sources.

6. The actual numbering of the stones is a compromise between the general north/south orientation and the relative nearness of stones. There is no ideal way.

7. Table 3 is a matrix that reveals the dramatically skewed nature of the pairing of *all* the different symbols (except *19/43*). Reciprocal pairs (X/Y and Y/X) are sometimes equated for simplicity's sake since *in principle* there should be equal numbers of both. For example, should there be just one case of *4/41*, then I have included this under *41/4*, rather than draw a new matrix. Ideally, there should be 16 matrices to cover all the combinations but, in fact, we only need 9 matrices to demonstrate the different pairs, which is the whole purpose of the table. The actually occurring combinations are given in Figure 2 but, again, only one of the reciprocals is shown.

An anomaly that needs to be explained is why the first two symbols in sets A and B (*viz* symbols *5* and *8* and symbols *3* and *6*) each self-combine? Theoretically this should not happen.

What is significant is that most of these anomalies occur within a restricted area: *Ross:* (Class I) No. 38 *(3/3?)*, No. 45 *(5/8/8)*, No. 42 *(5/5)*; (Class II) No. 10 *(8/8 II 5/8)*. *Moray* (Class I) No. 57 *(1?/8/8)*. *Fife* (Class I) No. 140 *(6/6)*.

The three examples of apparently multiple symbols all have *8/8* — could this be a local overemphasis on *8*? Could these represent an unusual pairing of the northern and southern branches of *8* (the two Brideis, cf. Part II, chapter 1)? As for the other self-combinations of *3*, *5* and *6*, perhaps they are not alliance stones. Obviously these anomalies need a special explanation, but these few exceptions do go to prove the rule of general pairing.

If we dismiss the totally ambiguous Wemyss Bay cave inscriptions from the rejected Class I designs of Table 2B, there are just 35 designs remaining, of which there are only 12 non-true symbols; 2(1), 22(1), 32(9+[25?]) and 36(1).

There are no designs at all in the rejected Class II stones in Table 2D. These exceptions prove the rule, since the 34 single bull designs *(32)* must have had a very special purpose — like votive offerings! The 40-odd Wemyss Bay engravings have absolutely nothing in common with the well-designed *symbols* in the Covesea cave (near Burghead), and so they must have represented something entirely different to them and the ordinary upright, paired symbol stones — if they were at all related!

8. Figure 2 shows all the different pairings of symbols (reciprocals are excluded), apart from *5/11*, *8/35d* and *35d/41* which were omitted because of the dubious standing of

designs *11* and *35d*. The numbers refer to the sequence numbers in Table 2; those in brackets are Class II. Hence double numbering indicates those dozen pairs common to both Class I and II — note that they contain either *8* or *31*. What is surprising is that these 90 pairs comprise the entire Pictish repertoire — a mere 12% of possible pairings. It will be seen that the symbol *8* is present in a third of the pairs and is only equalled in frequency by symbols *5* and *31*, combined. These frequencies are shown in Table 3.

The examples are copied from the original stones and show some of the *variations* in the designs but they are not all to the same scale, while some designs have been simplified for clearer reproduction. These are not necessarily the 'best' examples for they were just taken in the order they appeared in Table 2, but they do show a good cross-section of styles.

Chapter 3

9. It is instructive to compare Figure 2 with *ECMS* (pp79-127) where series of stereotyped symbols are misleadingly lined up in rows — ignoring the vital fact that *the pairs of symbols are actually arranged vertically and touching each other!* This mistaken presentation by Romilly Allen of rearranging the symbols to 'read' from left to right gives us the clue to his error: he believed (as have many others) that the symbols were, like the Oghams, a secret *language!* This is one source of all those fruitless attempts at trying to translate the symbols as if they were words. The true arrangement of the symbols was of course well-known but Romilly Allen's analysis still suggested that one should 'read' the stones from top to bottom — the delightful paradox being that the associated Oghams were always read from the bottom upwards! My own analysis shows, later, that it is indeed the bottom symbol which is the more important — it represents the man's lineage in the marriage alliance. So, yet again, Romilly Allen has unwittingly set scholars off in the wrong direction. Of course with hindsight it *seemed* reasonable at the time, but how disastrous have been the consequences of this primary analysis for Pictish studies!

Chapter 4

10. Van Gennep, the famous anthropologist who wrote that classic work *The Rites of Passage* (1909) about the ceremonies that marked birth, puberty, marriage and death, was at that time also intrigued by totemism. In 1919 he wrote that

totemism had already taxed the wisdom and ingenuity of many scholars and that it would continue to do so for many years. An apt parallel would be the contemporary debate on the Picts! However, van Gennep was wrong in his prediction, for interest in totemism rapidly waned as Lévi-Strauss points out in his own, brilliant, book on totemism. Here he declares: *Totemism is an illusion* that is the result of

> "a distortion of the semantic field to which belong phenomena of the same type. *Certain aspects of the field have been singled out at the expense of others, giving them an originality and a strangeness which they do not really possess; for they are made to appear mysterious by the very fact of abstracting them from the system of which, as transformations, they formed an integral part."*

> *Totemism* p. 86 (my italics)

This quotation exactly describes the so-called problem of the Picts.

Lévi-Strauss' book finally exploded the myth of totemism and he followed this up with his work *The savage mind* which attempts to explain the relationship between totems, clan organization, the rules of marriage, magic and ritual by examining the way people construct their systems of totemic classifications.

Clearly it is precisely these relationships that Lévi-Strauss is interested in that also concern my work on the Pictish symbols. I do not attempt to follow his style of analysis but the results are quite similar. In order to discern the system behind the symbols I have had to make certain assumptions which are the outcome of many years of trying out alternatives.

My prime objective has been to show that the paired symbol stones have nothing to do with the *dead* but only with the *living*. This *volte-face* from traditional approaches to the symbol stones is necessary if we are ever to understand what the symbol stones meant to the Picts. Too many Pictish scholars have been so obsessed with death that they could not see the obvious alternative! The Picts were concerned with this life, being pagan, and not bothered about the *next* life.

11. The following Tables 4-12 outline the steps which lead from the raw data (Table 3) via the hypothetical Figure 3 to the

important Table 13 and on to the final models in Tables 24-26. The aim is to demonstrate a basic consistency between the statistical frequency and importance of the primary symbols in their social significance. A comparison of these tables shows this similarity throughout. Indeed, in Lévi-Strauss' term, these tables are simply transformations of each other. The inserted frequency tables are a check that the transformed table is correct. No elaborate statistical correlation coefficients are employed, for, while appearing more scientific, they are more likely to confuse than help.

In practice there are *no* single (undamaged) symbol stones and this effectively removes all the *14* dubious (single-occuring) designs at one stroke — *viz 2, 11, 16, 20, 25, 26, 27, 28, 29, 30, 32b, 32c, 33 and 36l*. In Class II times, there are two new symbols: *38* and *35d*, which replace the *7* 'lost' Class I symbols: *1, 12, 14, 34, 37, 38* and *40g*. These various multiples of 7 are somewhat curious, just as the 21 symbols which represent *all* the lineages in Class II times for *42/3* has dropped out while *39d/39b* are conjoined! What *is* the significance of 7?

Chapter 5

12. An elementary book on kinship is Fox: *Kinship & marriage* which discusses some of the problems of unilinearity and cross-cousin marriage. More advanced arguments will be found in Lévi-Strauss 1969 and Needham 1962 & 1974.

13. The particular model of kinship and marriage advanced here is solely designed to account for the pairing of symbols, and must be regarded as tentative until a better model is devised. There is no necessity to prove the historical accuracy of the model *before* using it, since a model is independent of the data which it tries to explain. If the model works, *then* is the time to find the historical evidence. Given the obscurity surrounding Pictish kinship, one can only try to develop the best possible explanatory model.

Chapter 6

14. Table 13 is constructed on the basis of the genuine symbols listed in Table 2. It is assumed that the symbols combine with each other in pairs in a prescribed way determined by the structure of the macropit and that every macropit is different and composed of just four symbols. No prior

assumptions could be made about the actual composition or location of the macropits since they are a product of history and not of theory.

Given the binary nature of Pictish thought, it follows that the total number of macropits had to be a multiple of two in this symbol system. For Class I the number of macropits turned out to be $2^5 = 32$, while the total number of pairs should be $2^8 = 256$. The corresponding numbers for Class II is exactly half, i.e. 16 macropits and 128 pairs. This gives a grand total of 48 macropits and 384 pairs. It should be pointed out that this does not mean that there are 384 symbol *stones* because, occasionally, the Picts inscribed several pairs on one stone.

There was nothing to prevent the Picts creating extra-systemic inscriptions but these were quite distinct in purpose from the macropit symbol system which had as its sole aim: the regulation of alliances and inheritance. Failure to note this distinction has caused needless confusion between the ordered symbol system of the macropits and the use of symbols and other designs on objects, rocks and caves.

The actual arrangement given in the table was derived empirically by fitting in the symbol pairs as they occurred, starting from the geographical north. As can be seen, 95% of existent stones are neatly accomodated and they represent 56% of all the possible pairs. Those stones which are damaged and only have a single symbol have been included and have had their 'missing' symbol restored in the correct position — the commonest absentee is *8*, unsurprisingly. As this is an empirically derived table, it is only provisional since new finds may cause a change of composition of this array of macropits. More sophisticated techniques might improve the reliability of this table.

In the expansion of the macropits it is quite remarkable that ¾ of the macripits are half full and more, despite the fact that we have only found ½ the possible number of symbol pairs. Hence the future discovery of new stones by the turn of the century will fill up many of the macropits and significantly reduce the margin of error.

A new symbol stone has just come to my notice — a broken stone that has the symbol *8* upon it. It should be catalogued as Class I, No. 10a (Table 2) in Caithness, grid reference ND 3117 4076, bibliographical reference Gourlay (1984), and the place is Watenan. It could be placed in the 6th macropit of sub-table I in Table 14, under the pair *8/7*.

15. The results show there to be four main blocs. These have, somewhat provocatively, been given *real* provincial names: they correspond with what we know about these divisions. Now we can draw the actual boundaries! If the basic argument is found convincing, then historians are invited to consider its implications.

One interesting anomaly is that practically all moiety i of Class I Circind is in the 'wrong' area — in Ce territory. This is because the decision to erect the symbol stones was taken *before* Bridei reconquered Circind in 685 A.D. It is to be noted that these 'misplaced' symbol pairs are closer to Class II pairs than they are to other Class I pairs and this is related to that other anomaly — the small number of Class II stones in the Northern kingdom. This suggest that certain symbols (*read* lineages) had a foot in both camps. When Bridei settled in Circind, then moiety i returned home and later became Christian. However, while in exile, they had set up alliances with some of their northern companions, especially around the Moray Firth, which meant that they were possible heirs to the leadership there. After becoming Christian, they still had a legitimate claim in these places and so erected Class II stones there, which accounts for the similarity between the symbols of moiety i of the Circind stones and the Class II stones in the north. As ⅔ of these Class II stones have multiple symbol pairs, it suggests that these inheriting southerners banded together in face of the pagan Northern Picts.

This synoptic table is the hub of my argument, and from it there radiate many unexpected hypotheses concerning the unwritten history of the Picts and their social organization. I have not constantly qualified my assertions with 'maybes' since this makes for tedious reading, but they are still there! It is now up to others to convert these 'maybes' into facts or fantasies. What cannot be denied is that the macropit concept is not only a great generator of new ideas, like Lévi-Strauss' 'totemic operator', but it also demonstrates that the symbols *can* be translated and that their precise ordering and location *can* be accounted for, including the 'mirror and comb' element.

The notion of macropits gives us four important pieces of verifiable information:

1) the upper limit of the numbers of symbol pairs
2) the symbol pairs that are missing
3) the number of stones likely to be discovered

4) those stones that may have an undetected mirror/comb design

Theoretically there should be 384 symbol pairs (Class I and II) but there are only likely to be 320 *stones* because of multiple pairing: hence there are about 120 stones missing. As a quarter of existing stones are damaged to the extent of having just one symbol, it is quite likely that an equal number will have been completely destroyed. The implication is that there may be only 70 stones yet to be found, which, at the present rate of discovery, will take a century to recover.

Table 14 shows which pairs are missing and where they should be found. 98% of all the stones are accommodated in the macropits and they occupy 56% of the cells, but it is unlikely we will ever fill more than 75% of the cells because of destruction and this means we will only be really certain of 60% of the existing symbol *pairs*. Thus we are reaching the limits of our knowledge but the macropits do draw a definitive and reasonable boundary to work within, giving us a perspective on the symbols.

Earlier discussion had argued that there should be two leaders in every macropit per generation, the lineages alternating in turn. Hence one of each pair of reciprocals should represent a leader and have the bridewealth symbol attached at the bottom. This is shown in Table 14 where symbol *24* is given by *, + or ° — the last sign indicating an expected but yet undiscovered mirror and comb. It will be seen that many existing stones are marked ° and this suggests we should scrutinize these more carefully in case we have overlooked this design.

An interesting question is why Class II stones have so few mirror/comb designs? Obviously the strict requirement for FZD marriage was losing its force, as can be seen by the multiple symbol stones. Perhaps those lineages whose political control rested on mystical power were losing out against Christianity and could not enforce the marriage pattern. Ironically the only examples of bridewealth in Class II are with lineages *5, 31, 45 & 9* (the left-hand lineages) while the formerly strong Northern lineages: *8, 12, 40e & 17* (the right-hand side) who, alone, controlled ⅓ of all Class I symbol pairs, have utterly disintegrated. In terms of symbol frequencies in Class II times, then lineages *5 & 31* have drawn level with the powerful lineage *8*. This suggests that *45* is the royal Southern lineage, cf. pp 129-131.

These changes may be connected with the partial destruction of symbol pairs where one symbol is broken off the stone: it breaks the rigid marriage/alliance system with its hereditary leadership pattern, or, at least, denies it. These observations suggest that the Picts were becoming disenchanted with the inflexible marriage pattern although they still needed alliances with someone. The king-lists of this period suggest the same thing.

Despite a few minor descrepancies and omissions in this attempt to give a comprehensive explanation of the symbol pairs, it does provide the first working model to make sense of the symbols. The model will, of course, have to be revised since it is quite unlikely that I have got all the details correct. New discoveries will act both as a check and as a means of improving the table.

My hypotheses, stemming from the model, do not exhaust its possibilities since a finer-grained analysis might reveal the exact network of the individual macropits by correlating the position of the stones and the styles of the symbols. Other ideas may occur to people examining these distributions. The heartening result that the actual empirical facts fit the model almost perfectly suggests that this *must* be fairly close to what the Picts had in mind when they invented their system. It would be quite extraordinary that my relatively easily comprehensible model of a symbol system should give the same outcome in terms of symbol pairs in particular places as some *altogether different model* that the Picts really possessed! A comparison between those symbols which are present and those completely missing (not including the 51 damaged stones where one symbol has been lost) makes interesting reading.

The numbers of symbols present and absent (given in brackets) are to be found below:

3*	10 (19)	9	5 (3)	5	54 (20)	8	84 (52)
44*	9 (16)	40g*	3 (5)	45*	16 (21)	40e	14 (11)
6/7	21 (13)	21	10 (4)	23*	10 (18)	12	16 (15)
	41*	17 (23)			31	46 (17)	
	42/3	1 (—)			39b*	2 (8)	
1*	8 (9)	19	3 (2)	4*	11 (17)	17*	13 (16)
37	2 (—)	34	2 (2)	39b*	3 (5)	38	2 (2)
10*	3 (8)	46*	6 (10)	15*	3 (8)	14	3 (3)

The proportion in each set are:—

SET	PRESENT	ABSENT	% ABSENT
A	242	154	39%
B	81	83	51%
C	37	62	62%
D	25	31	57%

Well over half the symbols of the sets B, C and D are missing, but less than 2/5 of set A has been lost, despite the fact that it constitutes nearly half of the missing symbols. It stands to chance that the next symbol stones to be discovered will contain some of the 14 asterisked symbols (above), where there are *more* symbols missing than present. In terms of what we have and what is missing — it is level pegging! Interestingly enough, half the missing symbols just concern seven symbols: *8* (52), *41** (23), *45** (21), *5* (20), *3** (19), *23** (18) and *4** (17). These should be among the very *next* symbol stones to be discovered!

16. A simple comparison of the distribution maps of *pit*-names and Pictish monuments shows that there is an obvious overlap — with the single exception of the most northern counties and islands: Group W in my categorization. Furthermore, an interesting correlation appears regarding frequencies:

Area	All monuments		*pit*-names	
X & Y (Northern Kingdom)	103	45%	119	45%
Z (Southern kingdom)	128	55%	143	55%
X, Y & Z	231		262	

cf. Table 15

If every Pictish monument had appeared in a place with a *pit*-name, this would have provided an absolute link but, sadly, not even one such occurrence happens! Is not this rather odd? Actually the similarity of the above ratios disguises the fact that all classes of monument have been lumped together: no such similar ratio holds for the different classes, hence no conclusions on comparative dating can be reached on the basis of the class of monument. It therefore seems likely that the *pit*-names came into existence from pre-class I times *onwards*.

There are some paradoxes. Area Y has ⅓ of the *pit*-names and Class I stones but very few Class II, while Area Z has ½ the *pit*-names and ⅔ of the Class II but only ⅛ of Class I stones. If *pit*-names started with Class I, why are there none in Area W and so many in Area Z? If they began in Class II times, why are there so many in Area Y that has so few Class II stones? The only conclusion can be that there is no relation between the two sets of facts. *Pit*-names were probably just a feature of the Pictish naming system which constantly developed — their absence in the far north may be simply due to the fact that they were replaced by Norse names.

Although Watson has counted 323 *pit*-names, there are still 60 that cannot be pin-pointed on Map 6.

If *pit* or *pett* referred to a special (share) of land that belonged to a local household, then it may not be so surprising that the monuments are not found there but nearer the homestead or some other sacred place (later, a church). Perhaps they only erected stones on the *borders* of *pit*-named land, e.g. along the paths that surrounded the territory. Maybe a closer plotting of the stones and the *pit*-places might reveal some such connection. Unfortunately we do not know the size of a *pit* nor how many names have been lost, neither are we certain where all the stones originally stood.

Perhaps it could be enlightening to analyse all the meanings of the other component of the *pit*-name, e.g. Pit-meddan (middle share), Pit-arrow (corn share), Pit-gober (goat share). Such shares are unlikely to have been equal in area or symmetrically spaced. Also inheritance would diminish the size of holding *unless* the land was communally owned.

Summing up, one can assume that the *pit*-names indicate where the Picts used their land and that it coincides with the distribution of most of the monuments south of Sutherland. However there is no obvious connection between the two and hence these *pit*-names cannot directly help us to understand the symbols.

See Watkins (1984) for an interesting argument that the *pit*-names denoted the granting of estates during the consolidation of Pictish royal power.

17. The dualistic thesis that underlies my approach is well explored by Needham (1973), and also by Lévi-Strauss (1966), in establishing his case about the totemic operator.

18. The development of this argument stems directly from the statistical analysis given in chapter 4. The obvious parallels between pairs of symbols illustrated in Figure 2 needed to be explained. Malinowski, with his many books on the Trobrianders, provided a possible clue, for these people were also matrilineal, their chiefs practised FZD marriage, they have totems, believe in magic and the power of ancestral spirits, and they are also great traders in search of prestige.

    Of course the Trobriand cultural complex which makes total sense there, now, in quite different ecological conditions from the Picts, is not just transferable as a package. However the many similarities are suggestive. After all, the Picts must have had an equally integrated system and it *could* have been quite similar since the components of a culture tend to reinforce each other. The main parallel I would like to abstract is that the Picts were equally concerned about the ancestors and magic.

    Anna Ritchie (1972) has pointed out the existence of many painted pebbles which have come from broch sites and are probably Pictish. She suggests they might have been charm stones that had healing properties, and cites the contemporary evidence of St Columba's holy stone. What this indicates is that *stones* could be given special magical properties. However, none of the motifs on these pebbles are *true* symbols and so these patterns cannot be directly linked with the Pictish designs. It is just possible that such stones exist — resembling the *churinga* of the Australian aborigines — this, indeed, would be quite a find! However, it is dubious that they would ever have a pair of true symbols.

19. Tables 24-26 are an attempt to associate different levels of meaning with the various totemic pairs representing pairs of related lineages, always bearing the statistical frequencies in mind. This is the climax of my argument and it may come as something of a surprise to certain readers to be left staring at these models but *in fact one is now back at the beginning of the Picts!* With these models in mind it is now possible to reconstruct the development of the symbol system in a new way. This may be done by working *backwards* through the argument.

PART II

20. The chapters in Part II are independent of each other and are in no way affected by the truth or falsity of the conclusions reached in Part I. They all have a bearing on different aspects of Pictish research and may be thought of, simply, as being mutually complementary.

Chapter 1

21. The main purpose here is to suggest a new *type* of genealogical structure to explain the king-lists. No claim is made that the proffered genealogy is correct in all its details: it is a demonstration model. For further reading see Anderson 1973, Kirby and Miller. The adoption of a four lineage set in the genealogies would, I believe, make better sense of the data.

Chapter 2

22. This stone is more baffling than the symbol stones because *its* message is quite ambiguous, for its strip-cartoon story is not clear to us today. The critically important feature about the figures is their numbers. It is a shame that this magnificent stone is allowed to weather in the open.

23. The significance of the numbers is obscure to us but they are the only clue to its meaning.
    This account of Sueno's stone is an extremely compressed statement of this most noteworthy Class III stone, for this just summarises some of its extraordinarily complex compositional design. I merely point out some of the features that should be investigated further, since my sole purpose has been to show how it fits into the regnal sequence and relates to other Class III stones in date and composition, besides offering an account of why this tallest of Pictish monuments was ever erected! Although there is little relation to the symbol stones, it is connected to those scenes on Class II and III stones that depict armed aggression. What *is* the significance of those various groups of deer-hunters on horseback and those groups of armed horsemen? Are the numbers of horsemen involved important?

24. These suggestions may be maligning Kenneth, but if he did erect this monument after all the *realpolitik* I have ascribed to him, then he rises in my estimation as the only true master of the situation.

25. It is impossible to get completely accurate transcriptions of *all* the Oghams because of damage. I have not included a few grossly damaged fragments in the following analysis — these are identified in Table 28. It follows that there are problems with transliterations and, on the whole, I have accepted Padel's listing as the best compromise.

26. I have rendered all the strokes into one common form for comparison's sake.

27. The various interpretations of the Oghams now make the most hilarious reading, qv. Moore, Southesk and Diack. Their ingenuity and imagination equal that of Pennant who is quoted by Cruden as a horrid warning to the theorist. I trust that my attempt is on a sounder footing!

28. Referring back to the symbolic significance of numbers (Table 22), odd numbers (which include all the prime numbers) are associated with the sun and females, while even numbers are linked to the moon and males. Now the Pictish/Celtic festivals take place at intervals of 91 (7 × 13) days in the solar year, and so the first festival of the year is Bride which is connected with childbirth. The third festival is Lammas at which handfast (i.e. trial) marriages were arranged. Thus both these odd quarter-days are associated with women. It cannot be entirely coincidental that nine months after the festivities of Beltane, many women are in childbirth around the festival of Bride. Indeed, in an age where fertility had to be proved *before* marriage, it follows that Lammas would be the ideal time to try out marriage since one would then know if a woman was fertile. We might conclude that Beltane and Hallowmass were male-oriented, and it is interesting that May 1st and November 1st are still widely celebrated in Europe as folk festivals.

29. It is curious that only the prime numbers: 3, 7 and 13 have any mystical significance in Celtic and European thought generally. Is it because they all denote the end of some process?

>   a) Magical spells are always concluded after the 3rd
>   repeat
>   b) The week ends after 7 days
>   c) The year ends after 13 lunar months

d) The quarter-year Celtic festivals are celebrated after
   91 (7 × 13) days

The number 3 has no direct calendrical associations but it is
the basic unit of Celtic (Welsh) linear measurement: 3 barley-
corns/thumb, 3 thumbs/palm, 3 palms/foot, 3 feet/yard, etc.
This common, everyday usage might account for this
number receiving mystical significance since, like 7 and 13, it
is also based upon natural phenomena: barleycorns and the
body. It is also worth pointing out that another feature of
European thought is the three-fold gender division of nouns
into masculine, feminine and neuter. However, this does not
resolve the problem of why 3 should be used because, unlike
7 and 13 which are thrust into prominence by the
regularities of the sun and moon, there is no necessity for
using 3 in linear measurements. Elsewhere (Jackson, 1974) I
have argued that the proto-British measurement system was a
binary one, and this could have been the case for the Picts in
their dualistic universe. So it is interesting that the number 3
does not receive much emphasis in Pictish symbolism other
than the Oghams which, after all, were a loan from the Irish,
and that may have included a bias towards using groups of 3
to add extra mystical power to the strokes.

It is not quite true that the number 3 has *no* calendrical
associations but they are rather indirect. If one looks at Fig.
15, it can be seen that the periods between the four sets of
28 days which herald the solstices and equinoxes are filled
with *3* sets of 21 days. Likewise, in Fig. 6 on marriage, each
lineage is a member of a triad: itself and the lineages on
either side to whom and from whom they send and receive
women as wives. So while there are triadic elements present,
they are dependent on the four-fold structure which already
exists. Indeed, the common division of the day into two sets
of 12 hours, besides the division of the foot into 12 inches,
presupposes a basic four-part structure (the quarters) while
the intervals are equally divided *twice* — thus creating 3
'spaces' of time and length per quarter. it is this 'emergent'
property of 3 *out of a basic dualistic system* that is so
intriguing, for it can be simply seen if one adopts a circle as
a model: divide it twice and then divide the quarters, thus
formed, twice into equal portions — you get a total of 12
equal portions!
The mystic number, 7, obviously derives from the lunar
cycle of 28 days being divided into quarters — no further

subdivision is possible as 7 is a prime number. The same applies to mystic number 13 since this is the number of lunar cycles to the solar year, while the quarter days consist of 91 (7 × 13) days that cannot be further subdivided because of the two prime numbers.

It can be no mere coincidence that ALL the three major European mystical numbers — 3, 7 and 13 — arise directly out of the quadripartition of *time!* It is also worth noting that time intervals have *always* been set by ritual in all societies — hence the mystical association of these numbers with the 'rhythm' of the European universe is neither surprising or unexpected.

We might just pause to reflect that the extremely perverse system of Anglo-Saxon measurement is based upon *heavenly* principles, while the French metric system is based upon *human* principles — the 10 fingers and thumbs on our two hands (or our 10 toes) — with a little encouragement from that magnificent Arabic discovery of zero which so revolutionised mathematics. Ironically enough in our present computer age, we have reverted to binary counting — just like our ancestors — so, Nature triumphs in the end if she made our brains on the binary principle as Lévi-Strauss suggests! As a final point on numbers, consider the squares: $2^2 = 4$, $3 = 9$ (another mystic number), $4^2 = 16$, $5^2 = 25$ (¼ of 100), $10^2 = 100$, $12^2 = 144$ (gross). The other squares do not seem to be important to us, although $7^2 = 49$, $8^2 = 64$, $9^2 = 81$, $11^2 = 121$, $13^2 = 169$ are important in Buddhist societies! This symbolic importance of numbers is a universal feature of mankind and should be studied seriously.

It is possible that the Picts had their own 'megalithic yard' and so house-construction should be carefully examined — both in circular and rectangular measure — if they follow Anna Ritchie's Buckquoy Pictish house. This could be an important clue as to what is Pictish!

Chapter 4

Christianity undoubtedly had at least three major effects upon the Picts regarding their:

     i) belief system
     ii) marriage system
     iii) symbolism

Although our major concern is with the last point, it is still intimately tied in with the other two points.

31. The symbols themselves had two faces: a) a lineage/totem mark, b) magical potency. This last characteristic may well have been hidden from the Church or, if known, condemned as pagan. Either way the symbols did not challenge the authority of the Church.

This section on the influence of Christianity is far from comprehensive but I have only been concerned with the effect upon Class II stones. The other effects of Christianity are not our concern here.

32. The dating of the different classes of Pictish monuments is fraught with difficulty, as we have no reason to suppose that Classes I, II and III were chronologically sequential all over Pictland. The fact that Class I probably emerged first does not mean that all production ceased when Class II developed.

Similarity with Class III. So the following situation may have been the case:

Class I					
Class II					
Class III					
650	700	750	800	850	900

Thus while we may make a good guess at the beginning of these different classes there is no way of knowing when they ceased completely. Most likely they all began within the century: 675-775 but Class I could still be being made in 875! Although this goes against my thesis that the stones were all erected by 680, it does not follow that *replacement* stones were not carved later if they became damaged or households moved — the possibility must be borne in mind. Thus it is conceivable that in the pagan northern kingdom they put up new stones quite later in the Class I style. Similarly it is possible that the northern Class II stones are later than the southern ones because there was not the same pressing necessity as in Class I times. Hence it may well be that Sueno's Stone (c.840) was set up only shortly after the other northern Class II stones were carved; this makes better sense than to assume that the masons kept these patterns on cold ice for more than a century.

If we allow a generous fortnight for a single band of masons to travel to the various sites, find, cut and erect the Class I stones, then it would take them a decade to complete the theoretical total of 256 stones. On the other hand, six bands of masons could have completed the job between the edict of 683 A.D. and the battle of Nechtansmere in 685. If the Class II stones took a couple of months apiece, then it would take two decades to complete the work and the same length of time would be needed for the Class III stones. This gives us the following table:

Class	Period of erection	Interval	Reigning king
I	683-693		Bridei (671-692)
II	728-748	35 years	Oengus (728-760)
III	789-809	41 years	Constantine (789-820)
Sueno's stone	842	33 years	Kenneth (842-858)

The table shows that is is perfectly possible for knowledge and skill to be passed on during the intervals between these different phases of construction of these stones.

Conclusions

33. There is an archaeological puzzle about the souterrains. What was the function of these underground tunnels? Were they a refuge, storage chambers, or both? It is likely that they are a simple corollary of the brochs which mainly served the weaker communities defending herds and people against slave raiders. Going underground is a well-known technique for avoiding capture! Indeed this habit of building disguised shelters may account for the popular belief that the Picts were a small people who actually lived under the ground!

Watkins (1984) argues that souterrains were cereal stores and thus indicate the development of prosperous farming communities.

The close association of brochs and souterrains with the symbol stones in the same areas suggests that there is a link with the Picts. While the brochs and souterrains indicate a people on the defensive before 200 A.D., the symbol stones show they have "come out" and live freely without fear. After the unification of some of the Pictish tribes by 360 A.D., both the brochs and souterrains seem to have fallen into disuse. The main defensive structures remaining are the so-called vitrified forts south of the Moray Firth, about which we still know very little.

Archaeologists are prone to reject anthropological interpretations of their data on the grounds that they are only
arguments by analogy. This is true when we *compare*
artefacts between two different societies but is not so in the
present case where we examine the symbol stones in terms
of a theoretical model of kinship. There is no analogy since
the Picts had to have a kinship system — the only question
is whether I have chosen the right one. My model is likely
to be the only one that fits the facts concerning the pairing
of symbols and the use of the mirror and comb symbol at
the bottom. It might just be remarked that the suggestions
that the symbol stones are status messages and are funerary
monuments are *both* arguments by analogy!

34. Stevenson's analysis of the infilled decoration is a possible
lead in investigating the relations between the four branches
of lineage *8*. Is there a connection between the different
designs, their geographical location, their allies and the
kingship succession? Are there other similar examples? This
line of thought seems worth pursuing.

35. In his recently published history of Scotland: *Warlords and
Holy Men*, Smyth devotes a whole chapter to the Picts. His
purpose is to demystify the Picts and to show that they are
very much like, if not identical to, the Irish. To this end, he
chides the linguists for assuming a pre-Celtic language and
takes archaeologists to task for talking about proto-Picts and
for distinguishing too sharply between brochs and vitrified
forts. *Only* historians may define the *Picti!*
More than half this chapter of Smyth's book is reserved for
pouring scorn upon the matrilineal hypothesis. However, in
commenting on the alleged lack of a Pictish word for a son
(in the Oghams), he begins to trip up by saying that "even
matriarchs *(sic)* had male offspring" (p.58). Later, he
mentions that matrilineal succession went "from the mother
through a mother's son or through a sister's son" (p.59). The
implication that the Picts were matriarchal is utter nonsense,
since there are no matriarchal societies and, in any case,
matrilineal succession always goes from a *man* to his sister's
son. Of course women are involved, but they are not *that*
important and so no *mother* or sister is ever mentioned in
the king-lists! It is for the same reason that the fathers of
kings are also unimportant in the line of succession but they
would nevertheless appear significant to the Scottish
compilers of the Pictish king-lists — to answer Smyth's
question (p.58).

Smyth rejects all matrilineal genealogies based upon the king-lists on the grounds that there are no manuscripts *from within* Pictish society to corroborate these ideas. This is a ludicrous suggestion since we all know that the Picts never wrote on any manuscripts anyway.

The symbol stones are briefly dismissed as *art!* Smyth concludes that the designs were the result of contact with Iona, yet he previously suggests that they were possibly tattooed on the bodies of the Picts. Hence we receive the bizarre picture of groups of Picts trudging back from Iona with new tattoos emblazoned on their chests and then, later, engraving these designs on boundary and grave markers *all over Scotland* a century or so afterwards — a somewhat surprising spin-off from Columba's mission!

Smyth's attempts to claim the Picts for history *alone* are only partially successful. He is more effective against linguists and archaeologists than against his fellow historians. That said, the rest of the book is a welcome contribution to the background of the Picts — especially on the Viking impact wherein Kenneth conspires with the Norwegians to bring about the downfall of the Picts.

Like most historians, Smyth hopes for some *non-existent manuscript* to eventually prove his case and, at the same time, uses this postulated lack of evidence to dismiss other scholars' suggestions. This device is used as a smoke-screen to cast doubt upon the matrilineal hypothesis, yet the king-lists *do* exist! His own exegesis is very partial and quite fails to explain the lists.

36. There is scope for historians to use anthropological insights in building up an account of the Picts. Perhaps this attempt might spur them on.

37. Having criticised *ECMS* and *SSS* for employing Scotland in their titles, I also appear guilty of the same fault! My defence of the alliterative title is that the *only* symbol stones in Scotland are Pictish. The alternative of *Pictograms of Pictland* is too contrived.

38. Paradoxically, it is maintained here that Christianity was responsible for the origin *and* decline of the symbol stones. Masons, trained in carving Christian monuments, are likely to have suggested designs to the Pictish rulers and then executed them on commission. When the Church was firmly established (c 790 A.D.), it could forbid cross-cousin

marriage and insist on patrilineal succession — thereafter there were no more Class II stones and the lineage symbols disappeared. Thus the definitive century for the Pictish symbol was 685-785 A.D.

39. This is an attempt at a *holistic* interpretation which brings in *everything* we know into a single form. While there are still many debatable issues, the main patterns are reasonable clear from 683-843. These events are not simply the battles between kings, or their successes or defeats, but the changes in Pictish society under the influence of Christianity and the presence and pressure of outsiders.

40. It is worth noting the close interlinkages between those items in Pictish society which occur in multiples of 2 and of 7. Most of them emerged from the analysis given in this book.

The number 2
1. symbolic *designs* (totemic duos)
2. N & S Pictland (geometric and animal designs)
3. macropits (2 pairs of symbols and their location)
4. king list (2 pairs of lineages)
5. Newton stone (A and U designs)
6. Sueno's stone (Picts and Scots)
7. marriage alliances (2 lineages)

The number 7
1. symbol formation (sets of 7)
2. Pictish 'kingdoms' (traditionally 7)
3. king lists (groups of 7 kings)
4. Oghams (number of strokes)
5. Pictish calendar (number of days)
6. Pictish royal lineages (traditionally 7)
7. Sueno's stone (number of combatants)

Could such tight interlinkages in the Pictish world-view have been discovered if they were not true in some sense? All these holistic patterns could not just have arisen by accident.

41. This broad sweep through things Pictish has revealed some quite unexpected connections that relate to the origin and development of the symbol stones, the Oghams, various peculiar and hitherto unexplained Class III stones, besides the differently recorded Pictish king-lists. It is this *whole*

complex of puzzles that is a central issue that needs to be resolved by any *complete* explanation of the Picts. Partial explanations are not good enough since the Picts must, themselves, have had some convincing *overall* explanatory rationale for their behaviour in all these respects.

42. I *have* made a number of assumptions to make my models work — which they do quite successfully, I believe. This is the essence of scientific method: to make models, explaining the data. What alternative assumptions can better solve the combinations of symbols that are actually found? This is the real challenge — it does not simply concern the symbol stones alone but all the other aspects of Pictish Life.

43. The *only other* current hypothesis about the symbol stones is that they are some kind of funerary monument; yet, not even supporters of this idea are agreed amongst themselves because no symbol stone has yet been found in position above a burial.
    The main reasons for assuming that symbol stones are funerary monuments are:
      1) by analogy with Roman and Christian monuments over graves
      2) by analogy with Irish Oghams which state *plainly* to whom and by whom the stone was erected — again on Christian principles
      3) the occasional co-occurrence of symbol stones *near* burials.
      4) that symbols (hypothetically) represent statuses held by the dead.

None of these reasons is valid because they do not explain the extremely skewed combinations of pairs of symbols that *do* occur, their location and their very frequent *disassociation* with any burial, while the inexplicable nature of Pictish Oghams renders them quite meaningless, the *non*-presence of undamaged single symbol stones (if they represented a status) is unexplained, the meaning of the mirror and comb symbol and its presence *at the bottom of some symbol pairs* is not accounted for, while the fact that not a single particular combination of symbol pairs ever occurs *in the same place* is a very curious feature which is not explained at all! These grave and fundamental weaknesses do not *disprove* that thesis, even if such a modern individualistic notion would have been most unlikely in pagan, tribal society like the

Picts. There is simply *nothing* to be said in favour of this idea — so why has it been entertained? The answer has to be that it has been the *only* explanation to have been advanced so far! Consider its weaknesses, its lack of any proof, besides the fact that such an explanation would actually render any 'total explanation' of the symbol stones quite impossible, and you will see why this hypothesis has to be rejected lock, stock and barrel. Quite simply, this view of the symbol stones condemns us to utter ignorance of the symbols — consider what has happened so far this century!

Now, simply discrediting the *one and only* current explanation of the symbols does not, of course, in itself prove that my alternative must be correct. However, my thesis does happen to explain *all* the unanswered problems connected with the funerary monument idea, besides rendering the notion of status-adulation a totally ridiculous concept.

Leaving aside the actual symbol stones, my argument that dualism and the number 7 were *vitally* important to the Picts does explain much about the *unwritten* history of the Picts — the geometric and animal symbols, the binary nature of the symbol designs, the meaning of the symbols, the king-lists, Sueno's stone, the Oghams and the Pictish calendar — could this be mere chance?

44. The short, selective bibliography I give refers to those works that I have, personally, found helpful yet it also contains many references to other aspects of the Picts which I do not discuss. Although I am alone in putting forward the alliance/symbol stones hypothesis, it would not have been possible without the spadework done by these other scholars. While I am very critical of his findings, I am indebted to Thomas for his daring flights of fancy since they directly inspired my own! In addition, he has been instrumental in keeping the debate on the symbol stones alive for nearly a quarter of a century.

Select Bibliography

Alcock, L. 1980. Populi bestiales feroci animo: A survey of Pictish settlement archaeology, *British Archaeological Reports,* S71, 61-95.

Allen, J. R. 1887. *Early Christian symbolism in Great Britain & Ireland.* London.

Allen, J. R. & Anderson J. 1903. *The early Christian monuments of Scotland.* Edinburgh.

Allen, J. R. 1904. *Celtic art in Pagan & Christian times.* Edinburgh.

Anderson, J. 1881. *Scotland in early Christian times.* 2 vols. Edinburgh.

Anderson, J. 1883. *Scotland in Pagan times.* Edinburgh.

Anderson, A. O. 1908. *Scottish annals from English chronicles.* London.

Anderson, A. O. & Anderson, M. O. (eds). 1961. *Adomnan's Life of Columba.* Edinburgh.

Anderson, M. O. 1973. *Kings & kingship in early Scotland.* Edinburgh.

Backhouse, J. 1981. *The Lindisfarne Gospels.* Oxford.

Bain, G. 1951. *Celtic Art: The methods of construction.* London.

Bede. 1896. *Historia Ecclesiastica Gentes Anglorum,* in *Baeda Opera Historica,* ed. C. Plummer, 2 vols. Oxford.

Bannerman, J. 1974. *Studies in the history of Dalriada.* Edinburgh.

Brown, P. 1980. *The Book of Kells.* London.

Campbell, J. F. & Henderson, G. 1911. *The Celtic dragon myth.* Edinburgh.

Chadwick, H. M. 1949. *Early Scotland.* Cambridge.

Chadwick, N. K. 1958. Pictish & Celtic marriage in early literary tradition. *Scottish Gaelic Studies,* VIII Pt ii, 56-155.

Close-Brooks, J. 1984. 'Pictish and other burials' in Friell and Watson, 87-114.

Cottam, M. B. & Small, A. 1974. The distribution of settlement in southern Pictland. *Medieval Archaeology* 18, 43-65.

Cruden, S. 1964. *The early Christian and Pictish monuments of Scotland.* Edinburgh.

Curle, C. L. 1940. The chronology of the early Christian monuments of Scotland. *PSAS,* LXXIV, 60-116.

Diack, F. C. 1944. *The inscriptions of Pictland . . . with other writings & collections.* Aberdeen.

Douglas, R. 1934. Monuments: Sueno's stone, *Annals of the Royal Burgh of Forres.* Elgin, 306-13.

Dillon, M. & Chadwick, N. K. 1967. *The Celtic realms.* London.

Duncan, A. A. M. 1975. *Scotland, the making of the Kingdom.* Edinburgh.

ECMS cf. Allen, J. R. & Anderson, J. 1903.

Feachem, R. W. 1955. 'Fortifications' in Wainwright, 1955, 65-86.

Fox, R. 1967. *Kinship & marriage.* Harmondsworth.

Fraser, J. 1927. The question of the Picts. *Scottish Gaelic Studies,* II, 172-201.

Friell, J. G. P. & Watson, W. G. 1984 *Pictish Studies: Settlement, Burial & Art in Dark Age Northern Britain.* British Archaeological Reports, British Series 125.

van Gennep, A. 1960. *The Rites of Passage.* Chicago.

Goody, J. 1983. *The development of the family and marriage in Europe.* C U P.

Graham, A. 1947. Some observations on the brochs. *PSAS,* LXXI, 48-99.

Gordon, C. A. 1956. Carving technique on the symbol stones of north-east Scotland *PSAS,* 81, 40-60.

Gordon, C. A. 1966. The Pictish animals observed. *PSAS,* 98, 215-24.

Gourlay, R. 1984. 'A symbol stone and cairn at Watenan, Caithness' in Friell & Watson, 131-134.

Grimble, I. 1980. *Highland man.* Inverness.

Henderson, G. 1910. *The Norse influence on Celtic Scotland.* Glasgow.

Henderson, G. 1911. *Survivals in belief among the Celts.* Glasgow.

Henderson, I. M. 1958. The origin centre of the Pictish symbol stones. *PSAS,* 91, 44-60.

Henderson, I. M. 1967. *The Picts.* London.

Henderson, I. M. 1971a. 'Northern Pictland' in Meldrum 1971, 37-52.

Henderson, I. M. 1971b. 'The meaning of the Pictish symbol stones' in Meldrum 1971, 53-68.

Henderson, I. M. 1972. The Picts of Aberdeenshire & their monuments. *Archaeological Journal* 129, 47-73.

Jackson, A. 1971. Pictish social structure & symbol-stones. *Scottish Studies,* 15, 121-40.

Jackson, A. 1974. The megalithic yard reconsidered: rods, poles or barleycorns? *Northern Studies* 1974:4, 30-37.

Jackson, A. 1979. *Na-khi religion.* The Hague.

Jackson, K. H. 1955. 'The Pictish language' in Wainwright 1955, 129-66.

Kirby, D. P. 1976. '. . . per universas Pictorum provincias' in Bonner, G. (ed). *Famulus Christi,* London. 286-324.

Laslett, P. 1965. *The world we have lost.* London.

Le Roy Ladurie, E. 1974. *The peasants of Languedoc.* Illinois.

Lethbridge, T. C. 1954. *The painted men.* London.

Lévi-Strauss, C. 1966. *The savage mind.* London.

Lévi-Strauss, C. 1969. *Totemism.* Harmondsworth.

Lévi-Strauss, C. 1969. *The elementary structures of kinship.* London.

Macfarlane, A. 1978. *The origins of English individualism.* Oxford: Blackwell.

Mackinlay, J. M. 1914. *Ancient church dedications in Scotland.* 2 vols. Edinburgh.

McNeil, P. & Nicholson, R. (eds). 1975. *An historical atlas of Scotland c 400-c 1600.* St Andrews.

Magnusson, M. 1973. *Viking expansion westwards.* London.

Malinowski, B. 1922. *Argonauts of the Western Pacific.* London.

Marr, R. E. 1930. *Mac Beth.* Inverness.

Meldrum, E. (ed). 1971. *The Dark Ages in the Highlands.* Inverness Field Club.

Miller, M. 1978. Eanfrith's Pictish son. *Northern History* 14, 47-66.

Miller, M. 1979. The last century of Pictish succession. *Scottish Studies* 23, 39-67.

Miller, M. 1979. The disputed historical horizon of the Pictish king-lists. *Scottish Historical Review* LVIII, 1:165, 1-34.

Miller, M. 1980. 'Matriliny by treaty: the Pictish foundation legend' in MacKitterick, R. et al (eds) *Ireland in Early Mediaeval Europe.* Cambridge.

Moore, G. 1865. *Ancient pillar stones of Scotland.* Edinburgh.

Needham, R. 1962. *Structure & sentiment.* Chicago.

Needham, R. 1973. *Right & Left.* Chicago.

Needham, R. 1974. *Remarks and inventions.* London.

O'Rahilly, T. F. 1946. *Early Irish history & mythology.* Dublin.

Padel, O. J. 1972. *Inscriptions of Pictland.* Unpublished M. Litt. Edinburgh.

Piggott, S. (ed) 1962. *The prehistoric peoples of Scotland.* London.

PSAS : Proceedings of the Society of Antiquaries of Scotland.

Ralston, I. and Inglis, J. 1984. *Foul hordes: the Picts in the North-east and their background.* Aberdeen.

Ritchie, A. 1972. Painted pebbles in early Scotland. *PSAS* 104, 297-301.

Ritchie, A. 1974. Pict & Norseman in northern Scotland. *Scottish Archaeological Forum* 6, 22-36.

Ritchie, A. 1977. Excavation of Pictish & Viking-age farmsteads at Buckquoy, Orkney. *PSAS* 108, 174-227.

Ritchie, G. & A. 1981. *Scotland: Archaeology and early history.* London.

Ritchie, A. 1984. 'Orkney in the Pictish Kingdom' in C. Renfrew (ed): *The prehistory of Orkney.* Edinburgh.

Scott, A. B. 1918. *The Pictish nation its people and its church.* Edinburgh.

Skene, W. F. (ed) 1867. *Chronicles of the Picts, Chronicles of the Scots and other early memorials of Scottish history.* Edinburgh.

Skene, W. F. 1876-80. *Celtic Scotland.* 3 vols. Edinburgh.

Smyth, A. P. 1984. *Warlords and holy men.* London.

Southesk, Lord. 1885. *The Ogham inscription of Scotland.* Edinburgh.

Southwick, L. 1981. *The so-called Sueno's stone at Forres.* Elgin.

SSS cf Stuart 1856-67.

Stevenson, R. B. K. 1955. 'Pictish art' in Wainwright 1955.

Stevenson, R. B. K. 1959. The Inchyra stone and some other unpublished Early Christian monuments. *PSAS* XCII, 33-55.

Stuart, J. 1856-67. *Sculptured stones of Scotland.* 2 vols. Aberdeen & Edinburgh.

Thomas, A. C. 1961. The animal art of the Scottish Iron Age and its origins. *Archaeological Journal* 118, 14-64.

Thomas, A. C. 1963. The interpretation of the Pictish symbols. *Archaeological Journal* 120, 30-97.

Thomas, A. C. 1984. 'The Pictish Class I Symbol Stones' in Friell & Watson, 169-188.

Thomas, K. 1971. *Religion & the decline of magic.* London.

Wainwright, F. T. (ed). 1955. *The problem of the Picts.* Edinburgh.

Wainwright, F. T. (ed). 1962. *The Northern Isles.* Edinburgh.

Watkins, T. 1984. 'Where were the Picts?' in Friell & Watson, 63-86.

Watson, W. J. 1926. *The history of the Celtic place-names of Scotland.* Edinburgh.

Whittington, G. 1975. Place names and the settlement pattern of dark-age Scotland. *PSAS* 106, 99-110.

Index